Exploring Cross-Cultural Psychology
Exercises for Instructors and S

Exploring Cross-Cultural Psychology: Exercises for Instructors and Students is an accessible text that provides material for generating interactive discussion of a broad sampling of topics in cross-cultural psychology.

This new edition (previously *Interactive Exercises for Cross-Cultural Psychology*) expands the range of topics of cultural interest to psychology and connects cultural study to health, forensic, organizational, and other applied psychology fields. Each chapter offers suggestions for exposition, simulation, and confrontation of current cultural issues while allowing for creativity in instructional design. Topics covered include regional and Indigenous psychology; expression and play; language; identity; social perception and cognition; interpersonal interaction; emotion, motivation, and health; development and family; government and law; economics and work; environmental psychology; and animals and other species. This revised edition includes new coverage of WEIRD psychology, vaccination, well-being, tight vs. loose cultures, and home and homelessness.

Thoroughly and currently referenced, with connections to a wide range of accessible web-based and open-source materials, this user-friendly text is ideal for students and instructors of cross-cultural psychology across the spectrum of classroom and workshop applications.

David C. Devonis is a historian of psychology and a veteran instructor across a wide range of psychological areas, theoretical and applied. He is the author of the award-winning short history of modern psychology *History of Psychology 101* and is currently writing a book on psychology and the politics of equality.

Exploring Cross-Cultural Psychology Exercises for Instructors and Students

Second Edition

David C. Devonis

Routledge
Taylor & Francis Group
NEW YORK AND LONDON

Designed cover image: Leah Smith and Michael Townsend from Tape Art and Marwa Safa Azimi, Zuhra Nadem, Meetra Khamoosh, Abdullah Hafizi, and Negina Azimi from ArtLords.

Second edition published 2024
by Routledge
605 Third Avenue, New York, NY 10158

and by Routledge
4 Park Square, Milton Park, Abingdon, Oxon, OX14 4RN

Routledge is an imprint of the Taylor & Francis Group, an informa business

First edition published by Routledge 2018

Library of Congress Cataloging-in-Publication Data
Names: Devonis, David C., author.
Title: Exploring cross-cultural psychology : exercises for instructors and students / David C. Devonis.
Other titles: Interactive exercises for cross-cultural psychology
Description: Second edition. | New York, NY : Routledge, 2023. | Includes bibliographical references and index. | Summary: "Exploring Cross-Cultural Psychology is an accessible text that provides material for generating interactive discussion of a broad sampling of topics in cross-cultural psychology"—Provided by publisher.
Identifiers: LCCN 2023023021 (print) | LCCN 2023023022 (ebook) | ISBN 9781032291826 (hardcover) | ISBN 9781032291819 (paperback) | ISBN 9781003300380 (ebook)
Subjects: LCSH: Ethnopsychology.
Classification: LCC GN502 .D484 2023 (print) | LCC GN502 (ebook) | DDC 155.8/2—dc23/eng/20230620
LC record available at https://lccn.loc.gov/2023023021
LC ebook record available at https://lccn.loc.gov/2023023022

ISBN: 978-1-032-29182-6 (hbk)
ISBN: 978-1-032-29181-9 (pbk)
ISBN: 978-1-003-30038-0 (ebk)

DOI: 10.4324/9781003300380

Typeset in Sabon
by Apex CoVantage, LLC

A Note on the Cover

The lower of the two images on the cover is a mural of the well-known poem "Bani Adam" by Saadi Shirazi, created in Afghanistan by ArtLords, a collective of young Afghan artists (Marwa Safa Azimi, Zuhra Nadem, Meetra Khamoosh, Abdullah Hafizi, and Negina Azimi). This was destroyed by the Taliban when they reoccupied the country. The upper image is part of a collaborative mural created in Brattleboro, Vermont, USA in 2022, in tape and other materials by ArtLords and Tape Art of Providence, Rhode Island, USA (Leah Smith and Michael Townsend), symbolizing the restoration of the original mural.

Contents

Introduction and User Guide

"We Must Maintain Our Core Values and Culture"

Before beginning to read this introduction, reflect on the phrase above and write down the precise place where you think that this motto was found hanging framed on a wall.

If you guessed 'Costco, in West Des Moines, Iowa, U. S. A., you would be exactly right,

When I first saw it, my reaction was that it was incongruous. I didn't associate 'culture' and 'big-box retailers'. Others I asked suggested many other sources of organized institutional culture: churches of all sorts, military or police organizations, and nonprofit organizations and schools.

This example reveals the complications of the definition of culture. In 1952 the cultural anthropologists Ernest Kroeber and Clyde Kluckhohn identified over 150 different definitions (Kroeber & Kluckhohn, 1952). One of the preliminaries to the development of this book of exercises was my request, to an undergraduate class, to provide definitions of 'culture' in 10 words or less, The list eventually expanded to over 200 items. These sentence completions ranged from dismissive ("sacred superstition") through hostile or warlike ("what we will defend"), to philosophical, theoretical, or functional ("what we remember"; "a system of reinforcement"; "a religion"; "the sum of rights and privileges", "what is prohibited"; "what makes us uncomfortable"; "conferred by power"). Among these examples are not only connections to cognitive, emotional , and social dimensions of culture, but also to behaviorism, psychoanalysis (Freud, 1930), and anticolonialism (Said, 2003).

This tells me that even those naïve to cultural studies arrive with diverse ideas and unique personal characterizations of culture. This book is intended for students of all ages and all levels of expertise who want to examine the relation of culture and psychology in all its diversity and complexity. Its premise is that this relationship will emerge through discussion and questioning of the nature and multiple meanings of culturally significant ideas, objects, and practices. Students have played a primary role in its development. Its eighty-odd subjects have been winnowed out of more than twice that number of VICIs (Very Important Cultural Issues) generated by students. To these I added a couple of dozen concepts from applied psychology in the areas of industrial/organizational psychology, environmental psychology, sports psychology, and psychology and law. I also drew on the *Encyclopedia of Cross-cultural Psychology* (Keith,

DOI: 10.4324/9781003300380-1

2013), lists of cultural keywords (Williams, 1983; Grossberg, 2005), and several textbooks and news sources to round out the list, which ultimately grew to more than 150 separate potential topics. After that, I kept the following four criteria in mind: selectivity, feasibility, compatibility (with current textbooks), and practical usefulness. Regarding selectivity and compatibility, I compared the index terms in the first edition of this book with the list of terms and concepts contained in the *Encyclopedia of Cross Cultural Psychology* (Keith, 2013) and found about 20% agreement. This is the same percentage of agreement between the first edition and the indexed terms in a leading cross-cultural text (Shiraev & Levy, 2021), though the matching terms are different in both cases. This weak though consistent overlap is probably determined by the immensity of subjects and perspectives in the field, so a great deal of uniformity among sources shouldn't be expected. As one commentator put it, "knowledge is everywhere" (Montero, 2010) and any single book in this area fits into a mosaic of ideas. Regarding feasibility, I've included subjects that seemed most likely to promote active participation or simulation. Finally, a concern for practicality leads to some interesting but recondite terms, laughter, for example (Bryant & Bainbridge, 2022), being passed over in favor of terms attaching to larger social or environmental issues. This new edition, along with over 250 new or updated references, adds topics that have either become more prominent in the academic literature or that were not previously emphasized. Among these are specific consideration of WEIRD culture (Henrich, 2020, Muthukrishna et. al., 2020), 'tight' vs. 'loose' cultures (Gelfand, 2018); home and homelessness; COVID-related issues and vaccination, and well-being. This book is intended to expand the range of existing collections of interactive exercises, for instance the well-known U. S. Peace Corps training manual *Culture Matters* (Peace Corps, n.d.), the APA volume of *110 Exercises for Teaching Cross-Cultural Psychology* (Pedersen, 2004), and Susan Goldstein's *Cross-Cultural Explorations* (Goldstein, 2019). Some familiar subjects will be encountered (e.g., aging, back-translation) along with others that are rarely found in any of the standard collections of interactive exercises (e.g., friendship, rights, police and law enforcement, loyalty, and sports, among others). Beyond the core values of psychology represented in his book, openness to experience and reliance on evidence, no particular theoretical orientation is embodied or advanced.

The Structure of the Entries

Each entry contains

(1) **a TITLE:** usually a single word. If the word is somewhat unfamiliar in the context of cross-cultural psychology, or if it reflects only an aspect of what is contained in the entry, then a brief explanatory phrase will follow it. The word 'and' in the title indicates that the entry contains at least two separate but related areas of interest and interaction (e.g., Rights, Citizenship, and Voting). Entries with an 'and' will typically be at least twice as long as single-titled entries and will contain twice as many supporting references;

(2) **an INTRODUCTION** with a definition and description of the topic area, along with its relation to both psychology and culture. References mentioned in this section will usually be to sources that treat the subject comprehensively;

(3) **a section called EXPOSITION, CONFRONTATION, AND SIMULATION (ECS):** This section follows each introduction and contains suggestions for ways that interactive exercises can be planned. There are many paths to exploring the materials presented here. These

may include (but are not limited to) inventories, surveys, tests and other measurement instruments, articles describing scenarios or containing interactive components, and films and imaginative literature; and

(4) **REFERENCES AND SUGGESTED READINGS:** A set of entry-specific references follows the Introduction and ECS for each entry. These references have been chosen, for the most part, from currently available material at the time of writing and are, as far as possible, based on reliable journalism or open-source scientific publications. Occasionally there are some references to books or articles that are available only through an academic or professional library or by subscription, but even without these, acceptable substitutes of similar material can usually be easily found. I've kept in mind especially the needs of online course designers and teachers. If I could find it in a blog, I included it.

A Sample Entry

Title	→	**Vexillology, The Science Of Flags**
Introduction	→	One snap definition of a country or culture might be 'having a flag'. The history of regions and territories can be seen in the progression of their multiple flags over time, for instance that of Texas, which in its comparatively short life as a region has been under six (at least). Flags are symbolically and metaphorically rich. They are memorials to territorial conquest and to ownership, both terrestrial, extra-terrestrial (Fincannon, 2012), and commercial. They are communicative devices for everything from weather danger to, in Tibetan Buddhist culture, prayer. They convey messages of national solidarity (Smith, 2017) and also divisiveness. For example, the immediate replacement of the German national flag by the swastika banner overnight in 1933 was a symbol of menace and an alarm signaling the time to flee. Recently in the United States, alternatively-colored U. S. flags have emerged as symbols of political division (Chammah & Aspinwall, 2020). Above all, for purposes of an introduction to cultural psychology and cultural studies focusing on the communication of values and traditions, flags express values in a graphic and often highly emotional form. Sometimes, flags are worth dying for (Marshall, 2017). Flags are omnipresent shorthand for all of the levels of culture represented in this book—not only nations, but also indigenous and ethnic groups (Donella, 2017), individual cities and towns, corporations, religions, and schools; social movements (e.g., the graphically effective Equality flag of the US Human Rights Campaign for LGBTQ rights) and even the North American Vexillogical Association (NAVA, n.d.) assemble under their respective banners.
Exposition, Confrontation, and Simulation	→	Interactivity might be set up in the form of a contest to redesign an existing flag of a particular culture with known values. However, I've found it more interesting and entertaining to ask students to design a flag from scratch to represent the immediate culture of the class. This is an effective way of focusing the conversation, at the outset, on shared or divergent values. The task of designing a flag is often delegated to amateurs (for instance, legislators) and often flags that become the official symbols of regions, especially cities and states, can be pretty frightful (or humorous) from a design perspective. Some existing flags have been termed 'hot messes' (Spicuzza, 2016) and some have been, due to the confusing nature of their design, inadvertently flown upside down for some time (Monroe, 2017). But if the products of amateurs are messy, they also reverberate with cultural pulses, and a banner—or in the case of courses I've taught, usually six banners at least—is a natural rallying point.

(Continued)

(Continued)

		Another possibility for interactivity might be to introduce some graphic style into what might clearly reflect the phrase 'designed by committee'. One suggestion for this would be to examine and imitate flags that effectively express cultural and historical traditions, for instance the Lebanese flag with its cedar, the Canadian maple leaf, or—my own favorite—the flag of Nunavut with its indigenous stele. A further variation can be, along with the cultural flag, to adopt or create a shared cultural song.
References and Suggested Readings	→	References and Suggested Readings Chammah, M. & Aspinwall, C. (2020, June 8). The short, fraught history of the 'Thin Blue Line' American flag. The Marshall Project (online resource) Retrieved from https://www.themarshallproject.org/2020/06/08/the-short-fraught-history-of-the-thin-blue-line-american-flag [Accessed January 16, 2023]. Donella, L. (2017, July 14). On Flag Day, remembering the Red, Black, and Green. *National Public Radio Code Switch* (online broadcast transcript). Retrieved from https://www.npr.org/sections/codeswitch/2017/06/14/532667081/on-flag-day-remembering-the-red-black-and-green [Accessed March 30, 2023]. Fincannon, J. (2012). Six flags on the moon: What is their current condition? *Apollo Lunar Surface Journal* (US National Aeronautics and Space Administration) (online). Retrieved from https://www.hq.nasa.gov/alsj/ApolloFlags-Condition.html [Accessed March 30, 2023]. Marshall, T. (2017). *A flag worth dying for: The power and politics of national symbols.* New York: Scribner. *NAVA*. (n.d.). North American vexillogical association website. (online). Retrieved from https://nava.org/. [Accessed March 30, 2023]. Monroe, L. (2017, February 2). Nobody noticed Nebraska flag flying upside down on the Capital for over a week. Only In Your State Website. Retrieved from https://www.onlyinyourstate.com/nebraska/upside-down-flag-ne/ . [Accessed March 30, 2023}. Smith, A. (2017, August 21). Six Flags brings down Confederate flags. CNN Website. Retrieved from https://money.cnn.com/2017/08/21/news/companies/six-flags-confederate/index.html. [Accessed March 30, 2023]. Spicuzza, M. (2016, May 11). Design contest hopes to improve city's 'hot mess' of a flag. *USA Today* (online newspaper). Retrieved from https://www.usatoday.com/story/news/local/milwaukee/2016/05/11/design-contest-hopes-to-improve-citys-hot-mess-of-a-flag/84983134/ [Accessed March 30, 2023].

This book is designed to generate interest in cross-cultural psychology across the psychology curriculum, especially in applied areas. It intends to provide maximum creative range and flexibility, and thus does not prescribe too many highly specific instructions for activity design. It is intended to support, but it will not and should not supplant courses in cultural anthropology, race and ethnicity, privilege, sociology of the family, international business, intercultural communication, cultural health and counseling psychology, women's studies, gender and queer studies, sexuality, political psychology, and immigration, a selection of which should also be in the serious culture student's transcript. I hope to have provided ample material for constructing new thoughts and thoughtful cultural lessons. In light of the apparent impossibility of assimilating all culture, might I remind the users of this text, and myself, that the attempt is valuable and the returns, though incomplete and imperfect, are great.

References and Suggested Readings

Bryant, G. A. & Bainbridge, C. M. (2022). Laughter and culture. *Philosophical Transactions of the Royal Society B, 377*, 20210179. Retrieved from https://royalsocietypublishing.org/doi/10.1098/rstb.2021.0179. [Accessed March 31, 2023].

Freud, S. (1930). *Das unbehagen in der Kultur* (Civilization and its Discontents). Wien: Internationaler Psychoanalytischer Verlag.

Gelfand, M. (2018). *Rule makers, rule breakers: How tight and loose cultures wire our world.* NY: Scribner.

Goldstein, S. (2019). *Cross-cultural explorations: Activities in culture and psychology (3rd Ed.).* New York: Routledge.

Grossberg, L. (2005). *New keywords: A revised vocabulary of culture and society*. Hoboken, NJ: Wiley-Blackwell.

Henrich, J. (2020). *The WEIRDest people in the world: How the West became psychologically peculiar and particularly prosperous.* New York: Farrar, Straus, & Giroux.

Keith, K. (Ed.) (2013). *The encyclopedia of cross-cultural psychology* (3 vols.). Hoboken, NJ: Wiley-Blackwell.

Kroeber, A. , & Kluckhohn, C. (1952). *Culture: A critical review of concepts and definitions.* Chicago, IL: University of Chicago Press.

Montero, M. (2010). Community psychology's voyage into complexity: On liberation, change, and politics (pp. 519–532). In G. Nelson & I. Prilleltensky (Eds.), *Community psychology: In pursuit of liberation and well-being.* London & New York: Palgrave Macmillan.

Muthukrishna, M., Bell, A.V., Henrich, J., Curtin, C. M., Gedranovich, A., McInerney, J., & Thue, B. (2020). Beyond Western, educated, industrial, rich, and democratic (WEIRD) psychology: Measuring and mapping scales of cultural and psychological distance. *Psychological Science, 31*(6), 678–701. Open access at https://journals.sagepub.com/doi/full/10.1177/0956797620916782 https://doi.org/10.1177/0956797620916782

Peace Corps . (n.d.). *Culture matters: The peace corps cross-cultural workbook.* Washington, DC: US Government Printing Office (online). Retrieved from http://files.peacecorps.gov/multimedia/pdf/library/T0087_culturematters.pdf [Accessed November 4, 2017].

Pedersen, P. B. (2004). *110 experiences for multicultural learning.* Washington, DC: American Psychological Association.

Said, E. W. (2003). *Freud and the non-European.* New York: Verso.

Shiraev, E. B. & Levy, D. A. (2021). *Cross-cultural psychology: critical thinking and contemporary applications.* New York, NY and London (UK): Routledge.

Williams, R. (1983). *Cultural keywords: a vocabulary of culture and society.* London, UK: Fontana Press.

Boundaries

DOI: 10.4324/9781003300380-2

Boundaries and Maps

Immigration and the desire for refuge depend on boundaries, and the concept of boundaries also has interpersonal, intergenerational, and social connotations. Boundaries are sites for playing out the dynamics of cultural exchange and cultural friction. An example of only a small sliver of the territory covered by psychological studies investigating boundaries is the literature on sexual behavior. Recent psychological literature records dozens of articles dealing with sexual and gender boundaries—for example, between individuals in consensual sexual communities (Holt, 2016), between clients and therapist in contested sexual territory with the added complication of social media thrown in (Brown, 2011), and between gender-nonconformists and religious communities (Kashubeck-West, Whiteley, Vossenkemper, Robinson, & Deitz, 2017). In the United States, the arbitrary drawing of boundaries in election districts results in sharpened contrasts between antithetical political subcultures and leads to differential participation in elections by specific cultural groups (Amos, Smith, & Ste. Claire, 2017).

This pattern of psychic exclusion of groups by the erection of socially policed symbolic boundaries is also a feature of contested cultural spaces internationally. A recent study in Israel (Guetzkow, 2016) contrasts the immigrant-specific prejudices and attitudes directed against immigrant Ethiopian Jews with the entrenched, chronic discriminatory behaviors contributing to the perception on the part of Arab Palestinians that it is hopeless to expect changes in their status relative to the dominant culture.

Exposition, Confrontation, and Simulation

Boundary concepts can be integrated with discussions of immigration, sexuality, or any other area where ingroup and outgroup are foregrounded. Following Guetzkow's (2016) work cited earlier, an inventory might be constructed of the symbolic ways in which individuals are made to feel unwelcome in their immediate environment. Preliminary exploration might be directed in more objective ways toward an examination of the geography of boundaries and the physical constructions that establish and maintain them.

Pope and Keith-Spiegel (2008) offer numerous examples of situations in which boundaries may inadvertently be crossed in psychotherapy; compare these with boundary crossings between cultures generally. Cartographic exploration can be a starting point; search for data holes worldwide (e.g., Jacobs, 2017; Markstein, 2021) and suggest ways to conceptually examine the physical and virtual location of cultural differences. Programs exist to draw maps, and one might be employed to chart, for instance, the fluid boundaries of local social groups. Koeze, Lu, and Smart (2022) provide a brief effective simulation of *gerrymandering*, the artificial creation of voting districts by legislation. An excellent

DOI: 10.4324/9781003300380-3

set of basic exercises for understanding boundaries at the physical level is the *New York Times*' set of simple lesson plans for geography (Marshall & Gonchar, 2012). Students with a biological or neuropsychological sensibility may want to examine in detail both the blood-brain barrier and the immune system.

References and Suggested Readings

Amos, B., Smith, D. A., & Ste Claire, C. (2017). Reprecincting and voting behavior. *Political Behavior*, *39*(1), 133–156.

Brown, L. (2011). Everyone I know knows everyone I know: Boundary overlap in the life of one lesbian psychotherapist. In W. B. Johnson & J. P. Koocher (Eds.), *Ethical conundrums, quandaries, and predicaments in mental health practice: A casebook from the files of experts* (pp. 17–23). New York, NY: Oxford University Press.

Guetzkow, J. (2016). How symbolic boundaries shape the experience of social exclusion: A case comparison of Arab Palestinian citizens and Ethiopian Jews in Israel. *American Behavioral Scientist*, *60*(2), 150–171.

Holt, K. (2016). Blacklisted: Boundaries, violations, and retaliatory behavior in the BDSM community. *Deviant Behavior*, *37*(8), 917–930.

Jacobs, F. (2017, May 31). *The world's data holes, quantified: BigThink (online blog resource)* (online). Retrieved from http://bigthink.com/strange-maps/the-worlds-data-holes-quantified

Kashubeck-West, S., Whiteley, A. M., Vossenkemper, T., Robinson, C., & Deitz, C. (2017). Conflicting identities: Sexual minority, transgender, and gender nonconforming individuals navigating between religion and gender-sexual orientation identity. In K. A. DeBord, A. R. Fischer, K. J. Bieschke & R. M. Perez (Eds.), *Handbook of sexual orientation and gender diversity in counseling and psychotherapy* (pp. 213–238). Washington, DC: American Psychological Association.

Koeze, E., Lu, D., & Smart, C. (2022, January 27). Can you gerrymander your party to power? *The New York Times* (online newspaper). Retrieved from www.nytimes.com/interactive/2022/01/27/us/politics/congressional-gerrymandering-redistricting-game-2022.html

Markstein, E. (2021, October 27). The unmeasured world. *Mappenstance Website*. Retrieved from https://blog.richmond.edu/livesofmaps/2021/10/07/the-unmeasured-world/

Marshall, T., & Gonchar, M. (2012, December 4). All over the map: 10 ways to teach about geography. *The Learning Network: Teaching and Learning with the New York Times. Blog in The New York Times* (online resource). Retrieved from https://archive.nytimes.com/learning.blogs.nytimes.com/2012/12/04/all-over-the-map-10-ways-to-teach-about-geography/

Pope, K. S., & Keith-Spiegel, P. (2008). A practical approach to boundaries in psychotherapy: Making decisions, bypassing blunders, and mending fences. *Journal of Clinical Psychology, 64(5)*, 638–652. Retrieved from https://kspope.com/ethics/boundaryphp

Immigration and Refugees

At its root, migration is a biological phenomenon; the movement of populations of living beings, from birds to fish to plants, is ubiquitous in nature. Animal migrations are usually cyclic and often based on seasonal changes; hummingbirds return and leave on schedule every year. However, colonization occurs across all species as well (Onofri, 2008; Coutinho, Miller, & Macedo, 2015). Migration accompanied by conquest and colonization sets the pattern worldwide for the current arrangement of nation-states.

Viewed from a current vantage point in a mostly post-colonial world, the distinction between *immigrant* and *refugee* is not that large. Both groups cross borders and can be ranked on a scale of freedom of choice regarding their status. Immigrants are relatively voluntary refugees; refugees are involuntary or coerced immigrants. The political and social forces that impel movements of people to seek other places for either increased opportunity or safe refuge are essentially the same throughout history; relatively rarely is the immigrant or refugee journey taken as a caprice.

Science and psychology have some famous refugees in their history. Both Albert Einstein's and Sigmund Freud's flights, like thousands of others' during the 1930s, were contingent on their imminent execution had they stayed in Hitler's Europe. Persons of wealth and influence protected Einstein and Freud, as did their own perceived value to the cultures to which they migrated.

Often, however, both the refugee and the immigrant alike are relatively powerless and poor. Their journeys are often perilous and deadly. Established groups within nations and cultures resist, sometimes violently, those who they perceive as foreign or as enemies; the willingness of individuals to risk their lives to emigrate, as many from Africa do today in trying to reach Europe, is a testament to courage. Those immigrants and refugees who do succeed in their new cultures often have a history of victimization and trauma that is hard to share publicly. The APA acknowledges the severe psychological consequences to refugees and forcibly displaced persons, which now number between 60 and 120 million worldwide, and has developed an extensive network of resources for psychological professionals concerned with immigrants and refugees (American Psychological Association, 2023).

Exposition, Confrontation, and Simulation

At the very least, the subject of immigration and refugees can and should prompt consideration of the virtue of courage, which is often hidden in psychological discourse but is central to the preservation of culture (Lear, 2008). Some insight into the situation of forced emigration can be gained from participation in one of several dramatizations of

DOI: 10.4324/9781003300380-4

the scenario entitled "Five Minutes to Pack," which simulates the actual conditions under which many otherwise established persons suddenly become refugees. These simulations are part of many educational programs designed for preadolescents (and, thus, are very accessible and easy to demonstrate) available on the web for learning about refugees (e.g. Brown, 2021). The basic premise is that there are five minutes to pack, and bags or suitcases are stuffed with things that are perceived to be important, either from a prearranged list or from memory. This exercise can vary in its suddenness; compare a rationally composed list of necessaries and one that is assembled on the spot and under duress. Simulation of the totality of the refugee experience is also available, often from refugee aid organizations (Jesuit Refugee Service, 2022).

Voluntary immigration can be explored by visiting the websites of various countries' immigration services. Working through all aspects of an application for naturalization will be instructive and depressing at the same time (such as when discovering the length of residence time necessary to be considered a permanent resident or naturalized citizen). Note, for instance, that becoming a Japanese citizen by naturalization would involve being able to read and write Japanese at the level of an eight-year-old schoolchild, proving an income and tax payments, and also renouncing any other citizenships. How likely is it that a US citizen will comply with the latter? A challenging exercise would be to discover the reasons why the relative handful of US citizens renounce their citizenship yearly (Nesheim, 2022).

Pragmatic approaches to the successful cultural integration of immigrants and refugees might start with readings drawn from psychologists who empathize with this area of experience, such as Mary Pipher's book—now out of print but widely available in libraries and used—*The Middle of Everywhere: Helping Refugees Enter the American Community* (Pipher, 2003). This reading would be particularly instructive since its narrative centers on the refugee experience in the United States a generation ago, when borders and public attitudes were more open. Reading should also extend to stories by and about acculturative experiences (e.g., Nguyen, 2017).

Finally, seek out documentation of successful accomplishment of immigration or refuge—for example, that of an Egyptian man, Hatem El-Gamasy, who delivers a well-respected TV commentary on US politics for Egyptian TV out of the back room of the New York bodega and sandwich shop he's managed for more than 15 years and says, "The sky's the limit!" (Nir, 2017). Or that of Sudanese women, refugees arriving in Uganda (the country that, as of 2017, receives the most refugees in the world), reassembling their homes with their own hands on grants of bush land (Alexander, 2017). The documentary *Utica: The Last Refuge* (Phillipps, 2021) reflects on all aspects of the reception of refugees in a US city.

References and Suggested Readings

Alexander, R. (2017, September 15). Starting from scratch in Uganda. *BBC News Magazine* (online). Retrieved from www.bbc.com/news/magazine-41255233

American Psychological Association. (2023). Immigration and refugees. *American Psychological Association Website* (Topics section). Retrieved from www.apa.org/topics/immigration-refugees

Brown, M. (2021, August 27). How to talk to your kids about the refugee crisis. *Parents Magazine Website*. Retrieved from www.parents.com/news/how-to-talk-to-your-kids-about-the-refugee-crisis/

Coutinho, M. L., Miller, A. Z., & Macedo, M. F. (2015). Biological colonization and biodeterioration of architectural ceramic materials: An overview. *Journal of Cultural Heritage*, *16*(5), 759–777.

Jesuit Refugee Service. (2022). Walk a mile in my shoes. *Jesuit Refugee Services Website*. Retrieved from www.jrsusa.org/resource/walk-a-mile/

Lear, J. (2008). *Radical hope: Ethics in the face of cultural devastation*. Cambridge, MA: Harvard University Press.

Nesheim, C. H. (Ed.). (2022, October 28). Reported US citizenship renunciations in 2022 exceed last year's total already after 3rd quarter. *IMI (Investment Migration Insider) Website*. Retrieved from www.imidaily.com/intelligence/reported-us-citizenship-renunciations-in-2022-exceed-last-years-total-already-after-3rd-quarter/

Nguyen, V. T. (2017). *The refugees*. New York, NY: Grove Press.

Nir, S. M. (2017, September 16). Hold the egg sandwich: Egyptian TV is calling. *The New York Times Magazine* (online). Retrieved from www.nytimes.com/2017/09/16/nyregion/hatem-el-gamasy-bodega-television-egypt-pundit.html?mcubz=3&_r=0

Onofri, S. (2008). Colonization (Biological). In M. Gargaud et al. (Eds.), *Encyclopedia of astrobiology* (pp. 326–328). Berlin, DE: Springer.

Phillipps, L. (Director). (2021). *Utica: The last refuge* [Documentary Film]. New York, NY: Off Ramp Films.

Pipher, M. (2003). *The middle of everywhere: Helping refugees enter the American community*. New York, NY: Mariner Books.

Regional and Indigenous Psychology

Briefly, *regional* delimits a geographic area while *Indigenous* refers to the native people of that area and also to the conceptual framework of culture developed by those people (Pickren, 2015). Each of these, *regional psychology* and *Indigenous psychology*, can be a subject of study in its own right. A recent essay in the APA volume *Culture Reexamined* (Vandello, Hettinger, & Michniewicz, 2014) presents regional psychology as a specific and independent area of cross-cultural study. Indigenous psychology likewise has a separate presence in cross-cultural psychological research. But rather than two separate and autonomous areas, there is instead a spectrum of mixtures of the two.

At one extreme, there is pure regionality—that is, regions entirely void of peoples or cultures. The very farthest extreme in this direction would be the moon or the planets or, on Earth, Antarctica. Next, on the terrestrial globe, are regions where Indigenous tribes or groups have lived for many centuries. These places are of very high interest for anthropologists especially since there are now comparatively few of them due to the displacements contingent on expanding mega-cultures. Examples could be the grazing range of the reindeer of Sámi, the Himalayan regions populated by Tibetan natives, the remote regions where some Native American tribal groups in Canada and the Americas live, and the rainforests and plains of Amazonian and African Indigenous cultures. Even these, however, are hardly untouched by global expansion and technological change. Except for those that are most remote, most original Indigenous cultures of most global regions survive as remnants outside of their historical locations within regions that have taken on the primary cultural characteristics of their colonizers or settlers.

Indigenous may sometimes be equated with *static* or *unchanging*, and some Indigenous cultures are so. But, as Pickren (2015) notes, indigenization appears to be an ongoing evolutionary process in which cultures that were formerly native to a region or area are infused with the practices and ideas of newcomers. As the boundaries of the world shrink, the pressure to create new hybridizations of culture grows.

Little has been said here about specific psychological beliefs of Indigenous groups. In the United States, psychology as a field has recognized that all cultures have evolved particular sets of ideas and attitudes about human behavior and the mind such that all psychologies are, in a real sense, Indigenous (Marsella, 2013). Recently, there have been attempts to collect these; an example is the *Handbook of Arab American Psychology* (Amer & Awad, 2016). Indigenous psychology is intimately bound to ecopsychology. Indigenous communities' cultures are shaped by a history of repeated environmental invasion and depredation. Swanson (2022) provides a vivid example of the clash of car culture and Native American culture at a nickel mining site in Minnesota.

DOI: 10.4324/9781003300380-5

Exposition, Confrontation, and Simulation

As can be seen from the preceding short sketch, it can be difficult to tell when a culture is Indigenous, and preexisting templates do not capture the fluidity of cultural interchange and adaptation. The United States is a good example of the kind of patchwork of indigenousness and ongoing indigenizations that occur within geographically distinct regions. Perhaps a good starting point would be to contrast the range, scope, and focus of the organizational presentations of a conceptually regional group—for example, the Center for the Study of Southern Culture based at the University of Mississippi (CSSC, 2023) and a group that emphasizes its specific indigenousness, such as the Great Plains Action Society (Great Plains Action Society, 2023).

Indigenous identity is maintained in the face of ongoing incursions from surrounding or intruding cultures by demands for recognition, equality, and—sometimes—apologies or restitution. One example of this is the recent apology and request for forgiveness addressed by Amish groups living in Ohio to the descendants of Native American groups in the region for the way that their ancestors deprived the tribes of land (Brubaker, 2016). This is remarkable in the context of regionality and indigenousness as the Amish themselves can be taken as representative of a kind of regional indigenousness transplanted whole and maintained intact in a new region.

Organized psychology has recently made specific efforts to confront its longstanding silence on the mistreatment of Indigenous cultures. Discussion might start with the recent apology to people of color by the APA (American Psychological Association, 2021). An exercise that might prove useful in revealing the many interwoven strands of regionality and indigenousness could be to sketch out how many apologies might be delivered in such a meeting of groups in any region of a previously colonized area. A bonus would be if such an activity were, after such a plan were made, at least partially carried out.

References and Suggested Readings

Amer, M. M., & Awad, G. H. (Eds.). (2016). *Handbook of Arab American psychology*. New York, NY: Routledge.

American Psychological Association. (2021, October 29). Apology to People of Color for APA's role in promoting, perpetuating, and failing to challenge racism, racial discrimination, and human hierarchy in the U.S. *American Psychological Association Website*. Retrieved from www.apa.org/about/policy/racism-apology

Brubaker, J. (2016, August 1). The scribbler: Amish ask for forgiveness from native Americans. *Lancaster Online (online newspaper)*. Retrieved from https://lancasteronline.com/features/yesteryear/scribbler/the-scribbler-amish-ask-for-forgiveness-from-native-americans/article_4c4f8b02–54d1–11e6-a2ef-7b51a8d22c78.html

CSSC. (2023). *Center for the study of Southern culture: University of Mississippi (organizational website)*. Retrieved from https://southernstudies.olemiss.edu/

Great Plains Action Society. (2023). *Great Plains Action Society Website*. Retrieved from www.greatplainsaction.org/

Marsella, A. (2013, December). All psychologies are indigenous psychologies: Reflections on psychology in a global era. *Psychology International (online magazine, American Psychological Association Division 52)*. Retrieved from www.apa.org/international/pi/2013/12/reflections

Pickren, W. (2015). Indigenization. In K. Keith (Ed.), *The encyclopedia of cross-cultural psychology* (pp. 698–699). New York, NY: Wiley-Blackwell.

Swanson, A. (2022, August 30). This remote mind could foretell the future of America's electric car industry. *The New York Times (online newspaper)*. Retrieved from www.nytimes.com/2022/08/30/business/economy/electric-cars-us-nickel-mine.html

Vandello, J. A., Hettinger, V. E., & Michniewicz, K. (2014). Regional culture. In A. Cohen (Ed.), *Culture reexamined: Broadening our understanding of social and evolutionary influences*. Washington, DC: American Psychological Association.

Expression and Play

DOI: 10.4324/9781003300380-6

Dance and Music

Dance has been a focus of interest in varied ways in psychology since the beginnings of the field. Kate Gordon (later Kate Gordon Moore), preeminent in the establishment of principles of gender equity in the field (Young, 2010), viewed dance in an evolutionary context as an elaboration of movements involved in fighting and other forms of social interaction (Gordon, 1908). In the 1950s, Marian Chace and others began to engage with patients in mental institutions through dance (Chace, 1953) and established what is now dance therapy.

As psychology has evolved, both dance and music have been linked to the basic perceptual systems underlying language and also to social entrainment, the ability to form social bonds through imitative motion (Singer, 2017; Savage et al., 2020). Also in that time, dance has emerged as a factor in developing identity, individual and cultural. Hill, Sandford, and Enright (2016) challenge standard body images in the context of established ballet forms. Lee's dissertation (2015), which traces the development of queer Asianness in artistic opposition to mainstream Canadian culture, is particularly interesting for its examination of the many layers of cross-cutting identities in play in a world in which comfortable, established cultural stereotypes are dissolving.

Exposition, Confrontation, and Simulation

One way of entering the subject of dance theoretically could be to pursue the many metaphorical uses of the term *dance*—for example, in the title of Gary Zukav's now quite old but recently reprinted book *The Dancing Wu Li Masters* (Zukav, 1979/2009), which trades on Zukav's interpretation via tai chi of the Chinese term for physics (*WuLi*) as "patterns of organic energy." Building on this, a more directly interactive engagement with the subject could involve various forms of movement-based meditative activity—tai chi and yoga, for instance—contingent on the availability of local practitioners and experts. Further, there are nearly infinite possibilities for individual, partnered, and group dance across multiple cultures, and many internet sites and instructional videos for the same. Ideally the result would be an entire classroom engaging in organized (or disorganized) dance. Caution should be exercised with *hopak* (pull this up on YouTube). Speculative experimentation might be carried out to determine whether, for example, people otherwise randomly assorted into groups might feel better about both themselves and the group after dancing. Dance also has a history of cultural appropriation; Vainberg (2020) provides starting points for examining the cultural roots of several dance styles including ballet, hip-hop, and vogueing.

DOI: 10.4324/9781003300380-7

Dance rarely, if ever, exists without music, and a cultural tour through dance will inevitably involve contrasting cultural musical styles. Recent research in the psychology of music suggests more commonality than difference in music across cultures. Assembling examples of lullabies, for example, from several different cultures can illustrate the universality of music and serve as an introduction to the intensely quantitative analysis of the types and prevalence of music across cultures by Mehr and colleagues (Aggarwal-Schifellite, 2020; Mehr et al., 2019).

References and Suggested Readings

Aggarwal-Schifellite, M. (2020, October 19). Frère Jacques, are you sleeping? *The Harvard Gazette* (online magazine). Retrieved from https://news.harvard.edu/gazette/story/2020/10/research-shows-lullabies-in-any-language-relax-babies/

Chace, M. (1953). Dance as an adjunctive therapy with hospitalized mental patients. *Bulletin of the Menninger Clinic*, *17*, 219–225.

Gordon, K. (1908). Pragmatism in aesthetics. In E. L. Thorndike (Ed.), *Essays philosophical and psychological in honor of William James by his colleagues at Columbia University*. New York, NY: Longmans, Green (Available online at A Mead Project, Brock University, Canada). Retrieved from https://brocku.ca/MeadProject/sup/Gordon_1908.html

Hill, J., Sandford, R., & Enright, E. (2016). 'It has really amazed me what my body can now do': Boundary work and the construction of a body-positive dance community. *Sport in Society*, *19*(5), 667–679.

Lee, A. W. L. (2015). *Performing ManChyna: Unmapping promissory exaltation, multicultural eugenics, and the new whiteness* (or, 'call me Dr. ManChyna') (PhD Dissertation, Queen's University, Canada) (online). Retrieved from https://qspace.library.queensu.ca/bitstream/handle/1974/13741/Lee_Andrew_W_201509_PhD.pdf?sequence=1&isAllowed=y

Lee, E. (2013, June 24). Asian Americans break stereotypes through urban dance. *Voice of America News* (online resource). Retrieved from www.voanews.com/a/asian-american-break-sterotypes-through-urban-dance/1687837.html

Mehr, S. A., Singh, M., Knox, D., Ketter, D. M., Pickens-Jones, D., . . . Glowacki, L. (2019, November 22). Universality and diversity in human song. *Science*, *366*, eaax0868. Retrieved from https://mehr.cz/pdf/2019_MehrEtAl_Science.pdf

Savage, P. E., Loui, P., Tarr, B., Schachner, A., Glowacki, L., Mithen, S., & Fitch, W. T. (2020, August 20). Music as a coevolved system for social bonding. *Behavioral and Brain Sciences*, *44*, E59. Retrieved from https://doi.org/10.1017/S0140525X20000333

Singer, T. (2017). Does dancing just feel good, or did it help early humans survive? *Scientific American*, *317*(1), 67–71.

Vainberg, A. (2020, December 10). Appropriation of Black, LBGTQ + Club Dance styles. *Avital Vainberg Website*. Retrieved from https://storymaps.arcgis.com/stories/09c522debc204870b55d30c46aea742f

Young, J. L. (2010). Profile of Kate Gordon Moore. In A. Rutherford (Eds.), *Psychology's feminist voices multimedia internet archive (online resource)*. Retrieved from www.feministvoices.com/kate-gordon-moore/

Zukav, G. (1979/2009). *The dancing Wu Li masters: An overview of the new physics*. New York, NY: HarperOne.

Fashion and Dress

Clothing is one of the most immediate and tangible ways to encounter culture. Behind couture fashion, a huge international economic driver that sometimes descends into cultural appropriation, lie the multiple significances of dress. Dress is an indicator of economic position and social status; it serves as a cultural advertisement, signal, or flag; it commands authority; it is integral to ritual; it is specialized for occupations, sports, and leisure. Both anthropology (Dudley, 2011) and psychology (Pine, 2014) offer multiple contemporary perspectives on dress and the ways in which it interacts with human behavior. There are also numerous recent cross-cultural studies and episodes specifically connected to aspects of fashion. For instance, Natascha Radclyffe-Thomas, teaching in the London College of Fashion at the University of Arts in London (UK), observes that students from diverse cultures are attracted to the centers of creative fashion production located in major world cities yet find their particular cultural forms of creativity marginalized there (Radclyffe-Thomas, 2015). And some African countries, in order to develop their home clothing industries and support Indigenous designers, enacted bans on importing secondhand clothing from the United States, the major source of affordable apparel there, leading to unintended international consequences (Peralta, 2017; Dijkstra, 2020; Gbor, 2020).

Exposition, Confrontation, and Simulation

There's no end to web images of clothing. Search the internet for candid street scenes to prove that denim is really the choice of half the population anywhere on any given day (Hegarty, 2012). A fashion show would be awesome, though it would probably take as much time to set up as a negotiation simulation. It's worth examining the many guides for how to avoid looking like a tourist (pretty much one per country). Regarding clothing as a symbol of authority, beyond "dressing for success," examine—regardless of home country—the range of public opinion about commanders in chief wearing military uniforms. Some cultures want to keep the distinction between civilian and military explicitly distinct and assign the duty of chief military director to a civilian in mufti.

Clothing marks off cultural distinctions not only in the present but also in the past. Examination of films set in historical periods often can uncover inaccuracies not only in dress but also in cultural representation (Lipsitz, 2001). "Native" or traditional clothing is often exaggerated for effect in caricatures and in the popular imagination, but it is worth attempting to replicate the observation of Talha that members of some cultures—in her case, Pakistan—feel more secure and less anxious dressing in culturally traditional modes (Talha, 2012).

DOI: 10.4324/9781003300380-8

References and Suggested Readings

Dijkstra, A. (2020, October 1). Rwanda's clothing spat with the US helps China. *BBC World Service Website*. Retrieved from www.bbc.com/news/business-54164397

Dudley, S. H. (2011). Material visions: Dress and textiles. In M. Banks & J. Ruby (Eds.), *Made to be seen: Perspectives on the history of visual anthropology* (pp. 45–73). Chicago, IL: University of Chicago Press.

Gbor, N. (2020, July 14). Banning secondhand clothes by the Global South: A blessing or a curse for the local fashion industry? *Eco Styles* (environmental blog). Retrieved from www.ecostyles.com.au/blogs/2020/7/12/banning-secondhand-clothes-by-the-global-south-a-blessing-or-a-curse-for-local-fashion-industry

Hegarty, S. (2012, February 28). How jeans conquered the world. *BBC World Service News Magazine (Transcript of radio broadcast)* (online). Retrieved from www.bbc.com/news/magazine-17101768

Lipsitz, G. (2001). *Time passages: Collective memory and American popular culture*. Minneapolis, MN: University of Minnesota Press (Originally work published by 1990).

Peralta, E. (2017, July 21). Rwanda works to ban sale of secondhand clothes within 2 years. *NPR All Things Considered* (Transcript of radio broadcast) (online). Retrieved from www.npr.org/2017/07/21/538608486/rwanda-works-to-ban-sale-of-second-hand-clothes-within-2-years

Pine, K. (2014). Mind what you wear. *E-Book: Amazon Digital Services LLC*. Retrieved from http://karenpine.com/research/fashion-psychology/

Radclyffe-Thomas, N. (2015). Fashioning cross-cultural creativity: Investigating the situated pedagogy of creativity. *Psychology of Aesthetics, Creativity, and the Arts*, *9*(2), 152–160.

Talha, S. (2012). *Cross-cultural influences on female apparel selection: A comparison of Norway and Pakistan* (M.A. Thesis, Business Administration, University of Agder, Kristiansand). Retrieved from https://uia.brage.unit.no/uia-xmlui/bitstream/handle/11250/135843/Oppgave%20Sanaa%20Talha.pdf?sequence=1&isAllowed=y

Food and Art

A mashup of food and art—aside from being a bad pun—may seem almost impossible to achieve given the size and scope of each. Remarkably, these immense subjects are only weakly in evidence in cross-cultural psychology texts and reference works. Art, to many ways of thinking, is synonymous with culture, and food culture surely extends beyond yogurt. And while no one mistakes the Palace of Culture for the Chinese Palace Restaurant, every major art museum comes equipped with at least a café if not a full-scale fine dining establishment. (Whether its food is equal to the cultural diversity of the art is a matter for the critics to decide.)

On the art side, basic background reading might start with Khan Academy's introduction to its contribution to AP Art History (Harris & Zucker, n.d.), which asserts the direct connection between history and visual culture and which contains the usual basic iconographic prompts. The only limitation to assembling culture-related art materials for review and discussion is the degree of art historical sophistication of the instructor and students. In academic environments, artists and art historians are usually only too happy to oblige the psychologist with their collateral expertise. On the food side, comprehensive histories of cuisine like Civitello's (2011) along with Leon Rappoport's (2003) treatment of the psychological dimensions of eating are essential and yet not absolutely necessary given the infinite amount of web-based material available. Raw ingredients abound.

Exposition, Confrontation, and Simulation

The idea of a multicultural potluck might seem trite or in some way an instance of cultural appropriation, but most assuredly it is not—these are invariably delicious. Amateur outsiders should be encouraged to create specific cultural dishes with no more guidance than internet recipes. Arrange beforehand for critiques by knowledgeable experts. Depending on the environment, food is a natural impetus for field tripping—to markets or, if lucky, to intercultural festivals. Asian and African markets are particularly good sources for unusual vegetables; possibly insects could also be on the menu (Le Cam, 2017). Menus are available worldwide on the web, as are restaurant reviews—the more scathing, the more enjoyable, in some mysterious *schadenfreudliche* way (e.g., Rayner, 2017).

Alongside this culinary tour, take time to read and discuss accounts of the move of the largest Kosher slaughterhouse from New York City to Postville, Iowa (Bloom, 2000; Grey, Devlin, & Goldsmith, 2009). Up until 2008, Postville was considered by many a remarkably successful example of intercultural integration in the United States. Eventually, the town, previously heading for rural impoverishment, became home to not only strict Orthodox Jews but also Mexicans and Russians as well as Iowans—immigrants

DOI: 10.4324/9781003300380-9

only slightly further removed—who had lived there for generations. In 2008, a major immigration enforcement raid occurred, and, at the same time, extensive corruption and fraud were uncovered in the management of the slaughterhouse, which resulted in convictions and extensive jail time for those involved. The saga is still ongoing (Tapper, 2016) and lays bare the whole anatomy of US cultural relations as they have evolved to date. The story of Ibrahim Songne, who immigrated from Burkina Faso and evolved a unique pizza style, winning over an initially hostile surrounding culture (Brennan, 2022), can stimulate discussion of ways in which food plays a role in dissolving prejudice.

It was B. F. Skinner (1970) who observed many times that primitive humans' first forays into art were depictions of what they ate, or at least what they aimed at to eat. (You art what you eat!) Food and iconography have an intimate, multifaceted relationship. Start with still lifes. Barr (2015) observes that, for example, the eggplant has an advantage over the model because it smokes only when placed in oil. Collect, compose, create, and compare. Examine food photography; this occurs worldwide and is a specialized photographic craft. Many websites offer coaching in the basics (e.g., Serious Eats Staff, 2019). After gathering some examples, experiment—cellphones will do in lieu of more complicated equipment—and then compare with expert results. Also compare the content of food photography carried out in luxury vs. subsistence conditions—for example, Hong Kong vs. west-central Africa.

A simpler and fun way to begin thinking about food iconography is to distribute blank paper plates and markers or crayons and set the group the task of designing a plate for a restaurant in a specific culture. Commonalities emerge that are partly stereotypical, to be sure, but which also show significant awareness of the typical folk art of many cultures that is residually available in memory and only waiting for a prompt. If the group is lucky enough to live near an art museum, that will certainly be on the to-do list.

References and Suggested Readings

Barr, L. B. (2015). Still life: Theory and practice. *Cream City Review*, *39*(1), 84–91.

Bloom, S. (2000). *Postville: A clash of cultures in heartland America*. New York, NY: Mariner Books.

Brennan, J. (2022, September 3). Whatever happened to the African-born pizza chef that won over biased Italians? *Goats and soda: Stories of life in a changing world* (National Public Radio online news source). Retrieved from www.npr.org/sections/goatsandsoda/2022/09/03/1119943622/whatever-happened-to-the-african-born-pizza-chef-who-won-over-biased-italians

Civitello, L. (2011). *Cuisine and culture* (3rd ed.). New York, NY: Wiley-Blackwell.

Grey, M. A., Devlin, M., & Goldsmith, A. (2009). *Postville, U.S.A.: Surviving diversity in small-town America*. Boston, MA: Gemma Media.

Harris, B., & Zucker, S. (n.d.). A brief history of Western culture. *Khan Academy website* (online). Retrieved from www.khanacademy.org/humanities/ap-art-history/start-here-apah/brief-histories-apah/a/a-brief-history-of-western-culture

Le Cam, M. (2017, February 17). Can crunchy caterpillars help tackle malnutrition in Burkina Faso? *The Guardian* (online newspaper). Retrieved from www.theguardian.com/global-development/2017/feb/17/can-crunchy-caterpillars-help-tackle-malnutrition-in-burkina-faso

Rappoport, L. (2003). *How we eat: Culture, appetite, and the psychology of food*. Toronto, CA: ECW Press.

Rayner, J. (2017, April 9). Le Cinq, Paris: Restaurant review. *The Guardian* (online newspaper). Retrieved from www.theguardian.com/lifeandstyle/2017/apr/09/le-cinq-paris-restaurant-review-jay-rayner

Serious Eats Staff. (2019). The serious eats guide to food photography. *Serious Eats* (online blog). Retrieved from www.seriouseats.com/beginners-guide-to-food-photography

Skinner, B. F. (1970). Creating the creative artist. In A. Toynbee et al. (Eds.), *On the future of art*. New York, NY: Viking Press.

Tapper, J. (2016, February 2). Years after raid, Postville, Iowa's Jewish community is smaller, more self-reliant. *Jewish Telegraphic Agency* (online newspaper). Retrieved from www.jta.org/2016/02/02/news-opinion/united-states/years-after-raid-postville-iowas-jewish-community-is-smaller-more-self-reliant

Cultural Appropriation

Cultural appropriation is currently construed either as a violation of property law and rights (Baker, 2012; Nittle, 2021) or a form of oppression by a dominant group (Johnson, 2015). Typical quick-and-dirty examples of appropriation are a popular US vehicle named after an Indian tribe (Kierstein, 2021), party decorations such as sombreros for Cinco de Mayo celebrations, or a faux-Geisha or faux-African costume worn by a popular US singer. Sometimes, it is difficult to trace the true source of appropriation; the sombrero brought back from Mexico by a US tourist is likely to have been manufactured, along with appropriated symbols of other cultures, in China (Holcombe, 2016). Searching the subject heading of "cultural appropriation" in the psychological research literature uncovers a quite substantial amount of research considering the topic, ranging from consideration of appropriation as a means of developing cultural diversity via music (e.g., Schneider & Sippola, 2017) to description of the long-term harmful psychological effects of colonization (e.g., BigFoot & England-Aytes, 2016) to experimental demonstration of harm to intergroup relations (Mosley & Biernat, 2021).

Exposition, Confrontation, and Simulation

Discussion could start with consideration of all the points raised by Johnson (2015) and others about instances of cultural appropriation. An inventory of experiences, by both appropriators and their exploitees, would be appropriate. The subject lends itself well to case studies. Fashion often provides an entry into personal examples of conflict about whether a particular item of clothing would be considered offensive if worn; Friedman (2023) provides several case examples for discussion starters.

One instance that could be converted to a case study would be the continuing history of the name of the King Biscuit Blues Festival in Helena, Arkansas (King Biscuit Blues Festival, 2022). Scafidi (2005) provides the backstory up until 2005, when a corporation claimed rights to the name King Biscuit, itself the name of a radio program (*The King Biscuit Hour*) that popularized Delta blues from the 1940s onward. The case can be discussed as an example of corporate cultural appropriation. (The history of the Mississippi Delta itself is a good place to start for examination of the unstable equilibrium of cultures within the United States.)

References and Suggested Readings

Baker, K. J. M. (2012, November 13). A much-needed primer on cultural appropriation. *Jezebel* (Web magazine). Retrieved from https://jezebel.com/a-much-needed-primer-on-cultural-appropriation-30768539

DOI: 10.4324/9781003300380-10

BigFoot, D. S., & England-Aytes, P. J. (2016). Application: Cultural trauma in American Indian populations. In R. W. Summers (Ed.), *Social psychology: How other people influence our thoughts and actions*. Santa Barbara, CA: ABC-CLIO/Greenwood.

Friedman, V. (2023, February 13). Is it possible to wear clothes from other cultures without appropriation? *The New York Times* (online newspaper). Retrieved from www.nytimes.com/2023/02/13/style/cultural-appropriation-fashion.html

Holcombe, C. (2016, October 24). Balancing cultural appropriation with good business: The fine line between a fashion statement and political correctness. *South China Morning Post* (online newspaper). Retrieved from www.scmp.com/business/article/2039486/balancing-cultural-appropriation-good-business

Johnson, M. Z. (2015, June 14). What's wrong with cultural appropriation? These 9 answers reveal its harm. *Everyday Feminism* (online magazine). Retrieved from https://everydayfeminism.com/2015/06/cultural-appropriation-wrong/

Kierstein, A. (2021, February 23). Cherokee Nation to Jeep: It's time to change those names. *Motor Trend* (online magazine). Retrieved from www.motortrend.com/news/cherokee-nation-jeep-vehicle-naming/

King Biscuit Blues Festival. (2022). History. *King Biscuit Blues Festival Website*. Retrieved from https://kingbiscuitfestival.com/history/

Mosley, A. J., & Biernat, M. (2021). The new identity theft: Perceptions of appropriation in intergroup contexts. *Journal of Personality and Social Psychology, 121*(2), 308–331. https://doi.org/10.1037/pspi0000327

Nittle, N. K. (2021, February 4). What is cultural appropriation and why is it wrong? *ThoughtCo.* (Web magazine). Retrieved from www.thoughtco.com/cultural-appropriation-and-why-iits-wrong-2834561

Scafidi, S. (2005). *Who owns culture? Appropriation and authenticity in American law*. New Brunswick, NJ: Rutgers University Press.

Schneider, B., & Sippola, E. (2017). Introduction: Language ideologies in music. *Language and Communication*, *52*, 1–6.

Gambling: Fate, Play, Chance, and Luck

Although the forms it might take differ from familiar casino games, gambling is a widespread human activity (Binde, 2005). Games of chance (*alea*) are one part of a universal classification of games offered many years ago by Roger Caillois that still proves practically useful in classifying games in both their substance and purpose (Caillois, 2001). Bramham and Wagg (2014), from a leisure studies perspective, cite other anthropological work that suggests that preliterate cultures may engage in games of chance to the extent that beliefs in fate predominate in them (Sutton-Smith & Roberts, 1971; Sutton-Smith, 2001). Western-style casino gambling has spread its stereotyped and largely automated activities across much of the world, yet some primitive superstition remains along with more socially acceptable aspects of engaging in what might otherwise be seen as purposeless play (Kim, Ahlgren, Byun, & Malek, 2016).

Further evidence for gambling's universality is its resistance to regulation and prohibition. Islam and B. F. Skinner (Knapp, 1997) argue against gambling, both on moral grounds, to little use. Remarkably, horse racing (sans betting) is central to Saudi Arabian culture while Turkey, though it recently closed the window to horse racing and casino gambling as quickly as it opened it, still maintains a state lottery, as do other cultures that officially ban gambling.

Exposition, Confrontation, and Simulation

As the complicated title of this entry suggests, discussion could take many directions depending on the interests and tastes of the audience. Even though scientific psychological research is based on probabilistic principles and admits to being wrong 5 percent of the time or less, theoretical accounts of fate, luck, and fortune per se, although they have been adduced as topics in the field (Adler & Gielen, 2001), are mostly absent from current US and related psychology. One way to engage the science in this area directly would be to consider Albert Bandura's view on the role of chance in life direction (Bandura, 1982). Other paths might be derived from the literature on cross-cultural cognitive differences. These can include differences in probability estimation and their relation to logical vs. holistic modes of thought (Lechuga & Wiebe, 2011), differences in susceptibility to common statistical errors related to gambling (Ji, McGeorge, Li, Lee, & Zhang, 2015), or differences in the belief in luck (Harris, Milfont, & Hornsey, 2022). Simulation or replication of experiments in this domain could be attempted. In this connection, it may be interesting to think how cultures that are "anumeric" (Everett, 2017) participate in games of chance or understand probability. With regard to familiar US games of chance, the specific insights of Arthur Reber on gambling should not be ignored. Reber, by turns

DOI: 10.4324/9781003300380-11

cognitive psychologist and expert poker player and horse handicapper, has written extensively on the ways in which gambling and cognition interact (Reber, 2012).

Cross-cultural studies of children's play have been widely available for a long time, and children's games and toys contain much adaptable material for demonstrations (Edwards, 2000). Possibly an activity could be introduced where locally available toys could be modified to be more culturally universal—or, for that matter, how toys available in other cultures could be modified to be more Indigenous rather than representing the average corporate idea of toys. The "Burka Barbie" story could be a focus of discussion. A claim emerged in 2009 that the Mattel Toy Corporation had introduced a Burka Barbie as part of the 50th anniversary of the popular doll. Though this never happened and was debunked, there was at least a germ of truth in the assertion as an Italian artist/designer had clad a Barbie in traditional Islamic dress as part of an exhibit of several hundred differently decorated dolls being offered in a charity auction by the Save the Children foundation (Sandel, 2009).

Turning to gambling itself, surveys could be conducted to see how far, for instance, Peter Gray's observation of the over-representation of young males among gambling populations (Gray, 2004) or the observation of cross-cultural gender differences in risk perception (Lam, 2015) matches the local population. Discuss the effects of the legalization of casino gambling on Indigenous cultures (Chen, Walker, & Vogel, 2023). Games can be played without betting to get a feel for the cognitive and social aspects that, alongside avarice, propel players. Poker is easy to set up and learn while mah-jongg is a little more complicated; both of these—and more—are available online. Edgier approaches to interaction around this topic could involve examination and comparison of online gambling options, the preferred escape for those gamblers who are residents of cultures officially banning betting, such as China. Mention of these here does not constitute an endorsement!

References and Suggested Readings

Adler, L. L., & Gielen, U. P. (Eds.). (2001). *Cross-cultural topics in psychology*. New York, NY: Greenwood.

Bandura, A. (1982). The psychology of chance encounters and life paths. *American Psychologist*, *37*, 747–755.

Binde, P. (2005). Gambling across cultures: Mapping worldwide occurrence and learning from ethnographic comparison. *International Gambling Studies*, *5*(1), 1–27. Retrieved from https://ongambling.org/wp-content/uploads/2011/02/binde-gambling-across-cultures-2005.pdf

Bramham, P., & Wagg, S. (2014). *An introduction to leisure studies*. London, England: Sage.

Caillois, R. (2001). *Man, play, and games*. Champaign, IL: University of Illinois Press (Originally published in French by 1958).

Chen, D. W., Walker, M., & Vogel, K. P. (2023, February 10). How sports betting upended the economies of Native American tribes. *The New York Times* (online newspaper). Retrieved from www.nytimes.com/2023/02/10/sports/sports-betting-native-american-tribes.html

Edwards, C. P. (2000). Children's play in cross-cultural perspective: A new look at the six cultures study. *Cross-Cultural Research*, *34*(4), 318–338.

Everett, C. (2017, April 25). 'Anumeric' people: What happens when a language has no words for numbers? *The Conversation* (online magazine). Retrieved from https://theconversation.com/anumeric-people-what-happens-when-a-language-has-no-words-for-numbers-75828

Gray, P. (2004). Evolutionary and cross-cultural perspectives on gambling. *Journal of Gambling Studies*, *20*(4), 347–371.

Harris, E. A., Milfont, T. L., & Hornsey, M. J. (2022). Belief in luck and precognition around the world. *Journal of Cross-Cultural Psychology*, *53*(9), 1033–1053.

Ji, L. J., McGeorge, K., Li, Y., Lee, A., & Zhang, Z. (2015). Culture and gambling fallacies. *Springerplus* (online), *4*, 510. https://doi.org/10.1186/s40064-015-1290-2. Retrieved from www.ncbi.nlm.nih.gov/pmc/articles/PMC4573969/

Kim, J., Ahlgren, M. B., Byun, J. W., & Malek, K. (2016). Gambling motivations and superstitious beliefs: A cross cultural study with casino customers. *International Gambling Studies*, *16*(2), 296–315.

Knapp, T. (1997). Behaviorism and public policy: B. F. Skinner's views on gambling. *Behavior and Social Issues*, *7*(2), 129–139.

Lam, D. (2015). Gender differences in risk aversion among Chinese university students. *Journal of Gambling Studies*, *31*(4), 1405–1415.

Lechuga, J., & Wiebe, J. S. (2011). Culture and probability judgment accuracy: The influence of holistic reasoning. *Journal of Cross Cultural Psychology*, *42*(6), 1054–1065.

Reber, A. (2012). *Poker, life, and other confusing things*. Pittsburgh, PA: ConJelCo.

Sandel, A. (2009, December 10). Muslim world: Barbie's 50th anniversary Islamic makeover. *The Los Angeles Times: Babylon and Beyond Blog* (online newspaper). Retrieved from www.latimes.com/archives/blogs/babylon-beyond/story/2009-12-10/muslim-world-barbies-50th-anniversary-islamic-makeover

Sutton-Smith, B. (2001). *The ambiguity of play*. Cambridge, MA: Harvard University Press.

Sutton-Smith, B., & Roberts, J. M. (1971). The cross-cultural and psychological study of games. *International Review of Sport Sociology*, *6*, 79–87.

Sports and Spectators

Spectator sports were known in ancient China (Crowther, 2007); now, they are a modern industry. Sports and games are conceptually related in that they both are rule-governed and competitive, and both may be played individually or in teams. Perhaps the only difference is that sports involve more of the body and may also be more physically demanding and dangerous.

Sports participation and performance have attracted psychological interest for more than a century (Green & Benjamin, 2009) and have their own division in the APA (Division 47). Recently, sports has garnered attention from evolutionary psychological theorists who see in sports the outlines of processes of mate selection (Apostolou, 2015). Sports has been a pivotal force in bringing cultures and groups together. Jackie Robinson's signing a major league baseball contract in 1947 delivered a blow to racial segregation in the United States while Muhammad Ali, the US heavyweight boxing champion, became the public face of challenges to Anglo domination of all aspects of American culture. Internationally, the modern Olympic games have served as symbolic arenas for acting out cultural conflict. The triumph of Jesse Owens in the Berlin Olympics of 1936, the defiance of Black athletes at the Mexico City games in 1968, and the tragedy of terrorism at the Munich games in 1972 are among the most visible historical images of intercultural tragedy and triumph.

Sports has come to reflect globalization; the European Union has taken the integration of sports and migration seriously for some time (Gasparini & Cometti, 2010). Some sports have come to dominate and identify cultures (soccer in Brazil, for instance). But global expansion of sports has resulted in situations such as new soccer teams in China being populated by Brazilian stars bought up for the purpose (MacKenna, 2016), part of an experiment in cultural importation that may have been short-lived (Panja, 2023). Mangan and Hong (2013) describe the ways in which the Beijing Olympics in 2008 set the stage for China's ascent to modern superpower status.

Sports is just one of many cultural events that draw spectators. Spectators may seem like a passive background to the event (except for their noise), but theories of spectatorship, mostly emerging from film and theatre studies but applicable to sports as well (Kennedy, 2001), postulate that sports spectators are deeply psychologically engaged with what they watch. Their often strident loyalty to particular sports and teams puts them on a par with opera fans and other high-culture partisans. Sports spectatorship has been a means of examining selective attention related to prejudice (Hastorf & Cantril, 1954). Recent studies have examined different motivations for sports spectatorship across cultures. While collectivist cultures might emphasize community, family bonding, and team attachment in distinction to individualist cultures' focus on individual performance and

DOI: 10.4324/9781003300380-12

pleasure as motivations for attending sports events, there may be more sharing of these motivations than expected (Han, Mahony, & Greenwell, 2016). However, as evolutionary theories predict, there is a persistent sex difference across cultures in terms of who watches sports: men predominate (Bailish, Deaner, Rainham, & Blanchard, 2016).

Exposition, Confrontation, and Simulation

Access pre- and post-game interviews from different regions (for instance, interviews with cricketers from Pakistan) and compare across regions. Also compare the commentators at the Metropolitan Opera in New York, who also conduct play-by-play synopses and fan interviews at the intermissions. Sports, because of the diversity of its participants, especially in college settings, is a natural place for confronting issues of exclusion and privilege. Starting in the United States, construct a discussion around the acculturation issues raised in Anthony Kontos's (2009) contribution to the essential collection of studies of athletics and culture worldwide, *Cultural Sport Psychology* (Schinke & Hanrahan, 2009). Adopt a soccer or cricket team from another culture and follow its fortunes in the online standings (avoid betting!). Set up a test of sex discrimination as practiced by male fans hearing female sports announcers (Dicaro, 2017), and see if this extends to commentary delivered in other languages. Jessica Witt's research (Witt, 2021) has shown that the use of tools—and as she is an accomplished sport psychologist, she includes tennis rackets and golf clubs in this classification—alters perceptual responses, a modern variation on the claim that cultural experiences modify perception. Will a hockey puck (or street hockey ball) appear closer or larger when holding the stick? (An interesting challenge for classroom replication!)

References and Suggested Readings

Apostolou, M. (2015). The athlete and the spectator inside the man: A cross-cultural investigation of the evolutionary origins of athletic behavior. *Cross-Cultural Research*, *49*(2), 151–173.

Bailish, S., Deaner, R. O., Rainham, D., & Blanchard, D. (2016). Sex differences in sport remain when accounting for countries' gender inequality. *Cross-Cultural Research*, *50*(5), 395–414.

Crowther, N. (2007). *Sport in ancient times*. New York, NY: Greenwood Publishing Company.

Dicaro, J. (2017, September 18). Safest bet in sports: Men complaining about a female announcer's voice. *The New York Times* (online newspaper). Retrieved from www.nytimes.com/2017/09/18/sports/nfl-beth-mowins-julie-dicaro.html

Gasparini, W., & Cometti, A. (Eds.). (2010). *Sport facing the test of cultural diversity*. Strasbourg, France: Council of Europe Publishing (online). Retrieved from https://rm.coe.int/sport-facing-the-test-of-cultural-diversity-integration-and-intercultu/1680734be5

Green, C. D., & Benjamin, L. T. Jr. (2009). *Psychology gets in the game: Sport, mind, and behavior, 1880–1960*. Lincoln, NE: University of Nebraska Press.

Han, D., Mahony, D., & Greenwell, T. C. (2016). A comparative analysis of cultural value orientations for understanding sport fan motivations. *International Journal of Sports Marketing and Sponsorship*, *17*(3), 260–276.

Hastorf, A. H., & Cantril, H. (1954). They saw a game: A case study. *Journal of Abnormal Psychology*, *49*(1), 129–134.

Kennedy, D. (2001). Sports and shows: Spectators in contemporary culture. *Theatre Research International*, *26*(3), 277–284.

Kontos, A. (2009). Multicultural sport psychology in the United States. In R. Schinke & S. J. Hanrahan (Eds.), *Cultural sport psychology* (pp. 103–116). Champaign, IL: Human Kinetics.

MacKenna, E. (2016, February 1). China is latest destination for Brazilian stars. *The New York Times* (online newspaper). Retrieved from www.nytimes.com/2016/02/02/sports/soccer/in-the-brazilian-soccer-market-the-buyers-are-now-chinese.html?mcubz=3

Mangan, J. A., & Hong, F. (Eds.). (2013). *Post-Beijing 2008: Geopolitics, sport, and the Pacific Rim*. New York, NY: Routledge.

Panja, T. (2023, March 20). China's soccer experiment was a flop. Now it may be over. *The New York Times* (online newspaper). Retrieved from www.nytimes.com/2023/03/29/sports/soccer/china-soccer.html.

Schinke, R., & Hanrahan, S. J. (Eds.). (2009). *Cultural sport psychology*. Champaign, IL: Human Kinetics.

Witt, J. (2021). Tool use affects spatial perception. *Topics*, *13*(4), 666–683. Retrieved from https://onlinelibrary.wiley.com/doi/full/10.1111/tops.12563

Sacred Spaces and Holy Places

Sacred spaces and holy places anchor cultures to their surroundings, physical and social, and to family and ancestry besides. Sacredness and holiness are brain-deep and fuse emotion and reason, earthiness and heavenliness (Beck, 2012). Sacred sites are usually associated with religion: cathedrals, temples, pagodas, roadside shrines, and mosques are always high on the list of places to visit for new arrivals to a culture—at least for those who have the liberty and leisure to appreciate them. The experience of sacredness and holiness connects to a range of self-transcendent experiences (Yaden, Haidt, Hood, Vago, & Newberg, 2017), which include awe and mystical experiences. Awesomeness is experienced in connection with physical vastness, not only in human-made spaces such as cathedrals but in the sanctuaries of nature, which themselves often connote mystical or religious elements (e.g., the Garden of the Gods). Cemeteries and other memorials may be designed to create specific self-transcendent emotions (Petersson & Wingren, 2011).

Conversely, mystical experience occurs even in the most mundane places apart from specific religious connections. Arriving refugees who are simply grateful to have escaped the place where they previously were might kiss the earth itself, rendering even the architecture of an anonymous airport or an abandoned refugee camp sacred (Soeffer, 1997; Stonebridge, 2017). One instance of this is the spontaneous emergence of reverent commemorative behavior among modern nomads even in supermarkets in Britain (Walter, 2001); spontaneous candlelight vigils for mass shootings; or the appearance of bundles of flowers, crosses, and other tributes at the sites of fatal motor accidents or other significant deaths (Santino, 2006). It is entirely possible that, if sacredness may emerge in any deep emotional connection anywhere, wherever one currently stands may be someone's sacred space or place.

Exposition, Confrontation, and Simulation

It should not be difficult to find out the range of places sacred to individuals in any group; prompts might be to think of the place where a significant other was first met, where an important personal event occurred, or where family gathers for remembrance. Usually, too, there is some kind of public sacred space within walking distance of any classroom or meeting place, and this can be explored. This is lucky for anyone within walking distance of an actual cathedral! But graveyards can also be worthwhile to visit. The discussion might lead further toward consideration of personal experiences of awe or self-transcendence: the simple survey technique described by Jules Evans (2016) can be easily adapted and extended to reflect conceptions of spirituality across a range of cultures (e.g., Borislavova White, 2017).

DOI: 10.4324/9781003300380-13

References and Suggested Readings

Beck, R. (2012, April 2). The holiness of the F-word. *Experimental Theology (author blog, Richard Beck, Abilene Christian University)* (online). Retrieved from http://experimentaltheology.blogspot.com/2012/04/holiness-of-f-word.html

Borislavova White, D. (2017). *Being and beholding: A comparative analysis of joy and awe in four cultures* (Doctoral dissertation, James Madison University, Harrisonburg). Retrieved from https://commons.lib.jmu.edu/diss201019/150/

Evans, J. (2022, November 18). *The spiritual experiences survey: Philosophy for life (author blog of Jules Evans)* (online). Retrieved from www.philosophyforlife.org/blog/the-spiritual-experiences-survey-1

Petersson, A., & Wingren, C. (2011). Designing a memorial place: Continuing care, passage landscapes and future memories. *Mortality*, *16*(1), 54–69.

Santino, J. (Ed.). (2006). *Spontaneous shrines and the public memorialization of death*. New York, NY: Palgrave Macmillan.

Soeffer, H. G. (1997). *The order of rituals: The interpretation of everyday life* (pp. 88–89). Piscataway, NJ: Transaction Publishers.

Stonebridge, L. (2017, November 13). Sacred memory/prosaic history: Rivesaltes memorial camp. *Refugee History* (online blog). Retrieved from http://refugeehistory.org/blog/2017/11/13/sacred-memoryprosaic-history-rivesaltes

Walter, T. (2001). From cathedral to supermarket: Mourning, silence, and solidarity. *The Sociological Review*, *49*(4), 494–511.

Yaden, D. B., Haidt, J., Hood Jr., R. W., Vago, D. R., & Newberg, A. B. (2017). The varieties of self-transcendent experience. *Review of General Psychology*, *21*(2), 143–160.

Languages

DOI: 10.4324/9781003300380-14

Language and Accents

Conceptions of the role that language plays in psychological theorizing date to well before the time of Charles Darwin, who himself explored similarities between diverse languages at the beginning of his quest for a comprehensive theory of evolution (Darwin Correspondence Project, 2017). Darwin did not draw a firm distinction between the language of humans and the communication he observed in other species, nor did behavioristically oriented psychologists in the early 20th century, who also subscribed by and large to the idea that thought was internalized speech (Levelt, 2014). A modernized version of this theory attributes the origin of consciousness, and much more of human cultural heritage besides, to the internalization of external speech in connection with the perception of ongoing tasks (Kuijsten, 2016). Current theories of language development suggest that there are species-typical roots of language that can be intuited from the prelinguistic behavior of infants—for instance, common behaviors of pointing (Liszkowski, Brown, Callaghan, Takada, & de Vos, 2012).

Another level of cultural universality is indicated by research that suggests that infants acquire culturally universal musical and prosodic elements of language first (Brandt, Gebrian, & Slevc, 2012). It is certain that infants acquire, and embed neurologically, culturally specific features of language before their first year in a process termed "neural commitment" (Kuhl, 2010). Before this time, achieving multilingualism is relatively easy; after this, without specific attention to language learning and immersion, second-language learning becomes more arduous, and accents become more permanent.

Accents are another factor in early language development influencing the rate of language acquisition and are also one of the most prominent ways in which cultures encounter each other in everyday interaction (Johnson, van Heugten, & Buckler, 2022). Accents, like languages themselves, are a form of cultural boundary, fluid rather than geographically fixed, and reflect another way that cultures cohere internally while at the same time repelling outside influences. The ability to gauge cultural membership from accents is acquired soon after speech; from the age of four or five, cultural members can recognize each other as well as isolate and discriminate against outsiders automatically by accent (Chakraborty, 2007; Weatherhead, White, & Friedman, 2015). Accents may be used intentionally aggressively against members of other cultures or as a means of cultural appropriation (Nath, 2011; Alcido, McCallen, & Ramdeen-Chowdhury, 2022). Alternatively, accents may be adopted as camouflage by those who otherwise would experience this form of linguistic discrimination (Nath, 2011). Nor is this form of discrimination limited only to national origin. Sexual orientation may also be detected and attacked on the basis of perceived speech, as vividly expressed in the documentary film *Do I Sound Gay?* (Thorpe, 2015).

DOI: 10.4324/9781003300380-15

Exposition, Confrontation, and Simulation

Discussion might begin with surveying the number of languages in the world and then finding out how many are in use in the immediate area; a starting point can be the interactive graphic map of languages spoken in New York City (Perlin et al., 2021). The UNESCO Atlas of the World's Languages in Danger (UNESCO, 2011) shows how vulnerable many languages are to extinction. Interaction might occur around the question "Suppose you are the last speaker of ________. What would you most want to preserve about this language, and how would you go about doing it?"

As an entry into pre-linguistics, try to set up and perform a complex task entirely without using spoken language. A most effective interactive experience of the immigrant experience and also of the problems inherent in second language acquisition after the critical period for multilinguality can be set up by enlisting native speakers of another language to interact suddenly with a class (or individually via recording online) using their own language—unfamiliar to the group and spoken rapidly—to command a response to tasks to be performed in an intake area. Question members of the group during and after the experience regarding the meaning of what was said as well as their emotional reactions.

Accents are often encountered on the phone as many service workers are immigrants or members of different subcultures. A simulation of a call center can be set up with both native speakers and accented ones, and reactions to different voices may be surveyed. Discrimination based on accent is illegal in many places, and a search for and survey of the laws surrounding accents will be instructive. Finally, though language and accents may be a means of discrimination and exclusion, accents can be interesting and even beautiful in their own right. The Speech Accent Archive at George Mason University (Weinberger, 2015)—which offers a bountiful collection of speakers of dozens of languages, representing all ages and genders, saying the same paragraph-length phrase in English—might be explored to see which accents are most readily perceived and also which are judged pleasant (very likely all of them!).

References and Suggested Readings

Alcido, M., McCallen, M., & Ramdeen-Chowdhury, K. (2022, February 11). How 'Blaccents' appropriate Black culture, and why they've flown under the radar for decades. *theSkimm* (online news magazine). Retrieved from www.theskimm.com/news/how-blaccents-appropriate-black-culture-and-why-theyve-flown-under-the-radar

Brandt, A., Gebrian, M., & Slevc, L. R. (2012, September 11). Music and early language acquisition. *Frontiers in Psychology*, *3*, 327 (online open access). Retrieved from http://journal.frontiersin.org/article/10.3389/fpsyg.2012.00327/full (https://doi.org/10.3389/fpsyg.2012.00327).

Chakraborty, R. (2007). A short note on accent-bias, social identity, and ethnocentrism. *Advances in Language and Literary Studies*, *8*(4), 57–64.

Darwin Correspondence Project. (2017). The origin of language. *University of Cambridge, Darwin Correspondence Project* (online website for the Darwin Correspondence Project). Retrieved from www.darwinproject.ac.uk/commentary/human-nature/origin-language

Johnson, E. K., van Heugten, M., & Buckler, H. (2022). Navigating accent variation: A developmental perspective. *Annual Review of Linguistics*, *8*, 365–387. Retrieved from www.annualreviews.org/doi/10.1146/annurev-linguistics-032521-053717#:~:text=At%20approximately%2019%20months%20of,unfamiliar%20accents%20(Best%20et%20al

Kuhl, P. K. (2010). Brain mechanisms in early language acquisition. *Neuron*, *67*(5), 713–727.

Kuijsten, M. (Ed.). (2016). *Gods, voices, and the bicameral mind: The theories of Julian Jaynes*. Henderson, NV: The Julian Jaynes Society.

Levelt, W. (2014). *A history of psycholinguistics: The Pre-Chomskyan era*. New York, NY: Oxford University Press.

Liszkowski, U., Brown, P., Callaghan, T., Takada, A., & de Vos, C. (2012). A prelinguistic gestural universal of human communication. *Cognitive Science*, *36*(4), 698–713.

Nath, V. (2011). Aesthetic and emotional labor through stigma: National identity management and racial abuse in offshored Indian call centres. *Work, Employment, and Society*, *25*(4), 709–725.

Perlin, R., Kaufman, D., Lampel, J., Daurio, M., Turin, M., & Craig, S. (Eds.). (2021). *Languages of New York City (digital version)*. New York, NY: Endangered Language Alliance. Retrieved from https://languagemap.nyc/Info/About

Thorpe, D. (Director). (2015). *Do I sound gay? (film)*. Brooklyn, NY: Impact Partners/Little Punk/Think Thorpe.

UNESCO. (2011). *UNESCO atlas of the world's languages in danger* (online atlas, United Nations Educational, Scientific, and Cultural Organization). Retrieved from https://unesdoc.unesco.org/ark:/48223/pf0000187026

Weatherhead, D., White, K. S., & Friedman, O. (2015). Where are you from? Preschoolers infer background from accent. *Journal of Experimental Child Psychology*, *143*, 171–178.

Weinberger, S. (2015). *Speech accent archive* (online open-source archive). Retrieved from http://accent.gmu.edu/

Imaginative Literature and Translation

Imaginative writers have always intuitively understood culture. Expatriate novelist Jean Rhys explicitly compared reading to immigration. T. S. Eliot (1949) addressed culture directly. Some channeled other cultures so completely that their transformation was acknowledged by critics, for instance Franz Kafka, who, many say, metamorphosed into a person with a Chinese outlook (Hsia, 1996; Zeng, 2022). Social science has long observed a lack of attention to the role of imaginative literature and its cognates, drama and screenplay, in the understanding of culture (Albrecht, 1954), and it is true that theory and the experimental attitude dominate. But this is paradoxical, since the intimate relation of literature and culture in all their varieties is attested to in psychology, both theoretically (Rieber & Kelly, 2014) and in practice in psychology and its cognate fields. Those wishing to put the reading and analysis of texts for their cultural character into a theoretical frame may avail themselves of the idea of the "social imaginary" (Taylor, 2004), the totality of social relations and practices internalized by members of a society in order to make sense of their collective existence, which concept has been expanded to the "cultural imaginary" (Vandevoort, Clycq, &Verschraegen, 2018). Searching for specific types of literature or film will lead to reservoirs of attractive material. Ethnographic films, for instance, are available and underutilized (Lemelson, 2014). More attention has been given to translation within cross-cultural psychology. This occurs most often in connection with the process of "back-translation," a process designed to enable, as far as possible, English-language materials and the concepts they embody to be utilized in non-English speaking countries (World Health Organization, n.d.). However, the question of translation extends well beyond the exporting of Western science. From a historical perspective, many of the founding documents of psychology were written in languages other than English and persuasive cases can be made for their having been mistranslated or culturally misconstrued (Kermode, 1983). The deep intertwining of culture and translation (Cutler, 2017) and the persistent idea that some texts and ideas are untranslatable should suggest caution to anyone venturing into literature as a way of understanding culture. Nonetheless, much vividness will be missed by not doing so.

Exposition, Confrontation, and Simulation

More specific exercises can be sketched for practice in translation and back-translation than for the introduction of literature into the cross-cultural curriculum. Short measurement instruments with a cultural purpose can be readily translated if there are some bilingual members in the class or group to translate and explain their translations. Some

DOI: 10.4324/9781003300380-16

attention can be given to the idea of untranslatability: suggestions can be solicited of words, ideas, or experiences that are hard to describe and then matched up with various lists of untranslatable words readily available on the internet and also in a recent *Scientific American* article (Lomas, 2016). Turning to literature, enlistment of experts in literary studies would be essential in seeking suggestions for how to get psychologists to engage with imaginative texts. Design of a regional reading list will lead to better understanding of the region as well as the reading. But the first choice of text will sometimes obviate the need for specific motivators for engagement. While I was searching for information on Max Graf, the Austrian musicologist who was a friend of both Freud and Gustav Mahler, the indefatigable Google provided, through the medium of Google Books, two captivating chapters of the autobiography of Lotfi Mansouri (1929–2013) co-authored with Donald Arthur, *Lotfi Mansouri: An Operatic Journey* (Mansouri & Arthur, 2010). Mansouri was an ebullient opera impresario who was born in Iran and eventually made himself at home in cultures worldwide. His storytelling—for instance of his trip back to Iran in 1970 after an absence of 23 years, including the episode of having to run through jammed traffic to rescue his two passports from a traffic jam pickpocket (!)—is hilarious. His poignant and accurate account of the psychic terrors he experienced in not having a home culture, even as a widely successful man, and the therapy that pulled him through those, give insight into the level at which culture and the psyche interact that can't be understood except in the near-face-to-face encounter that narrative provides. Of course, I'm an opera fan: I would gravitate to this serendipitous find. But other finds await regardless of taste: see for example Norman Van Aken's account of his chef's career and its intersections with the polyglot cultures of the US food scene (Van Aken, 2013). All that is creative is cultural.

References and Suggested Readings

Albrecht, M. C. (1954). The relationship of literature and society. *American Journal of Sociology, 59*, 425–436.

Cutler, S. (2017, March 9). What the act of translation reveals. *Brigham Young University Humanities Department Website* (online). Retrieved from https://humanities.byu.edu/what-the-act-of-translation-reveals/ [Accessed February 24, 2023].

Eliot, T. S. (1949). *Notes toward the definition of culture*. New York, NY: Harcourt, Brace, & Co. Retrieved from https://ia801501.us.archive.org/22/items/in.ernet.dli.2015.159230/2015.159230.Notes-Towards-The-Definition-Of-Culture.pdf [Accessed February 20, 2023].

Hsia, A. (Ed.). (1996). *Kafka and China*. Bern: Peter Lang AG.

Kermode, F. (1983, February 6). Freud is better in German. *The New York Times* (Online Newspaper). Retrieved from https://archive.nytimes.com/www.nytimes.com/books/00/06/25/specials/kermode-betterlheim.html?mcubz=. [Accessed February 24, 2023].

Lemelson, R. (2014, February 12). 20 Ethnographic and documentary films psychological anthropologists should be teaching. *Psychocultural Cinema* (Online Resource). Retrieved from http://psychoculturalcinema.com/20-ethnographic-and-documentary-films-psychological-anthropologists-should-be-teaching/ [Accessed March 25, 2023].

Lomas, T. (2016, July 12). The magic of "untranslatable" words. *Scientific American* (Online Magazine). Retrieved from www.scientificamerican.com/article/the-magic-of-untranslatable-words/ [Accessed February 24, 2023].

Mansouri, L., & Arthur, D. (2010). *Lotfi Mansouri: An operatic journey*. Boston, MA: Northeastern University Press.

Rieber, R. W., & Kelly, R. J. (2014). *Film, television, and the psychology of the social dream*. New York, NY: Springer-Verlag.

Taylor, C. (2004). What is a “social imaginary”? In C. Taylor (Ed.), *Modern social imaginaries* (pp. 23–29). Durham, NC: Duke University Press.
Van Aken, N. (2013). *No experience necessary: The culinary Odyssey of Norman Van Aken*. New York, NY: Taylor Trade.
Vandevoort, R., Clycq, N., & Verschraegen, G. (2018). Studying culture through imaginaries: Some reflections on the relevance of imaginaries for the social sciences. In H. Alma & G. Vanheeswijck (Eds.), *Social imaginaries in a globalizing world* (pp. 167–192). Berlin: De Gruyter.
World Health Organization. (n.d.). WHODAS 2.0 Translation Package. *World Health Organization Disability Assessment Schedule Website*. Retrieved from https://terrance.who.int/mediacentre/data/WHODAS/Guidelines/WHODAS%202.0%20Translation%20guidelines.pdf. [Accessed March 25, 2023].
Zeng, Y. (2022). *Franz Kafka and Chinese culture*. London, England: Palgrave Macmillan.

Dystopias and Utopias

Dystopias and utopias are underutilized probes for gaining a synoptic view of cultures everywhere. In the same way that war is more interesting than peace, dystopias are often more arresting and attractive than accounts of cultures working well. Classic literary dystopias, such as *Brave New World* (Huxley, 1932), vie with films old, for example *Metropolis* (Lang & Von Harbou, 2002), and new, for example *The Hunger Games* (Ross, 2012), to reveal the seamy side of cultures. A range of cultural observers have characterized recent US history as dystopian (or utopian, depending on their political alignment) (Brodman & Doan, 2019). I confess that, as an observer of US culture, my all-time favorite cultural portrait of at least some parts of the United States is *Idiocracy* (Judge, 2006), though it is only of middling tomato rank on the Rotten Tomatoes film-rating website (there's no accounting for (my) bad taste). There's a shortage of humor in dystopia (and in cross-cultural studies generally); this less-serious film can be a springboard for entering the world of cross-cultural comedy and humor as well.

Exposition, Confrontation, and Simulation

Gendler (2016) provides a useful brief overview of the utopia/dystopia dichotomy. Dystopias are preeminently cinematic, and many lists of dystopian films are available online (e.g., Santoni, 2018, lists mostly pre-2000 classics). There purport to be gaming simulations of both utopias and dystopias; exercise care when accessing. Likewise, there are many lists of dystopian fiction, modern and classic, typically created in WEIRD cultures (Western, Educated, Industrialized, Rich, and Democratic) (Pan Macmillan, 2023). An approach could be to find, read, and compare the many dystopian authors not well known in the United States (e.g., Bina Shah).

Dystopias are often centered in cities; culturally contrastive readings in this vein might be selected from Prakash's (2010) collection of essays connected to contemporary city life. Also consider reading Boo (2012) on the realities of life in a Mumbai slum or the various accounts of the planned futuristic utopian Saudi line city, Neom (e.g., Heathcote, 2022).

Finally, all is not lost. After a showing of your favorite dystopic film, design a utopian antidote using the template in Bufe and Hubbard's *Design Your Own Utopia* (Bufe & Hubbard, n.d.). Will a utopia contain one or many cultures?

References and Suggested Readings

Boo, K. (2012). *Behind the beautiful forevers: Life, death, and hope in a Mumbai undercity*. New York, NY: Random House.

DOI: 10.4324/9781003300380-17

Brodman, B., & Doan, J. E. (Eds.). (2019). *Utopia and dystopia in the age of Trump: Images from literature and visual arts*. Lanham, MD: Rowman & Littlefield.

Bufe, C., & Hubbard, L. (n.d.). Design your own utopia (Pamphlet posted on). *See Sharp Press website* (online resource of See Sharp Press, Tucson, AZ). Retrieved from www.seesharppress.com/utopia.html

Gendler, A. (2016). How to recognize a dystopia. *TedEd* (online video resource). Retrieved from https://ed.ted.com/lessons/how-to-recognize-a-dystopia-alex-gendler

Heathcote, E. (2022, August 1). Saudi's Neom is dystopia portrayed as Utopia. *Financial Times* (online news magazine). Retrieved from www.ft.com/content/04fcb9d4-5907-45b0-9388-f84b34bc4bea

Huxley, A. (1932). *Brave new world*. London, England: Chatto & Windus.

Judge, M. (Director and Screenplay). (2006). *Idiocracy* (film). Los Angeles, CA: 20th Century Fox/Ternion Pictures.

Lang, F. (Director) & Von Harbou, T. (Screenplay). (2002). *Metropolis* (film). New York, NY: Kino on Video (Originally produced by UFA in 1927).

Pan Macmillan. (2023, January 13). 22 of the best dystopian novels of all time. *Pan Macmillan Website* (corporate website). Retrieved from www.panmacmillan.com/blogs/literary/the-best-dystopian-novels-of-all-time

Prakash, G. (Ed.). (2010). *Noir urbanisms: Dystopic images of the modern city*. Princeton, NJ: Princeton University Press.

Ross, G. (Director). (2012). *The hunger games* (film). Vancouver, British Columbia, Canada: Lionsgate.

Santoni, E. (2018, December 12). 20 great dystopian films that are worth your time. *IMDb* (online). Retrieved from www.imdb.com/list/ls047658484/?ref_=otl_5

Silences

"Whereof one cannot speak, thereof one must be silent."
—Ludwig Wittgenstein, *Tractatus Logico-Philosophicus 7.1* (trans. Caws, 2006)

Exposition, Confrontation, and Simulation

See references.

References and Suggested Readings

Austin, D. (2021, March 26). What you're saying when you give someone the silent treatment. *The Atlantic* (online magazine). Retrieved from www.theatlantic.com/family/archive/2021/03/psychology-of-silent-treatment-abuse/618411//

Caws, P. (2006, November–December). Tractatus 7.1: Translation and silence. *Philosophy Now: A Magazine of Ideas*, p. 58 (online magazine). Retrieved from https://philosophynow.org/issues/58/Tractatus_71_Translation_and_Silence

Daniels, D. (2016). Silence and void: Aesthetics of absence in space and time. In Y. Kaduri (Ed.), *The Oxford handbook of sound and image in Western art* (online reference). New York, NY: Oxford University Press. Retrieved from https://doi.org/10.1093/oxfordhb/9780199841547.013.11

Finkel, D. (2000). *Teaching with your mouth shut.* Portsmouth, NH: Heinemann.

Kolb, R. (2017, November 3). Sensations of sound: On deafness and music. *The New York Times* (online newspaper). Retrieved from www.nytimes.com/2017/11/03/opinion/cochlear-implant-sound-music.html?_r=0

Krajewski, S., & Schröder, H. (2008). Silence and taboo. In G. Antos & E. Ventola in Cooperation with T. Weber, *Handbook of interpersonal communication* (pp. 595–621). Berlin, Germany and New York, NY: Mouton De Gruyter.

Mannion, R., & Davies, H. T. (2015). Cultures of silence and cultures of voice: The role of whistle-blowing in healthcare organisations. *International Journal of Health Policy and Management*, *4*(8), 503–505.

Noelle-Neumann, E. (1991). The theory of public opinion: The concept of the Spiral of Silence. In J. A. Anderson (Ed.), *Communication yearbook* (Vol. 14, pp. 256–287). Newbury Park, CA: Sage.

Novic, S. (2022, July 19). Silence brought me a community and an escape. *The New York Times* (online newspaper). Retrieved from www.nytimes.com/2022/07/19/magazine/silence-deafness.html

Shakespeare, W. (1609). *Sonnet 30.* Retrieved from https://www.poetryfoundation.org/poems/45091/sonnet-30-when-to-the-sessions-of-sweet-silent-thought

Spaeth, D. (2014, September 25). Silence, shunning, and shying away: Destroying personhood and connection through preserving the peace. *New Existentialists Posts, Saybrook University* (online). Retrieved from www.saybrook.edu/2014/09/25/09-25-14/

DOI: 10.4324/9781003300380-18

Identity

DOI: 10.4324/9781003300380-19

Globality, Biculturality, and Multiculturality

Often, cross-cultural psychology emphasizes differences between cultures and preservation of cultural identity, for instance the identity and practices of indigenous peoples. The concepts identified in this entry's title challenge the idea of separate and preservable cultures (to say nothing of permanent social or racial differences) and suggest that—perhaps not at present but soon—there will be more de-differentiation, intermingling, and cultural blending. An approach to this set of concepts from a specifically cross-cultural psychological direction can begin with consulting the work of Angela-Minh Tu D. Nguyen, who has written extensively on the conceptual foundations of biculturalism (including the entry in the *Encyclopedia of Cross-Cultural Psychology*, Nguyen, 2013) and also on the relation between bilingualism, socialization practices, and biculturality (Nguyen & Ahmadpanah, 2014).

Exposition, Confrontation, and Simulation

This can be a naturally confrontational topic, since it directly opposes strident monoculturalism and monolingualism. The bigotry associated with these positions can be contextualized historically in psychology by consulting and directly discussing accounts of it, personal and professional (e.g., Sue, 2001). A less direct way of addressing specifically monocultural and often racist undertones to ordinary everyday reference to other people can be unpacked by designing a revised "identity" question for the demographic section of research or census questionnaires. This survey of the myriad of cultures each individual carries with them—gender, ancestry, tastes, activities, occupations, and also national identity/ies—would also be desirable as an opening exercise in any course (United States Census Bureau, 2020). Alongside this, use of the historically racist term "Caucasian" as an indicator of—whatever it indicates—can be challenged and hopefully demolished (Khan, 2011, Shamambo & Henry, 2022). From a psychological measurement perspective, several biculturality and multiculturality scales might be constructed from the items on the wide variety of cultural-specific scales developed over the past several decades (e.g., Davis & Engel, 2011; Basilio et al., 2015; Mezzich, Ruiperez, Yoon, Liu, & Zapata-Vega, 2009; Tropp, Erkut, Coll, Alarcon, & Vazquez-Garcia, 1999), utilizing the Multicultural Ideology Scale (Lefringhausen, Berry, Grigoryev, & Stogianni, 2022) as a theoretical starting point.

References and Suggested Readings

Basilio, C. D., Knight, G. P., O'Donnell, M., Roosa, M. W., Umaña-Taylor, A. J., & Torres, M. (2015). The Mexican American Biculturalism Scale: Bicultural comfort, facility, and advantages for adolescents and adults. *Psychological Assessment*, *26*(2), 539–554.

DOI: 10.4324/9781003300380-20

Davis, L. E., & Engel, R. (2011). *Measuring race and ethnicity*. New York, NY: Springer-Verlag.

Khan, R. (2011, January 22). Stop using the word "Caucasian" to mean white. *Discover Magazine (Gene Expression blog)* (Online). Retrieved from http://blogs.discovermagazine.com/gnxp/2011/01/stop-using-the-word-caucasian-to-mean-white/#.Wc_oYORhjIU [Accessed February 25, 2023].

Lefringhausen, K., Berry, J., Grigoryev, D., & Stogianni, M. (2022, November 24). Validation of the Revised Multicultural Ideology Scale (MCI-r) in the UK. *Psychological Reports* (Online First). Retrieved from https://journals.sagepub.com/doi/epub/10.1177/00332941221142002 [Accessed February 25, 2023].

Mezzich, J. E., Ruiperez, M. A., Yoon, G., Liu, J., & Zapata-Vega, M. I. (2009). Measuring cultural identity: Validation of a modified Cortes, Rogler, and Malgady Bicultural Scale in three ethnic groups in New York. *Culture, Medicine, and Psychiatry*, *33*(3), 451–472.

Nguyen, A. M. D. (2013). Biculturalism. In K. Keith (Ed.), *Encyclopedia of cross-cultural psychology* (pp. 132–134). New York, NY: Wiley-Blackwell.

Nguyen, A. M. D., & Ahmadpanah, S. S. (2014). The interplay between bicultural blending and dual language acquisition. *Journal of Cross-Cultural Psychology*, *45*, 1215–1220.

Shamambo, L. J., & Henry, T. L. (2022, February 25). Rethinking the use of "Caucasian" in clinical language and curricula: A trainee's call to action. *Journal of General Internal Medicine* (online). Retrieved from https://link.springer.com/article/10.1007/s11606-022-07431-6 [Accessed February 25, 2023].

Sue, D. W. (2001). Surviving monoculturalism and racism: A personal and professional journey. In J. G. Ponterotto, J. M. Casas, L. A. Suzuki, & C. M. Alexander (Eds.), *Handbook of multicultural counseling* (2nd ed., pp. 45–54). Thousand Oaks, CA: Sage.

Tropp, L. R., Erkut, S., Coll, C. G., Alarcon, O., & Vazquez-Garcia, H. A. (1999). Psychosocial acculturation: Development of a new measure for Puerto Ricans on the U.S. mainland. *Educational and Psychological Measurement*, *59*, 351–357.

United States Census Bureau (2020). Decennial census of population and housing questionnaires & instructions. *United States Census Bureau Website*. Retrieved from www.census.gov/programs-surveys/decennial-census/technical-documentation/questionnaires.2020_Census.html [Accessed February 25, 2023].

WEIRD

Weird can mean strange, but, in cultural psychology at present, WEIRD—an acronym for "Western, Educated, Industrialized, Rich, and Democratic"—has become a widely prominent concept. It was originally proposed by Joseph Henrich and colleagues in 2010 (Henrich, Heine, & Norenzayan, 2010) as a mnemonic describing a collection of features of societies, especially the United States, overrepresented in samples used in cross-cultural research. Originally, it was directed toward correcting this research bias, but since that time, Henrich has extended WEIRD to represent an underlying sociohistorical dynamic that has propelled those societies to dominant positions in the world (Henrich, 2020). Though this formulation is not without critics (e.g. Syed, 2021), an attempt at explicating WEIRD has led an international group of researchers, Henrich among them, to construct a metric of cultural difference based on the fixation ratio in population genetics, treating individual responses to surveys of cultural perceptions and values as analogous to alleles (Muthukrishna et al., 2020). The resulting table of differences (calculated between countries) ramifies the WEIRD concept but also suggests that this combination of elements has more widely diffused across the world than its creators may have originally imagined. At the very least, this explicatory project combines several major theoretical elements (including the 2014 World Values Survey and subscales (Inglehart et al., 2014) and its morally-debatable scale, Hofstede's cultural dimensions, Schwartz's cultural values, tight vs. loose cultures, the NEO 5-factor personality system, a corruption scale, linguistic relatedness, and geographic proximity) and can serve as a ready reference for these.

Exposition, Confrontation, and Simulation

The WEIRD concept and the Muthukrishna et al. cultural distance scale are both intuitive and, as such, readily lend themselves to speculative discussion. Muthukrishna et al.'s research report cited here provides calculated distances relative to the United States and China. They also, however, provide R code to enable the calculation of a distance measure between any countries, and those with moderate statistical competence could create these comparisons and discuss their face and ecological validity. Discussion of WEIRD could start by examining the premise that sampling in cross-cultural research studies is preponderantly drawn from societies with those characteristics. Examine sampling in published studies in available cross-cultural psychology journals or as open-source on the web; tabulate and describe the sample compositions. Critiques of WEIRD can be simulated by suggesting alternatives to the letters of the acronym. For example, Clancy and Davis (2019) replace "W" with "white." Another approach could be to consider whether WEIRD is similar to another five-letter acronym of historical importance in

DOI: 10.4324/9781003300380-21

clinical psychology, YAVIS (Howes, 2009). YAVIS (Young, Attractive, Verbal, Intelligent, and Successful) was said to represent the ideal psychotherapy client; perhaps WEIRD similarly describes an ideal individual in Western (or US) culture or possibly specifies a preferred combination conferring the opposite of weird or strange—normality and rationality.

References and Suggested Readings

Clancy, K. B. H., & Davis, J. L. (2019). Soylent is people and WEIRD is white: Biological anthropology, whiteness, and the limits of the WEIRD. *Annual Review of Anthropology*, *48*, 169–186.

Henrich, J. (2020). *The WEIRDest people in the world: How the West became psychologically peculiar and particularly prosperous*. New York, NY: Farrar, Straus & Giroux.

Henrich, J., Heine, S. J., & Norenzayan, A. (2010). The weirdest people in the world? *Behavioral and Brain Sciences*, *33*, 61–83.

Howes, R. (2009, December 30). The ideal psychotherapy client: Are you a YAVIS? *Psychology Today* (online magazine). Retrieved from www.psychologytoday.com/us/blog/in-therapy/200912/the-ideal-psychotherapy-client

Inglehart, R., Haerpfer, C., Moreno, A., Welzel, C., Kizilova, K., Diez-Medrano, J., Lagos, M., Norris, P., Ponarin, E., & Puranen, B. (Eds.). (2014). *World values survey: Round six – Country-pooled datafile version*. Madrid, Spain: JD Systems Institute. Retrieved from www.worldvaluessurvey.org/WVSDocumentationWV6.jsp

Muthukrishna, M., Bell, A. V., Henrich, J., Curtin, C. M., Gedranovich, A., McInerney, J., & Thue, B. (2020). Beyond Western, Educated, Industrial, Rich, and Democratic (WEIRD) psychology: Measuring and mapping scales of cultural and psychological distance. *Psychological Science*, *31*(6), 678–701. Retrieved from https://journals.sagepub.com/doi/full/10.1177/0956797620916782

Syed, M. (2021, June 10). WEIRD times: Three reasons to stop using a silly acronym. *Get Syeducated* (professional blog). Retrieved from http://getsyeducated.blogspot.com/2021/06/weird-times-three-reasons-to-stop-using.html

Names and Naming

Names have profound connections to the roots of all cultures. Some names are sacred, so much so that they are surrounded by mystery and secrecy and are not to be pronounced. Many names have origins in religious traditions, connecting to figures less secret but no less honored. Some names confer power—for instance, titles attached to names. At the most mundane level, names can be pointers, not necessarily absolute, to at least the following important information: family membership, nationality, linguistic community, conformity or nonconformity to social norms, religious affiliation, subgroup or subculture membership (e.g., Amish names), age cohort, gender, criminality (e.g., mob nicknames), and geographical position within a region (e.g., Varnum & Kitayama, 2011). In cultural studies, naming and cultural linguistics are linked. In psychology, naming leads mainly to studies of neurocognitive performance or deficit, but a little digging can uncover interesting cross-cultural connections (e.g., Watzlawick, Guimarães, Han, & Jung, 2016).

Exposition, Confrontation, and Simulation

Many interactive demonstrations of the cultural power and complexity of naming are possible. Luckily, the materials for these are portable and easily accessible—individuals' names! Tracing the origin of names can lead to genealogy and immigration history. Distribution of names can be viewed with an eye to understanding how rapidly populations are merging worldwide—for instance, via Forebears.io (Hopkins, 2017; Nguyen, 2015) or other websites that provide world maps of surnames.

The question of whether a name can be changed, and how, can also be investigated. Ask individuals to suggest a name that they would choose if they had to "pass" in another culture and describe the reasons for the choice of that particular name. Examine the gender-specificity of names in the immediate environment, and extend this to cultures worldwide (Oyewumi, 1998). The power of elevating as well shaming by naming can also be examined, in local contexts as well as in the larger world political environment (Pizano, 2014), with examples given of both honoring and dismissing politically and socially significant individuals. Discussion of whether and how to use a first name instead of a formal title can be an interesting exercise in tracing power relationships and levels of respect (Lawrence-Lightfoot, 2000). Who in your immediate environment would you never call by a first name?

The discussion of naming need not be focused only on humans and human cultures; pets, countries, behavioral practices, and products need names too. Experiment with naming new sandwiches, businesses, or furniture that will be distributed worldwide—

DOI: 10.4324/9781003300380-22

trying to choose names that will be culturally universal and also culturally inoffensive (Gabler, 2015; Quito, 2017). Relatively recently, pronouns—grammatical replacements for names—have become prominent as symbols of gender identity (BBC, 2019). Discussion might turn on whether publicly declaring one's pronouns ought to be compulsory or whether controversies about gender and pronouns cross cultural boundaries (e.g., Bonnin & Coronel, 2021).

References and Suggested Readings

BBC. (2019, September 22). A brief history of gender neutral pronouns. *BBC Newsbeat (British Broadcasting Corporation Website)*. Retrieved from www.bbc.com/news/newsbeat-49754930

Bonnin, J. E., & Coronel, A. A. (2021, March 15). Attitudes toward gender-neutral Spanish: Acceptability and adoptability. *Frontiers in Sociology (Section Gender, Sex, and Sexualities)*, 6 (online). Retrieved from www.frontiersin.org/articles/10.3389/fsoc.2021.629616/full

Gabler, N. (2015, January 15). The weird science of naming new products. *The New York Times* (online). Retrieved from www.nytimes.com/2015/01/18/magazine/the-weird-science-of-naming-new-products.html

Hopkins, D., et al. (2017). *Forebears website* (genealogical source) (online). Retrieved from http://forebears.io/surnames

Lawrence-Lightfoot, S. (2000). *Respect: An exploration*. Cambridge, MA: Perseus Books.

Nguyen, C. (2015, November 2). Here's a global heatmap of people with your last name. *Vice Motherboard* (online magazine). Retrieved from www.vice.com/en/article/mg7qwb/heres-a-global-heatmap-of-people-with-your-last-name

Oyewumi, O. (1998). Making history, creating gender: Some methodological and interpretive questions in the writing of Oyo oral traditions. *African History*, *25*, 263–305.

Pizano, P. (2014, August 5). The power of naming and shaming. *Foreign Policy* (online magazine). Retrieved from https://foreignpolicy.com/2014/08/05/the-power-of-naming-and-shaming/

Quito, A. (2017, January 30). The secret taxonomy behind IKEA's product names, from Billy to Poang. *Quartz* (online magazine). Retrieved from https://qz.com/896146/how-ikea-names-its-products-the-curious-taxonomy-behind-billy-poang-malm-kallax-and-rens/

Varnum, M. E. W., & Kitayama, S. (2011). What's in a name? Popular names are less common on frontiers. *Psychological Science*, *22*(2), 176–183.

Watzlawick, M., Guimarães, D. S., Han, M., & Jung, A. J. (2016). First names as signs of personal identity: An intercultural comparison. *Psychology & Society*, *8*(1), 1–21.

Sexuality

Sex and sexuality can be daunting in terms of the sheer bulk of references to them in both general psychology (114 separate terms refer to sex or sexuality in the *APA Dictionary of Psychology*) and cross-cultural psychology (there are 14 separate index headings and 8 separate entries for sex-related material in the *Encyclopedia of Cross-Cultural Psychology* or ECCP). For comparison, aggression (probably at least as important in terms of interpersonal relations) has only a single ECCP entry. Sexuality intersects with aggression (sexual assault, rape) and also with feeling (ranging from pain and pleasure during sex activity to the absence of sexual feeling or sexual anesthesia). On the sociocultural side, sexuality connects to social roles and individual identity, positive and negative attitudes toward sex (Gregerson, 2013), and sexual value systems. On the biopsychological side, sexuality connects to cognitive processing differences, genetically linked behaviors across species including specific courtship rituals, and evolutionarily determined mating strategies (Buss, 2006). Some overtones of the older Freudian psychology still hover around the topic as well.

Probably the most pressing issue in sexuality within culture currently is the conflict between thinking of sex and sexuality as expressions of an underlying mutually exclusive gender dichotomy between *male* and *female* and thinking in terms of gender fluidity within a proliferating range of intermediate forms of both gender membership and sexual expression. Some psychologists and psychiatrists consider this class of *nonbinary* or *genderqueer* individuals as a group subject worldwide to marginalization and repression (Richards et al., 2016), as indeed it is. While discrimination against sexual orientation is officially prohibited in several African countries, for instance, persecution of gender-nonconforming behavior is frequent and often cruel and can be a cause for flight and applications for asylum (Ghelli, 2014).

Exposition, Confrontation, and Simulation

Obviously, real interactive education in the physical dimensions of sexuality would be difficult to specify in a series of lesson plans. However, theoretical attention might be directed to any of the many areas to which sexuality connects. Exploration of the variety and nuance of sexual self-definition is a first priority; information on definition and on scale composition is readily available (e.g. Ferguson, 2020; McGuire, Beek, Catalpa, & Steensma, 2019). Rebecca Merkin (2008) has a brief, adaptable questionnaire that could be used for exploration of the question of the relation of sexual aggression to cultural characteristics in the perception of sexual harassment.

DOI: 10.4324/9781003300380-23

More positively, the concept of intimacy may be a good place to start a discussion that indirectly contacts the more physical dimensions of sexuality. William Jankowiak's (2008) edited volume on intimacy traces multiple aspects of universal romantic love (and its violations) across a wide spectrum of cultures. Included in it are, among many others, studies of infidelity in Papua New Guinea, intimacy and masculinity in Nigeria, and Indonesian wedding night stories, all of which should prove to be interesting departure points for conversation about personal experiences with intimacy and other aspects of sexuality.

References and Suggested Readings

Buss, D. (2006). Strategies of human mating. *Psychological Topics*, *15*(2), 239–260.

Ferguson, S. (2020, January 29). What does the Kinsey Scale have to do with your sexuality? *Healthline* (online health information source). Retrieved from www.healthline.com/health/kinsey-scale#origin

Ghelli, T. (2014, December 16). UNHCR helps gay Congolese rejected by his mother find a new home. *UNHCR (The United Nations Refugee Agency) Website* (online). Retrieved from www.unhcr.org/en-us/news/makingdifference/2014/12/54905cf39/unhcr-helps-gay-congolese-rejected-mother-find-new-home.html

Gregerson, M. (2013). Sex: Cultural context. In K. Keith (Ed.), *Encyclopedia of cross-cultural psychology* (pp. 1157–1161). New York, NY: Wiley-Blackwell.

Jankowiak, W. R. (Ed.). (2008). *Intimacies: Love and sex across cultures*. New York, NY: Columbia University Press.

McGuire, J. K., Beek, T. F., Catalpa, J. M., & Steensma, T. D. (2019). The Genderqueer Identity (GQI) Scale: Measurement and validation of four distinct subscales with trans and LGBQ clinical and community samples in two countries. *International Journal of Transgenderism*, *20*(2–3), 289–304. Retrieved from www.ncbi.nlm.nih.gov/pmc/articles/PMC6830987/

Merkin, R. S. (2008). Cross-cultural differences in perceiving sexual harassment: Demographic incidence rates of sexual harassment/sexual aggression in Latin America. *North American Journal of Psychology*, *10*(2), 277–290. Retrieved from www.researchgate.net/publication/259220569_Cross-cultural_differences_in_perceiving_sexual_harassment_Demographic_incidence_rates_of_sexual_harassmentsexual_aggression_in_Latin_America

Richards, C., Bouman, W. P., Seal, L., Barker, M. J., Nieder, T. O., & T'Sjoen, G. (2016). Non-binary or genderqueer genders. *International Review of Psychiatry*, *28*(1), 95–102. https://doi.org/10.3109/09540261.2015.1106446

Women's Roles and Rights

Neither of the two terms in the title of this entry is indexed in the most recent *APA Dictionary of Psychology*. It seems a reasonable starting point to assert that rights are rights, irrespective of gender or sex, and have been seen so ever since Olympe de Gouges, who should be read at the start, and Mary Wollstonecraft. Some cultural theorists, however, reinforce ideas of specific, and often derogatory, inequality between women and others (e.g., by emphasizing the universality of relatively greater frequency of involvement in direct childcare by women or by describing cultures in terms of *masculine* and *feminine* values—drive for success, for example, for the former; nurturance for the latter). These asymmetries—which easily become inequalities in popular as well as academic discourse—are in themselves worth discussing. More to the point for this particular topic would be discussion about why the fundamental right to vote was awarded to women in the United States nearly 150 years after the country was founded and why proposed constitutional amendments guaranteeing equal rights for women and men have foundered since that time at both state and national levels. A discussion of this history would be in keeping with the feminism of current psychology (Isanski, 2009; Rutherford & Pettit, 2015).

Exposition, Confrontation, and Simulation

Mostly confrontation is recommended here. Spirited discussion can be had, more so if the surrounding culture is high in power distance (i.e., inequality) and highly masculine in the Hofstede system. The following two suggestions are offered to start:

1 In all countries, work is necessary and a primary form of self-definition and self-regard. Regarding compensated work only, it is also a worldwide phenomenon that women's work is compensated, on average, at about 65–70 percent of men's. Leaving aside for the moment the question of how to define woman and man (which can itself be the basis of another spirited discussion and apposite to parallel courses in women's studies, psychology of gender, or the like), the issue can be raised for explanation and theorizing. Although there may be weak evidence for the effect of personality traits on the gender pay gap (Roethlisberger, Gassmann, Groot, & Martorano, 2022), the results of study and discussion will likely reveal reasons no less superstitious than any others explaining and defending inequality. For a start, consult the World Bank's summary of issues impeding women's equality worldwide (World Bank, 2022).
2 Should the discussion prompted by Option 1 prove too tame, shift to a more macroscopic view and compare the status of women in the immediate ambient culture with

DOI: 10.4324/9781003300380-24

that of women in Ghor, Afghanistan (Mashal & Nader, 2017). Examples this strong may shock, but what else is a cross-cultural course for?

References and Suggested Readings

Isanski, B. (2009, July–August). The history of women in psychology. *APS (American Psychological Society) Observer* (online newsletter). Retrieved from www.psychologicalscience.org/observer/the-history-of-women-in-psychology

Mashal, M., & Nader, Z. (2017, July 8). No justice, "no value" for women in a lawless Afghan province. *The New York Times* (online). Retrieved from www.nytimes.com/2017/07/08/world/asia/afghanistan-women-honor-killings.html

Roethlisberger, C., Gassmann, F., Groot, W., & Martorano, B. (2022, March 28). The contribution of personality traits and social norms to the gender pay gap: A systematic literature review. *The Journal of Economic Surveys* (open access). Retrieved from https://onlinelibrary.wiley.com/doi/full/10.1111/joes.12501

Rutherford, A., & Pettit, M. (2015). Feminism and/in/as psychology: The public sciences of sex and gender. *History of Psychology*, *18*(3), 223–237. Retrieved from https://pubmed.ncbi.nlm.nih.gov/26375152/

World Bank. (2022). The World Bank in gender. *World Bank Website*. Retrieved from www.worldbank.org/en/topic/gender/overview

Brooms (Animism, Anthropomorphism, and Dehumanization)

Animism and anthropomorphism are conceptually close: both imply the presence of lifelike or human-like characteristics in nonhuman or inanimate objects. One benign psychological interpretation of animism is to see it as related to pantheism, panentheism, or pan-spiritualism. Some see religion as an outgrowth of the fusion, by distant early ancestors, of animistic or anthropomorphic traits to the idea of a single creator god (Peoples, Duda, & Marlowe, 2016). A more mundane interpretation is reflected in purchasers' imparting lifelike qualities to consumer products, for instance perceiving a certain car as an embodiment of love (Avis, 2011). Other somewhat more negative views of animism connect it, via the theories of Piaget and other developmentalists, to cognitive immaturity (Drescher, 2013). Recently, Lasana Harris and Susan Fiske (Harris & Fiske, 2008, 2011) have drawn attention to the role that animism plays in dehumanization. Animism, they claim, referring as an example to the transmutation of the animated brooms in the early Walt Disney film *Fantasia* from willing helpers to conspiring killers, is a visible embodiment of cognitive processes related to making dispositional attributions about other humans. These ease the process of divesting groups of humans—including entire cultures—of their human characteristics, while also activating the amygdala, making them easier to hate and kill.

Exposition, Confrontation, and Simulation

Collect examples of characters and objects that reflect animism in both children and adults. These could range from Hello Kitty through Transformers to "cute" products in the IKEA catalog. Likewise, collect, from as many cultural sources as possible, animations that embody the characteristics that make killing acceptable (these could be entirely innocent: my wife suggests Bugs Bunny). A search for violent animation across cultures, in gaming and elsewhere, should be an interesting voyage. In an attempt to draw the line between benign and dehumanizing varieties of imagery, Haslam & Loughnan's (2014) review offers a comprehensive set of features of dehumanization and infrahumanization. Sunglasses worn by the randomly assigned "guards" were a memorable prop in the well-known Stanford Prison Experiment (Haney, Banks, & Zimbardo, 1973). A replication of Zhong, Bohns, and Gino's study (2010) in which wearing sunglasses decreased prosocial behavior should be easy to do and effective in conveying the essential features of the concept of dehumanization. Further, expand outward from Harris and Fiske to examine concepts of depersonalization, dehumanization, and distancing from moral responsibility as expressed in other comprehensive psychological theories, for example Albert Bandura's (2016) work on moral disengagement.

DOI: 10.4324/9781003300380-25

References and Suggested Readings

Avis, M. (2011). Anthropomorphism and animism theory in branding. In Z. Yi, J. J. Xiao, J. J. Cotte, & L. Price (Eds.), *AP-Asia Pacific advances in consumer research* (Vol. 9, pp. 313–319). Duluth, MN: Association for Consumer Research.

Bandura, A. (2016). *Moral disengagement: How people do harm and live with themselves.* New York, NY: Worth Publishers.

Drescher, C. F. (2013). Animism. In K. Keith (Ed.), *Encyclopedia of cross-cultural psychology* (pp. 66–69). New York, NY: Wiley-Blackwell.

Haney, C., Banks, C., & Zimbardo, P. (1973, September). A study of prisoners and guards in a simulated prison. *Naval Research Review, 9,* 1–17.

Harris, L. T., & Fiske, S. T. (2008). The brooms in Fantasia: Neural correlates of anthropomorphizing objects. *Social Cognition*, *26*(2), 210–223.

Harris, L. T., & Fiske, S. T. (2011). Dehumanized perception: A psychological means to facilitate atrocities, torture, and genocide? *Zeitschrift für Psychologie*, *219*(3), 175–181.

Haslam, N., & Loughnan, S. (2014). Dehumanization and infrahumanization. *Annual Review of Psychology*, *65*, 399–423. Retrieved from www.annualreviews.org/doi/10.1146/annurev-psych-010213-115045 [Accessed March 25, 2023].

Peoples, H. C., Duda, P., & Marlowe, F. W. (2016). Hunter-gatherers and the origins of religion. *Human Nature*, *27*(3), 261–282.

Zhong, C.-B., Bohns, V. K., & Gino, F. (2010). Good lamps are the best police: Darkness increases dishonesty and self-interested behavior. *Psychological Science*, *21*, 311–314.

Social Perception and Cognition

DOI: 10.4324/9781003300380-26

Color and Skin Color

Psychologists address the question of whether people perceive or understand color differently due to their culture mostly from the perspective of language. Languages differ in the number of basic color categorizations, so some languages have only a few—as few as two (light and dark)—and some have upwards of 10. Evidence exists to support both the view that humans all see color in the same way due to the identity of eye and brain structures and the view that language acquisition and learning create different color experiences across and within cultures. Until some reliable method of objectively observing and comparing phenomenal visual experience (or that of hearing, tasting, smelling, or feeling) emerges, this uncertainty will persist. Color symbolism differs across cultures and relates to language and learning as well as to the capability of humans to create arbitrary color categories—that is, colors that are purely symbolic. For instance, a particular shade of green may identify a political party. Color's connection to emotion is likewise variable and appears to depend on regional or national culture (Adams & Osgood, 1973; Hupka, Zaleski, Otto, Reidl, & Tarabina, 1997; Jonauskaite et al., 2020).

Even though one group of vision scientists in the past speculated on the possibility that brown is as elemental a color as yellow or red (Fuld, Werner, & Wooten, 1983), skin color remains without doubt the most divisive concept in all of society all across the world, producing hot and defensive emotions. (For a recent example, observe the case of the too-light Beyoncé (Fortin, 2017)). Skin color is an objective factor in computer face recognition, a complex problem that has not yet been fully solved. A decision is still pending on the optimal color space system for skin color discrimination (Shaik, Ganesan, Kalist, Sathish, & Jenitha, 2015) as well as on the optimal methods for doing so (Pujol, Pujol, Jimeno-Morenilla, & Pujol, 2017; Samson & Lu, 2021). Recently, a 10-tone skin scale, the Monk Skin Tone Scale (McHugh-Johnson, 2022) has been adopted as a simplified way of improving accuracy of recognition and representation of skin tone in AI-related applications. Also recently, genetic research has uncovered genetic instructions for skin color that are shared worldwide, suggesting, again, that skin color is a relative and graded series rather than a set of discrete categories (Zimmer, 2017; Naik & Farrukh, 2022). But that does not stop humans from wielding skin color as a blunt discriminatory instrument unconnected to actual color theory and vision science, computer science, genetics, or science of any sort.

Exposition, Confrontation, and Simulation

At the very least, have fun with some of the color issues that this area of cross-cultural psychology uncovers. For theory's sake, review hue, brightness, lightness, and saturation; review the difference between light and pigment primaries (additive and

DOI: 10.4324/9781003300380-27

subtractive mixtures); and get used to ranges within hues. The sensation and perception chapters in any introductory psychology textbook can serve as a basic guide. Using simple craft materials, mix pigments to create an unusual color (e.g., rust), and show how it varies along a continuum of lightness by adding pure white (tinting) or pure black (shading). Be as creative when making colors as you can be—my favorite is chrome, and you might like colors with mixed glitter—but do include rust (and, if inclined to extra effort, produce a rust-colored light using mixed lights rather than pigments). Discuss emotionality regarding color; inventory everyone's favorite and least favorite colors in terms of the emotions that they evoke, collate these, and seek commonalities. Using Hupka et al.'s list of emotions, compare your local results. Discuss arbitrary color categories; would the red, white, and blue of the US or French flags (among many others) be as meaningful if they had originally been copper, eggshell, and licorice? (And which shade of eggshell?) Could they be changed, now, at will? Investigate the skin-color reasoning behind the blue of the Blue Man Group (Langmuir, 2022); compare this with the approach of Glenn Ligon to Blackness (Cotter, 2017). Compare and discuss colors of the human body that have little variance among people, for instance, the color of blood or the color of the liver. After doing that, do the following: Cut squares of white copier paper, 92 or greater brightness, about 50 mm square, with an aperture about 20 mm square in the middle. Lay these squares on two human forearms or other places where skin is exposed and where a photograph (a cellphone is satisfactory) can be made of both surfaces together. Next, compare the colors showing in the apertures with each other and with the surrounding paper square. Only one of these items will be *white*—ever. Establish the hue name for the colors in the apertures; someone who is adept at manipulating computer images should, if possible, collect all the images and cut and arrange the aperture colors in a sequence from lightest to darkest. Compare this range of hues with the many iterations of skin color scales available online—for example, the Monk Scale mentioned above—and also with the selection of 24 colors offered by Crayola in crayons and color pencils in its "Colors of the World" series (Crayola.com, n.d.). There is a science of the variation in skin tone hue and lightness, and it's worth discussing and reading the elementary education materials available (e.g., Smithsonian Institution, n.d.) to confirm with physical and theoretical certainty that the variance is one of degree, not kind.

It may be, however, that raising the topic of skin color at all will prompt a shift in the conversation away from science and toward prejudice. As mentioned in the introduction, this book, and any cross-cultural psychology course to which it might be connected, calls for complementary courses in human diversity, social relations, racism, and the like as well as encountering the eloquence of contemporary figures in the humanities (Gates & Curran, 2022) and the arts (Allman, 2023) about discrimination by color. If it is necessary in the context of the material in this section to go further in probing the roots of discrimination by color, one approach could be to discuss the experience of albinism in South Africa (Ross, 2017), where the full range of superstition in the absence of science is on vivid display. Another way could be to discuss self-identification by skin-color emojis (Janse, Jarenwattanon, & Khalid, 2022). Another could be to consider recent controversy over the term *BIPOC* (Black, Indigenous, and People of Color) (Meraji, Escobar, & Devarajan, 2020) and examine whether it is a cultural help or hindrance. If the discussion progresses even farther toward race, Jackson (2016) provides a framework to examine the claims of evolutionary psychologists of a universal human cognitive facility for classification of humans on the basis of superficial characteristics.

References and Suggested Readings

Adams, F. M., & Osgood, C. E. (1973). A cross-cultural study of the affective meanings of color. *Journal of Cross-Cultural Psychology*, *4*(2), 135–156.

Allman, R. (2023, January 16). George Shirley: A life in music. *The 1-A* (online news magazine/podcast, WAMU/National Public Radio). Retrieved from https://the1a.org/segments/george-shirley-a-life-in-music/

Cotter, H. (2017, August 10). Glenn Ligon rethinks the color line in the show "Blue Black." *The New York Times* (online newspaper). Retrieved from www.nytimes.com/2017/08/10/arts/design/glenn-ligon-rethinks-the-color-line-in-the-show-blue-black.html

Crayola.com. (n.d.). Colors of the world. *Product website.* Retrieved from www.crayola.com/product-feature/colors-of-the-world

Fortin, J. (2017, July 21). Beyoncé statue at Madame Tussaud's is 'adjusted' after criticism. *The New York Times* (online newspaper). Retrieved from www.nytimes.com/2017/07/21/arts/music/beyonce-madame-tussauds-wax-statue.html?mcubz=3&_r=0

Fuld, K., Werner, J. S., & Wooten, B. R. (1983). The possible elemental nature of brown. *Vision Research*, *23*(6), 631–637.

Gates, H. L. Jr., & Curran, A. S. (2022, March 3). We need a new language for talking about race. *The New York Times* (online newspaper). Retrieved from www.nytimes.com/2022/03/03/opinion/sunday/talking-about-race.html

Hupka, R. B., Zaleski, Z., Otto, J., Reidl, L., & Tarabina, N. V. (1997). The colors of anger, envy, fear, and jealousy. *Journal of Cross-cultural Psychology*, *28*(2).

Jackson, J. P. (2016). Cross-cultural research, evolutionary psychology, and racialism: Problems and prospects. *Philosophy, Theory, and Practice in Biology*, *8*(2) (Michigan Publishing. Open access online at https://quod.lib.umich.edu/cgi/t/text/text-idx?cc=ptb;c=ptb;c=ptpbio;idno=6959004.0008.002;rgn=main;view=text;q1=Collaboration;xc=1;g=ptpbiog). http://dx.doi.org/10.3998/ptb.6959004.0008.002

Janse, A. M., Jarenwattanon, P., & Khalid, A. (2022, February 9). Which skin color emoji should you use? The answer can be more complex than you think. *NPR Code Switch* (online blog/podcast, National Public Radio). Retrieved from www.npr.org/2022/02/09/1078977416/race-chat-emoji-skin-tone-colors

Jonauskaite, D., Abu-Akhel, A., Nele, D., Oberfeld, D., Abdel-Khalek, A., . . . Mohr, C. (2020). Universal patterns in color-emotion associations are further shaped by linguistic and geographic proximity. *Psychological Science*, *31*(10), 1245–1260. https://doi.org/10.1177/0956797620948810

Langmuir, M. (2022, March 28). How Blue Man blew up: The wild success of a show starring strange bald men painted in Yves Klein blue. *Vulture* (online magazine). Retrieved from www.vulture.com/article/blue-man-group-oral-history.html

McHugh-Johnson, M. (2022, May 11). A closer look at the research to help AI see more skin tones. *The Keyword* (Google in-house blog). Retrieved from https://blog.google/technology/research/ai-monk-scale-skin-tone-story/

Meraji, S. M., Escobar, N., & Devarajan, K. (2020, September 30). Is it time to say R.I.P. to P. O. C.? *NPR Code Switch* (online blog/podcast, National Public Radio). Retrieved from www.npr.org/2020/09/29/918418825/is-it-time-to-say-r-i-p-to-p-o-c

Naik, P. P., & Farrukh, S. N. (2022). Influence of ethnicities and skin color variations in different populations: A review. *Skin Pharmacology and Physiology, 35*(2), 65–76. Retrieved from www.karger.com/Article/FullText/518826

Pujol, F., Pujol, M., Jimeno-Morenilla, A., & Pujol, M. J. (2017). Face detection based on skin color segmentation using fuzzy entropy. *Entropy*, *19*, *26* (MDPI).

Ross, E. (2017, June 4). Being black in a white skin: Students with albinism battle prejudice. *The Conversation* (online news magazine). Retrieved from https://theconversation.com/being-black-in-a-white-skin-students-with-albinism-battle-prejudice-78368

Samson, G. L., & Lu, J. (2021). PKT: Fast color-based spatial model for human skin detection. *Multimedia Tools and Applications*, *80*, 32807–32839. Retrieved from https://link.springer.com/article/10.1007/s11042-021-10955-4

Shaik, K. B., Ganesan, P., Kalist, V., Sathish, B. S., & Jenitha, J. M. M. (2015). Comparative study of skin color detection and segmentation in HSV and YcbCr color space. *Procedia Computer Science*, *57*, 41–48.

Smithsonian Institution. (n.d.). Human skin color variation. *On: What Does It Mean to Be Human? (website page, Smithsonian Museum of Natural History)*. Retrieved from http://humanorigins.si.edu/evidence/genetics/human-skin-color-variation

Zimmer, C. (2017). Genes for skin color rebut dated notions of race, researchers say. *The New York Times* (online newspaper). Retrieved from www.nytimes.com/2017/10/12/science/skin-color-race.html?_r=0

Eye Contact

Traditionally, cultures venerate the gaze; adages like "The eyes are the windows of the soul" or the refrain "Drink to me only with thine eyes" from Ben Jonson's "Song: To Celia" testify to the pervasiveness of the idea that sight projects power. Add to this the tradition in many cultures of the belief in the evil eye. Blue and white glass bull's-eye amulets—themselves called "evil eyes" and said to have power to avert malevolent rays of gaze and often interwoven with the hand-like symbol of the Hamsa—are readily available in shops and online from vendors catering to clientele from the Middle East and Africa. I received my first one from a friend from Turkey, and I have anecdotal evidence for its effectiveness.

Not everyone agrees about the positive importance or the value of gaze. The conceptual artist Robert Smithson, writing to his wife about an exhibit of his paintings in 1961, said that he was distressed by the public exposure of his art. "But what can I do?" he said.

> This is the 20th century and the whole world is on a tour inspecting the rotting remains of a vanished age . . . . People want to stare with aggressive eagerness or they feel they must stare in order to grant approval. There is something indecent about such staring.
>
> (Tsai, 2004, p. 41)

The neuropsychology of gaze reveals a widely distributed collection of brain regions and response systems that cooperate in social perception (Itier & Batty, 2009; Jarick & Bencic, 2019). Sensitivity to gaze may be a feature of some forms of neurodiversity as well (Cañigueral & Hamilton, 2019). Gaze may be at least unconsciously aimed at objects of affection, and individuals who are asked to gaze into each other's eyes report feeling heightened feelings of desire after the experience (Bolmont, Cacioppo, & Cacioppo, 2014). Frequently, gaze is cited as a primary physical and social marker of cultural membership and cultural difference. For example, an averted or indirect gaze in the United States may be interpreted as evasive or dishonest while a similar downcast or avoidant gaze may be understood as a sign of respect in Asian and Middle Eastern cultures.

Exposition, Confrontation, and Simulation

Discussion may emerge from tabulation of gaze experiences or by listing places where staring is expected and where it is not at all acceptable (e.g., New Jersey: "Whaddya lookin' at?"). The "power of gaze" demonstration is simple to replicate (Catron, 2015).

DOI: 10.4324/9781003300380-28

Cross-cultural examples of eye contact are embedded in the multitudinous sites offering cultural travel advice. Likewise, many examples of watching and being watched can be discovered in literature, art, and film. With some patience, it may be possible to construct a simulation of stimuli measuring sensitivity to gaze (e.g., as used in Lasagna, McLaughlin, Deng, Whiting, & Tso, 2020).

References and Suggested Readings

Bolmont, M., Cacioppo, J. T., & Cacioppo, S. (2014). Love is in the gaze: An eye-tracking study of love and sexual desire. *Psychological Science*, *25*, 1748–1756.

Cañigueral, R., & Hamilton, A. F. de C. (2019, March 15). The role of eye gaze during natural social interactions in typical and autistic people. *Frontiers in Psychology (Sec. Perception Science)*, *10*. Retrieved from www.frontiersin.org/articles/10.3389/fpsyg.2019.00560/full

Catron, M. L. (2015, January 9). To fall in love with anyone, do this. *The New York Times* (Modern Love Blog) (online). Retrieved from www.nytimes.com/2015/01/11/style/modern-love-to-fall-in-love-with-anyone-do-this.html

Itier, R. J., & Batty, M. (2009). Neural bases of eye and gaze processing: The core of social cognition. *Neuroscience and Biobehavioral Review*, *33*(6), 843–863.

Jarick, M., & Bencic, R. (2019, June 4). Eye contact is a two-way street: Arousal is elicited by the sending and receiving of eye gaze information. *Frontiers in Psychology (Sec. Perception Science)*, *10*. Retrieved from www.frontiersin.org/articles/10.3389/fpsyg.2019.01262/full

Lasagna, C. A., McLaughlin, M. M., Deng, W. Y., Whiting, E. L., & Tso, I. F. (2020, March 13). Deconstructing eye contact perception: Measuring perceptual precision and self-referential tendency using an online psychophysical eye contact detection task. *PLOS One* (Open access). Retrieved from https://journals.plos.org/plosone/article?id=10.1371/journal.pone.0230258

Tsai, E. (Ed.). (2004). *Robert Smithson*. Berkeley, CA: University of California Press.

Privacy

Privacy is a nexus term in psychology and culture; the concept intersects directly with ideas of boundaries, openness, secrecy, and rights. Within the United States, from an economic perspective, it ties into the question of public vs. private services, a politically fraught border in virtually all areas of government and commerce (e.g., the question of private vs. public hospitals or proposals to privatize essential services such as air traffic control or the funding of road infrastructure construction). A substantial change in cultural expectations of privacy in the United States occurred when the US Supreme Court reversed its holding in *Roe v. Wade* (Totenberg & McCammon, 2022).

Privacy is central to psychology's self-definition as a science. Questions of whether thought is ultimately private and inward and, therefore, not directly observable have fueled debates about whether psychology can be a science based on publicly observable and replicable data. Cognitively and socially, privacy turns on questions of expectations. Exclusion and segregation link to the idea of a place that is personally private and inviolate. Ultimately, there are deep connections between privacy and shame (Schneider, 1977). From a cultural perspective, there are interesting variations as well. Cultures that are more demonstrative and open may have less expectation and demand for privacy. On the other hand, some remarkably well-regulated and sober cultures allow public nudity, for example, or periods of time when regulations are relaxed (e.g., Carnival times), and the private becomes momentarily publicly accessible for enjoyment. Altman (1977) and Newell (1998) together provide a panoramic view of the history of cultural differences in perceptions of privacy. Recent research tends to focus on privacy vs. exposure across social media (e.g., Ostendorf, Müller, & Brand, 2020) and on the potential for technological intrusion into private affairs (Knijenburg et al., 2022). Karniel and Lavie-Dinur (2015) examine how concepts of privacy in Israel are affected by the shift toward a more open, communicative, and individualistic society.

Exposition, Confrontation, and Simulation

List actions that can and cannot be done in public; list and discuss laws and areas of regulation specifically directed at ensuring privacy—for instance, expectations of privacy on the internet. Read Nathaniel Simmons's account of his big blue health secret (Simmons, 2014) for an idea of how different the experience of privacy can be in another culture. Historically, trace the evolution of modern privy councils from the groups of retainers who served and controlled access to medieval kings in their private rooms. Survey to find experiences of privacy violations in earlier educational and family environments; grade and junior-high teachers in the United States are sometimes quite intrusive in their

DOI: 10.4324/9781003300380-29

management of electronic communications, and parents' transgressions into personal space increase during adolescence. Rather than engaging in any direct violations of personal privacy or space, take a more design-oriented approach. For example, sketch out how privacy would be managed and maintained in various situations (hospital, climbing expedition, traveling). Form groups, and, after discussing the relative need for privacy among each, have each group design a living space that would accommodate both socialization and privacy.

References and Suggested Readings

Altman, I. (1977). Privacy regulation: Culturally universal or culturally specific? *Journal of Social Issues*, *33*, 66–84.

Karniel, Y., & Lavie-Dinur, A. (2015). *Privacy and fame: How we expose ourselves across media platforms*. Lanham, MD: Lexington Books.

Knijenburg, B. P., Page, X., Wisniewski, P., Richter Lipford, H., Proferes, N., & Romano, J. (Eds.). (2022). *Modern socio-technical perspectives on privacy*. New York, NY: Springer (Open Access). Retrieved from https://link.springer.com/book/10.1007/978-3-030-82786-1

Newell, P. B. (1998). A cross-cultural comparison of privacy definitions and functions: A systems approach. *Journal of Environmental Psychology*, *18*(4), 357–371.

Ostendorf, S., Müller, S. M., & Brand, M. (2020, October 27). Neglecting long-term risks: Self-disclosure on social media and its relation to individual decision-making tendencies and problematic social-networks-use. *Frontiers in Psychology (Sec. Cognition)*, *11*. Retrieved from www.frontiersin.org/articles/10.3389/fpsyg.2020.543388/full

Schneider, C. D. (1977). *Shame, exposure, and privacy*. New York, NY: W. W. Norton & Company.

Simmons, N. (2014). My "big" blue health secret: My experience with privacy, or lack thereof, in Japan. *Health Communication*, *29*, 634–636.

Totenberg, N., & McCammon, S. (2022, June 24). Supreme Court overturns Roe Vs. Wade, ending right to abortion upheld for decades. *All Things Considered (National Public Radio Website)*. Retrieved from www.npr.org/2022/06/24/1102305878/supreme-court-abortion-roe-v-wade-decision-overturn

Safety and Danger

Maslow's motivational framework slots safety, next to basic survival needs, as essential. The two main divisions of psychological theories of safety and danger are environmental and interpersonal. At the beginning of the 20th century, accidents were mostly explained, psychologically, with reference to the habits or personality of the unlucky victim (Burnham, 2010), summarized in the idea that some individuals were more likely to be "accident prone." Over the past hundred years, the development of a science of human–machine systems has removed the stigma of accident proneness and replaced it with systems engineered to guide and reinforce safe operation of vehicles and machinery. But as vehicles have become more predictable, humans worldwide have remained prone to unsafe behavior. Partly this is due to environmental and economic factors. Rapid increases in car ownership in China and India, where roads are often unimproved and are crowded with pedestrians and motorized small craft, lead to fatality rates several times higher than in Europe. Unsafe behaviors are also determined by individual and cultural patterns of risk approach and avoidance. For instance, Chinese, Japanese, and US accident rates vary; Japanese accident rates are lower because the culture is more risk-averse than the others (Atchley, Shi, & Yamamoto, 2014). Also, cultures vary in the amount of safety devices they deploy and maintain. Guardrails, for instance, are placed along roads in both Denmark and Uganda. In Denmark, they are a permanent part of the roadscape, but in Uganda, they rapidly fall victim to economic necessity and are regularly stolen and turned into saucepans or privy supports (Tabaire, 2021). Cultural attitudes and behaviors toward alcohol also play a role in motor safety.

Exposition, Confrontation, and Simulation

Motor safety is only one small area in which safety behaviors are culturally modulated. Building outward from this, discussion could turn on the ways in which highly regimented safety cultures—air travel has many examples—can be defeated by cultural factors. Instructions to pilots may be misunderstood due to linguistic errors; disruption of flights by passengers claiming entitlements based on their place in a social hierarchy may occur (Borowiec, 2015). A checklist that includes all potential sources of danger in air travel could be generated and compared with official protocols—for instance, those of the US Transportation Security Administration or the safety agencies in other countries (TSA, 2023). It should not be ignored that individuals are perceived as unsafe based on specific appearance or mode of dress; this form of rapid cognitive typing could also be extended to other factors that may incite suspicion (Kane, Jacobs, & Hawkins, 2015). There are many lists of relatively safe vs. unsafe countries, and these can also be launching points

DOI: 10.4324/9781003300380-30

for discussion of practical ways to keep safe as well as of the metrics used to arrive at the definitions of countries or regions as "safe." One of the most successful classroom demonstrations I have experienced was given by a student from Venezuela who used a combination of personal experience and YouTube videos incorporating surveillance footage of armed robbery and kidnapping to demonstrate the environment in which street smarts would need to be quickly learned (see e.g., Casey, 2016). If students are intending to travel abroad on internships or for enrichment, some cautionary tales could be told about the relative amounts of supervision and safeguards in remote locations. Finally, interpersonal and emotional safety can be discussed and dramatized in the contexts of cultural safety (Richardson & Williams, 2007) and *safe spaces* for discourse.

References and Suggested Readings

Atchley, P., Shi, J., & Yamamoto, T. (2014, September). Cultural foundations of safety culture: A comparison of traffic safety culture in China, Japan, and the United States. *Transportation Research, Part F: Traffic Psychology and Behavior*, *26*, Part B, 317–325.

Borowiec, S. (2015, February 12). Ex-Korean air executive sentenced to prison in 'nut rage' case. *Los Angeles Times* (online). Retrieved from www.latimes.com/world/asia/la-fg-south-korea-nut-rage-case-20150212-story.html

Burnham, J. (2010). *Accident prone: A history of technology, psychology, and misfits in the machine age*. Chicago, IL: University of Chicago Press.

Casey, N. (2016, January 21). Q & A: Is it safe to visit Venezuela? In Moving to Venezuela, a land in turmoil. *The New York Times* (World: Reporter's Notebook) (online). Retrieved from www.nytimes.com/interactive/projects/cp/reporters-notebook/moving-to-venezuela

Kane, M. N., Jacobs, R. J., & Hawkins, W. E. (2015). Beliefs about safety and religious and cultural diversity. *Journal of Social Service Research*, *41*(5), 622–641.

Richardson, S., & Williams, T. (2007). Why is cultural safety essential in health care? *Medicine and Law*, *26*(4), 699–707.

Tabaire, B. (2021, January 30). Some steal money, others steal guardrails and we're all happy. *Daily Monitor* (online newspaper, Uganda). Retrieved from www.monitor.co.ug/uganda/oped/commentary/some-steal-money-others-steal-guardrails-and-we-re-all-happy--1708540

TSA (Transportation Security Administration). (2023). Security screening. *TSA website* (online). Retrieved from www.tsa.gov/travel/security-screening

Surveillance and Eyewitnessing

Historically, all cultures have had systems of surveillance and eyewitnessing. Watchtowers were built for observation and signaling; armies have always posted sentries. Seafarers, faced with the necessity of constant surveillance, evolved a complex system of watches designed to balance out hours on deck and night work (Lindsay, 1874). Since then, via technology, surveillance has become a ubiquitous presence in daily life in some cultures (Qian, Xiao, Mozur, & Cardia, 2022).

All legal systems rely on eyewitness testimony, which has a complex history itself. In the 17th century, English law broke with traditions of Continental law that apportioned weights to witnesses based on their number and reliability (Wigmore, 1901); today, there is still significant cultural variation in who can count as an eyewitness. For instance, in Yemen, a woman's testimony counts half as much as a man's (Basha, Ghanem, & Abdulhafid, 2005; Hoffman, 2016). Eyewitnessing also includes historic prophetic and cultural narrative traditions and extends to current queer-theoretical accounts of surveillance and control of gender and sexuality across cultures (McCormack, 2014).

Exposition, Confrontation, and Simulation

From a practical and current standpoint, surveillance and eyewitnessing come together in US and cross-cultural contexts regarding surveillance technology. In instructional settings, the following pathways are starting points for discussion:

1 Examine differential acceptance of surveillance across cultures plus acceptance of surveillance based on social acceptability. Various questionnaires can be created on the spot to evaluate group opinions about surveillance. Specifically, discussion could center on situations in which surveillance would be rated as acceptable (e.g., in the aftermath of terroristic events, e.g., Landler & Sussman, 2013). O'Donnell, Jetten, and Ryan (2010) suggest that identification with a group under threat will lead to surveillance being perceived as more acceptable; this would be an easy result to replicate and test. Further discussion could extend ideas in the Privacy entry in this book. A survey of the areas in which surveillance cameras would be acceptable or not could be done in conjunction with a survey of situations rated as least to most private. Internet and social media privacy, very prominent in social science research recently as well as a focus of many legislative interventions (NCSL, 2022), would be an area in which many individuals would have had direct experience.
2 Examine eyewitness testimony research. Body cameras for police are being implemented worldwide (e.g. Chin, 2017) and were a crucial element in the conviction of

DOI: 10.4324/9781003300380-31

several police officers in Minneapolis in 2020 for their conduct during the arrest of a citizen, George Floyd (Stanley, 2020). These devices can be obtained fairly cheaply, and getting one would be good investment. Simulation of a pursuit and arrest could be done, and comparisons between eyewitness accounts and the body camera input could be made. Discussion can turn on the inherent weaknesses in eyewitness testimony, well documented over the past 50 years by cognitive and forensic psychologists and implemented practically in programs to reverse convictions based on inaccurate eyewitness testimony (e.g. The Innocence Project, n.d.).

3 In conjunction with Item 2, extend eyewitness testimony issues to the cross-ethnicity effect (Stepanova, 2013). Set up cross-ethnic/cross-gender simulations, film with the body camera, and discuss. In the absence of a body camera, photo decks for comparing faces can easily be assembled from published photos in news magazines or other sources online. A method for training the technique suggested by the studies of McDonnell, Bornstein, Laub, Mills, and Dodd (2014) of focusing more on the lower parts of the face in recognition tasks can be designed.

References and Suggested Readings

Basha, A., Ghanem, R., & Abdulhafid, N. (2005, October 14). Women's rights in the Middle East and North Africa—Yemen. *RefWorld Website (UNHCR)*. Retrieved from www.refworld.org/docid/47387b712f.html

Chin, J. (2017, May 7). China puts body cameras on troubled security force. *The Wall Street Journal* (online newspaper). Retrieved from www.wsj.com/articles/china-puts-body-cameras-on-troubled-security-force-1494154800

Hoffman, C. (2016, March 14). Yemen. *Women Around the World* (Weblog, Penn State University). Retrieved from https://sites.psu.edu/chloehoffmanciblog/2016/03/14/yemen/

Innocence Project. (n.d.). Eyewitness identification reform. *Innocence Project Website*. Retrieved from https://innocenceproject.org/eyewitness-identification-reform/

Landler, M., & Sussman, D. (2013, April 30). Poll finds strong acceptance for public surveillance. *The New York Times* (online). Retrieved from www.nytimes.com/2013/05/01/us/poll-finds-strong-acceptance-for-public-surveillance.html

Lindsay, W. S. (1874). *History of merchant shipping and ancient commerce*. London, England: S. Low.

McCormack, D. (2014). *Queer postcolonial narratives and the ethics of witnessing*. New York, NY: Bloomsbury.

McDonnell, G. P., Bornstein, B. H., Laub, C. E., Mills, M., & Dodd, M. D. (2014). Perceptual processes in the cross-race effect: Evidence from eyetracking. *Basic and Applied Social Psychology*, *36*(6), 478–493.

NCSL. (2022). State laws related to internet privacy. *National Conference of State Legislatures (NCSL) website* (online). Retrieved from www.ncsl.org/technology-and-communication/state-laws-related-to-digital-privacy#anchor9072

O'Donnell, A. T., Jetten, J., & Ryan, M. K. (2010). Who is watching over you? The role of shared identity in perceptions of surveillance. *European Journal of Social Psychology*, *40*(1), 135–147.

Qian, I., Xiao, M., Mozur, P., & Cardia, A. (2022, July 26). Four takeaways from a Times investigation into China's expanding surveillance state. *The New York Times* (online newspaper). Retrieved from www.nytimes.com/2022/06/21/world/asia/china-surveillance-investigation.html

Stanley, J. (2020, June 25). Body cameras and the George Floyd protests. *ACLU Website*. Retrieved from www.aclu.org/news/privacy-technology/body-cameras-and-the-george-floyd-protests

Stepanova, E. V. (2013). Cross-ethnicity effect (Face recognition). In K. D. Keith (Ed.), *Encyclopedia of cross cultural psychology* (pp. 286–288). New York, NY: Wiley-Blackwell.

Wigmore, J. H. (1901). Required numbers of witnesses: A brief history of the numerical system in England. *Harvard Law Review*, *15*(2), 83–108.

Stupidity and Intelligence

Stupidity is practiced more than it is studied. It is probably a human cultural universal though not celebrated as such. The economic historian Carlo Cipolla sketched a framework for locating stupidity in the universe of human behavior using a 2 × 2 graph (Pomeroy, 2016). The *x*-axis extends continuously from "harmful to self" to "helpful to self" and the *y*-axis from "harmful to others" to "helpful to others." Those who are helpful to self but harmful to others are, of course, bandits; those who are both self- and other-harmful are, according to this scheme, stupid. Stupidity is the B side of intelligence, and it is not unexpected that a highly credentialed generalist in the intelligence field assembled a comprehensive set of academic essays on the subject (Sternberg, 2003), examining the foibles of managers, politicians, and other foolish creatures. Stupidity also twines around the roots of humor, a rich vein of cross-cultural interplay (Yue, Jiang, Lu, & Hiranandani, 2016).

Exposition, Confrontation, and Simulation

Students can, and should, share and document experiences of stupidity. This might extend from cultural faux pas through beginners' ignorance and even to interpersonal relations. "Stupid is as stupid does," as Forrest Gump said, and there are lots of videos of pratfalls and epic fails across cultures. Patricia Greenfield's *American Psychologist* article on the vagaries of intelligence and ability testing across cultures (Greenfield, 1997) neatly synthesizes, with several cogent examples, the ways in which tests can portray intelligence incompletely and inaccurately across cultures. The well-known Kpelle object-sorting study (Cole, Gay, Glick, & Sharp, 1971) and Greenfield's own studies of Piagetian conservation and collective vs. individualistic problem solving could be briefly replicated as examples for discussion and possible extension of cognitive and developmental studies across cultures. Taking tests of out-of-domain knowledge can stimulate feeling stupid in testing situations. Provide yarn and needles and see how many individuals are and are not fluent in a common task! Many tests for pilots, truckers, and other highly skilled professions, crafts, and trades are also readily available for practice on the internet. Review and replicate as far as possible Krys et al.'s (2016) study of the perception of intelligence or stupidity from facial expression; this study additionally introduces the GLOBE project as another cross-cultural typology (GLOBE, 2020). Beyond this, Cipolla's taxonomy of stupidity could be explored with case studies, locating the actors in each of the four cells and, after identifying those who fall into the "stupid" cell, examining each in more detail.

DOI: 10.4324/9781003300380-32

References and Suggested Readings

Cole, M., Gay, J., Glick, J., & Sharp, D. W. (1971). *The cultural context of learning and thinking*. New York, NY: Basic Books.

GLOBE. (2020). *GLOBE project (Global Leadership and Organizational Behavior Effectiveness) website*. Retrieved from https://globeproject.com/about

Greenfield, P. M. (1997). You can't take it with you: Why ability assessments don't cross cultures. *American Psychologist*, *52*(10), 1115–1124.

Krys, K., Vauclair, C. M., Capaldi, C. A., Lun, V. M. C., Bond, M. H., . . . Yu, A. (2016). Be careful where you smile: Culture shapes judgments of intelligence and honesty of smiling individuals. *Journal of Nonverbal Behavior*, *40*, 101–116. Retrieved from https://link.springer.com/article/10.1007/s10919-015-0226-4#Sec7

Pomeroy, R. (2016, September 14). The basic laws of human stupidity. *RealClear Science* (blog) (online). Retrieved from www.realclearscience.com/blog/2016/09/the_basic_laws_of_human_stupidity.html

Sternberg, R. J. (Ed.). (2003). *Why smart people can be so stupid*. New Haven, CT: Yale University Press.

Yue, X., Jiang, F., Lu, S., & Hiranandani, N. (2016, October 4). To be or not to be humorous? Cross-cultural perspectives on humor. *Frontiers of Psychology*, *7*. Retrieved from www.frontiersin.org/articles/10.3389/fpsyg.2016.01495/full https://doi.org/10.3389/fpsyg.2016.01495

Interpersonal Interaction

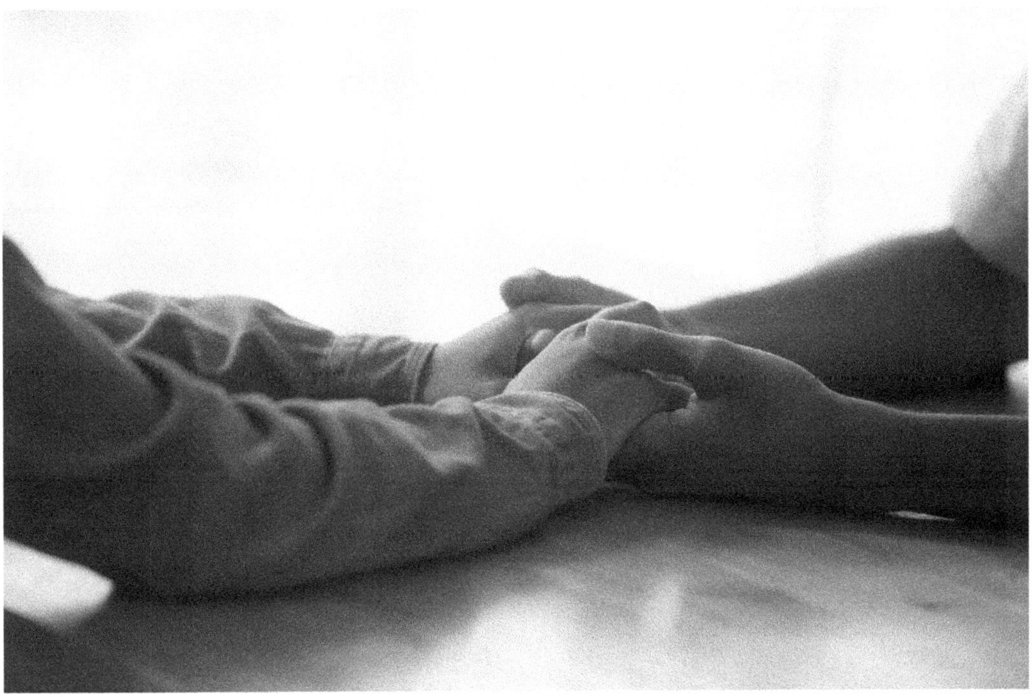

DOI: 10.4324/9781003300380-33

Charity

Charity is prescribed by all major world religions and is essential for economic functioning. For instance, donated care by physicians is built in as an expected contribution to economic models of health care even in cultures such as the Netherlands where private insurance and public support of health expenses have reached a steady equilibrium (White & Eijkholt, 2015). Likewise, pro bono contributions are expected from other professions including law and psychology.

Charity as a specific form of prosocial behavior has only recently received detailed attention in the scientific literature of psychology. The results of recent studies suggest that the determinants of charitable actions are nuanced across cultures. Peter Smith of the University of Sussex (UK), drawing on several global databases including the World Values Survey, recently analyzed data from 135 nations to test hypotheses about the effects of various structural variables (national wealth, relative income equality or inequality, trust, absence of corruption, in-group favoritism, and uncertainty avoidance) on the prosocial behaviors of charitable giving, helping a stranger, and volunteering time (Smith, 2015). He found that low in-group favoritism and low uncertainty avoidance most strongly predicted charitable giving. Interestingly, in view of the stress placed on charitable giving in all major world religions, he found that there was significantly more giving in less-religious nations. Klein, Grossman, Uskul, Kraus, and Epley (2015) performed an experiment across seven national cultures (Austria, China, Denmark, Turkey, Russia, the United Kingdom, and the United States). They presented participants with a scenario in which one of two participants in a hypothetical experiment, provided with an endowment standardized to $6 across cultures, was free to donate from 0/6 to 6/6 to the other person, described as a stranger the giver had never met. Klein et al. asked participants to evaluate the prosociality of the giver and also his warmth and his competence. (Note: Only men were represented in the scenarios.) They found an asymptotic result; after 3/6 of the endowment was shared, sharing of greater amounts did not increase the perceptions of prosociality, warmth, or competence. In fact, in some cases, they found that the evaluation of the giver's competence decreased with greater hypothetical generosity, suggesting links to evaluations of rationality and intelligence accompanying charitable actions.

Exposition, Confrontation, and Simulation

Both Smith and Klein et al. are excellent sources to consult to identify major cross-cultural data sources and to get an idea of how they can be used to construct variables for multivariate research. Klein et al.'s study is simple and could be replicated with or

DOI: 10.4324/9781003300380-34

without variations in small or large classes. For instance, the factors of gender, cultural membership, and religious affiliation, among other variables, could be introduced. Examination of mutual-sharing insurance practices such as Muslim *takaful* and Amish community support for health expenses can be examined as forms of charity (Rohrer & Dundes, 2016). For instance, the benefits of working in a community-building charitable role, as a volunteer, or as a salaried person taking on, in effect, a voluntary vow of relatively less affluence (though not poverty) are well described in the *Community Tool Box* produced by the Center for Community Health and Development at the University of Kansas (Center for Community Health and Development, 2017). Chapter 28 especially is a rich source of motives and strategies for innovative participation in community charity and for discussion and simulation. Cultures of begging should also be considered, perhaps in the context of discussing whether DSGs (Diverted Giving Schemes) depersonalize the relation between beggar and giver (Pérez-Muñoz, 2018).

References and Suggested Readings

Center for Community Health and Development (U. of Kansas). (2017). Community tool box (Chapter 28: Spirituality and community building). *Community Tool Box website of the KU CCHD* (online). Retrieved from https://ctb.ku.edu/en/table-of-contents/spirituality-and-community-building/being-charitable-towards-others/main

Klein, N., Grossman, I., Uskul, A. K., Kraus, A. A., & Epley, N. (2015). It pays to be nice, but not really nice: Asymmetric reputations from prosociality across 7 countries. *Judgment and Decision Making*, *10*(4), 355–364.

Pérez-Muñoz, C. (2018). Beneficence, street begging, and diverted giving schemes. *Political Research Quarterly*, *71*(4), 923–935.

Rohrer, K., & Dundes, L. (2016). Sharing the load: Amish healthcare funding. *Healthcare*, 4(4), pii E92 (online). Retrieved from www.ncbi.nlm.nih.gov/pmc/articles/PMC5198134/

Smith, P. B. (2015). To lend helping hands: In-group favoritism, uncertainty avoidance and the national frequency of pro-social behaviors. *Journal of Cross Cultural Psychology*, *46*(6), 759–771.

White, B. D., & Eijkholt, M. (2015). Physician charity care in America: Almost always an illusion, ever more commercial. *Laws*, *4*, 201–215 (Open access online). Retrieved from www.mdpi.com/journal/laws

Compromise and Tolerance

Compromise is an idea that is often, especially recently in the United States, in ill repute. From the viewpoint of the basic definition of culture in this book, it may seem that engaging in a compromise is a downrating or even an outright betrayal of values. Especially in the political arena, compromise may seem to threaten otherwise healthy competitiveness and thus may be vigorously resisted on that principle.

Serious students of social and political polarization endorse strengthening aspects of government that promote compromise (e.g. Haidt, 2022). From a theoretical psychological standpoint, compromise connects to ideas in the areas of negotiation, behavioral optimization, and satisficing (Brown, 2004). It is related to ideas of *good enough* that surface from time to time in the field in connection with the ability to accept less than perfection or completeness in problem solutions. There is a natural conceptual tie between compromise and studies of tolerance. Theories of coalition building are also in play (Fine & Halkovic, 2014). Interpersonal relations are a fertile ground for theoretical examination of compromise; marriage and family counseling has a strong stream of ideas about bringing mutually conflicting parties together as do legal psychology and the psychology of conflict resolution. A recent study (Kaplan et al., 2017) confronted US, Chinese, and Iranian individuals with narratives that activated core personal values that are resistant to compromise, analyzing brain activity while doing so. More intensive processing occurred in areas of the brain connected to understanding and interpreting narrative when core values were foregrounded, differing in strength across national groups. This heightened activity may correlate with the intensity with which compromise across cultures is resisted when negotiations touch on core values, resistance that may be moderated with more attention to cultural differences (Marsella, 2015).

Exposition, Confrontation, and Simulation

Gather personal examples of compromise, interpersonal and social, attending to the circumstances in which a need for compromise arose and the ways in which it was (or was not) achieved. For more confrontation, select a controversial issue that doesn't seem to admit compromise and discuss. Sites aimed toward secondary school students in history and government often contain materials with which historic situations of compromise can be regenerated and, as far as possible, reenacted. Extensive materials for a psychologically based course on dealing with conflict are available on the *Beyond Intractability* website (Burgess & Burgess, 2017). Consider also examining the Interpersonal Tolerance Scale (Thomae, Birtel, & Wittemann, 2016) for which materials are available for inspection online.

DOI: 10.4324/9781003300380-35

References and Suggested Readings

Brown, R. (2004). Consideration of the origin of Herbert Simon's theory of "satisficing," 1933–1947. *Management Decision*, *42*(10), 1240–1256.

Burgess, G., & Burgess, H. (Eds.). (2017). Dealing constructively with intractable conflicts. *Beyond Intractability Knowledge Base* (program website) (online). Retrieved from www.beyondintractability.org/educationtraining/dealing-constructively-intractable-conflicts

Fine, M., & Halkovic, A. (2014). A delicate and deliberate journey toward justice: Challenging privilege: Building structures of solidarity. In P. T. Coleman, M. Deutsch & E. C. Marcus (Eds.), *The handbook of conflict resolution: Theory and practice* (3rd ed., pp. 56–75). San Francisco, CA: Jossey-Bass.

Haidt, J. (2022, April 11). Why the past 10 years of American life have been uniquely stupid. *The Atlantic* (online magazine). Retrieved from www.theatlantic.com/magazine/archive/2022/05/social-media-democracy-trust-babel/629369/

Kaplan, J. T., Gimbel, S. H., Dehghani, M., Immordino-Yang, M. H., Sagae, K., . . . Damasio, A. (2017). Processing narratives concerning protected values: A cross-cultural investigation of neural correlates. *Cerebral Cortex*, *27*(2), 1428–1438.

Marsella, A. (2015). Reflections on the cultural contexts of conflict resolution via truth and reconciliation processes. In M. Galluccio (Ed.), *Handbook of international negotiation: Interpersonal, intercultural, and diplomatic perspectives* (pp. 287–295). Cham, Switzerland: Springer International Publishing.

Thomae, M., Birtel, M. D., & Wittemann, J. (2016, July 13–16). *The Interpersonal Tolerance Scale (ITPS): Scale development and validation.* Paper presented at the 2016 Annual Meeting of the International Society of Political Psychology, Warsaw, Poland (online). Retrieved from https://manuelathomae.files.wordpress.com/2016/07/the-interpersonal-tolerance-scale-ipts.pdf

Friendship

The title of a recent comprehensive cross-cultural psychological treatment of friendship (Harré & Moghaddam, 2013) reflects friendship's implication of a corresponding dark side of enmity. Friendships may differ in depth and intensity across cultures; Lu et al. (2021) provide evidence for the differential importance of friendship worldwide. Certainly, there are differences. For instance, the Chinese conception of *friend* is less inclusive than the Western term and is limited to a "long-time close friend" (Chen, 2013). Likewise, it is more likely that people will say that they have specific personal enemies in Ghana than in the United States (Stambor, 2005). However, friendship's historic and cultural universality may outweigh these region-specific differences. Friends add to, and sometimes supplant, the social support afforded by families. Friendship, including self-friendship (Krakovsky, 2012), is a mainstay of mental health. Friendship may span species (Dunbar, 2014) and, through the medium of cultural and educational exchange, is one of the surest routes to intercultural understanding in humans (Gareis, 2017; US Department of State, n.d.).

Exposition, Confrontation, and Simulation

Examine the texture of friendships in the immediate environment by creating sociograms of friend networks. Set criteria for deciding the degree to which these cross cultural or ethnic boundaries and discuss those that do. Extend the findings of Lessard, Kogachi, and Juvonen (2019) about in- and outside-of-classroom friendships among adolescents to other areas of differential contact, such as work settings. Also, become familiar with psychological measurements of friendship—for example, the Hawthorne Friendship Scale (Hawthorne, 2006) and the McGill Friendship Questionnaire (Mendelson & Aboud, 2012). Use these to reveal other dimensions of friendship and, if possible, compare results across cultures.

Exchange student experiences are more frequent than might be supposed. Survey to see how prevalent these are. Individuals who have been exchange students themselves or who are members of families who have been exchange hosts often have formed durable friendships, and their stories can illustrate the successes as well as the challenges of friendship across borders. For a more macrocultural approach, look into the history of bridges bearing the specific name Friendship Bridge (hint: two of these connect North Korea with neighboring countries). For an artistic approach, curate and discuss the role of friendship as represented in examples of art celebrating international friendship—for instance, the Statue of Liberty.

DOI: 10.4324/9781003300380-36

References and Suggested Readings

Chen, F. F. (2013). Construct equivalence. In K. Keith (Ed.), *Encyclopedia of cross cultural psychology* (pp. 235–236). New York, NY: Wiley-Blackwell.

Dunbar, R. (2014, May 21). Friendship: Do animals have friends too? *New Scientist* (online). Retrieved from www.newscientist.com/article/mg22229700-400-friendship-do-animals-have-friends-too/

Gareis, E. (2017). Intercultural friendships. *Oxford Research Encyclopedias Online: Communication*. Retrieved from http://communication.oxfordre.com/view/10.1093/acrefore/9780190228613.001.0001/acrefore-9780190228613-e-161

Harré, R., & Moghaddam, F. M. (2013). *The psychology of friendship and enmity: Relationships in love, work, politics, and war* (Vol. 2). New York, NY: Praeger.

Hawthorne, G. (2006). Measuring social isolation in older adults: Development and initial validation of the Friendship Scale. *Social Indicators Research*, *77*, 521–548.

Krakovsky, M. (2012, July 1). Self-compassion fosters mental health. *Scientific American* (online magazine). www.scientificamerican.com/article/self-compassion-fosters-mental-health/

Lessard, L. M., Kogachi, K., & Juvonen, J. (2019). Quality and stability of cross-ethnic friendships: Effects of classroom diversity and out-of-school contact. *Journal of Youth and Adolescence*, *48*(3), 554–566. Retrieved from www.ncbi.nlm.nih.gov/pmc/articles/PMC6469703/

Lu, P., Oh, J., Leahy, K. E., & Chopik, W. J. (2021, January 18). Friendship importance around the world: Links to cultural factors, health, and well-being. *Frontiers in Psychology (Sec. Personality and Social Psychology)*, *11*. Retrieved from www.frontiersin.org/articles/10.3389/fpsyg.2020.570839/full

Mendelson, M. J., & Aboud, F. (2012). McGill Friendship Questionnaire: Respondent's Affection (MFQ-RA). *Measurement Instrument Database for the Social Sciences MIDSS* (website) (online). Retrieved from www.midss.org/sites/default/files/mfq-ra.pdf

Stambor, Z. (2005, June). Perceptions of enemies differ across cultures. *Monitor on Psychology (American Psychological Association)*, *36*(6), 18. Retrieved from www.apa.org/monitor/jun05/perceptions

US Department of State. (n.d.). Why participate? *Bureau of Educational and Cultural Affairs Exchange Programs, U.S. Department of State* (US Federal Government website). Retrieved from https://exchanges.state.gov/non-us/why-participate

Interpersonal Trust

One of the mottos of the United States blazoned on its currency (discounting the intervention of the supernatural) emphasizes the indispensability of trust in many cultures. Trust is a bedrock element in Erik Erikson's theory of development and, as such, is said to be essential for carrying out human interchanges: economic, romantic, and therapeutic. As a variable in cross-cultural studies, interpersonal trust is increasingly studied across areas of psychological interest. For instance, in a case study of team building in virtual environments (Cheng et al., 2016), interpersonal trust varied depending on the degree of multicultural makeup of teams. Language and task clarity were factors that influenced trust levels. Ward, Mamerow, and Meyer (2014) found some support as well as some contrary evidence for the theoretical differentiation between *high-trust* and *low-trust* societies advanced by political scientist Francis Fukuyama (1996). Persons less likely to express trust include those with lower incomes, those who are younger, and those in poor health. Along with its being an essential element for commerce and the maintenance of social institutions, trust is also basic to more intimate interpersonal relations. A recent study carried out in Ethiopia (John, Tsui, Seme, & Roro, 2017) validates this claim and affirms the consensus that trust scales developed in Western cultures are cross-culturally valid.

Exposition, Confrontation, and Simulation

Seek out and become familiar with interpersonal trust scales, e.g., the Rotter Interpersonal Trust Scale (Rotter, 1967), many versions of which are available gratis online. Save time and experiment with the three-item Interpersonal Trust Short Scale (Niessen, Beierlein, Rammstedt, & Lechner, 2020). Examine the trust variables included for the first time in the sixth and seventh waves of the *World Values Survey* (available at www.worldvaluessurvey.org/WVSOnline.jsp) and compare by country. These include "trust in people you have met for the first time," "trust in neighborhood," "trust in people of another nationality," "trust in family," and "trust in people of another religion."

A classic trust story from Ireland can be adapted for a simulation. In 1970, during a six-month strike of the Irish banks, a network of interpersonal financial trust emerged to keep the country's economy flowing more or less normally. Personal checks were exchanged, and pub owners—nodes of trust in their communities who were well acquainted with the habits of their customers and could accurately judge their trustworthiness—became intermediaries and facilitators of the process (Brancaccio, 2017; Haque, 2010; Smith & Chang, 2017). Based on this episode, conjure a scenario in which some essential element of social life is lost: a food shortage, a natural disaster, a war, a failure of government, or similar.

DOI: 10.4324/9781003300380-37

Discuss who would be the persons most likely to be trusted to fulfill various necessary roles (communicators, expert advisors, resource providers, interpersonal supporters, etc.) and sketch out systems of trust that might potentially emerge. Could a world of Irish pubs be the future of intercultural trust?

References and Suggested Readings

Brancaccio, D. (2017, September 18). Using stories to teach economics. *National Public Radio Marketplace* (online broadcast transcript). Retrieved from www.marketplace.org/2017/09/18/economics-education/

Cheng, X., Fu, S., Sun, J., Han, Y., Shen, J., & Zarifis, A. (2016). Investigating individual trust in semi-virtual collaboration of multicultural and unicultural teams. *Computers in Human Behavior*, *62*, 267–276.

Fukuyama, F. (1996). *Trust: The social virtues and the creation of prosperity*. New York, NY: Simon & Schuster.

Haque, U. (2010, November 29). The Irish banking crisis: A parable. *Harvard Business Review* (online). Retrieved from https://hbr.org/2010/11/the-irish-banking-crisis-a-par

John, N. A., Tsui, A. O., Seme, A., & Roro, M. A. (2017). Understanding the meaning of marital relationship quality among couples in peri-urban Ethiopia. *Culture, Health, & Sexuality*, *19*(2), 267–278.

Niessen, D., Beierlein, C., Rammstedt, B., & Lechner, C. M. (2020, November 17). An English-language adaptation of the Interpersonal Trust Short Scale (KUSIV3). *Measurement Instruments for the Social Sciences*, 2, 10. Retrieved from https://measurementinstrumentssocialscience.biomedcentral.com/articles/10.1186/s42409-020-00016-1#Abs1

Rotter, J. B. (1967). A new scale for the measurement of interpersonal trust. *Journal of Personality*, *35*(4), 651–665.

Smith, R., & Chang, A. (2017, April 12). Episode 764: Pub in a box. *National Public Radio Planet Money Podcast* (online podcast/broadcast transcript). Retrieved from www.npr.org/sections/money/2017/04/12/523653040/episode-764-pub-in-a-box

Ward, P. R., Mamerow, L., & Meyer, S. B. (2014). Interpersonal trust across six Asia-Pacific countries: Testing and extending the 'high trust society' and 'low trust society' theory. *PLoS ONE*, *9*(4). Retrieved from https://journals.plos.org/plosone/article?id=10.1371/journal.pone.0095555

Loyalty

Loyalty is a primary virtue in the Boy Scout Law (second on the list after trustworthiness) though for some reason it's not mentioned in the Girl Scout Law. In psychology, it's not featured in personality theories, though it is specifically mentioned in the 24 character strengths of positive psychology (VIA Institute, 2017) in connection with justice and teamwork. Possibly, this lack of attention to loyalty stems from psychology's stance as a science based on statistical decision, ready to change hypotheses based on new data. Possibly, too, it reflects an underlying cultural attitude in which life is characterized by change and it's considered necessary to act according to one's self-interest as conditions alter. Choices of job, place of residence, and relationship partners aren't meant to be permanent. There is substantial variation in marriage longevity and divorce rates worldwide (World Population Review, 2023). Unequivocal statements on the relative latent loyalty of gay marriages are difficult to find, though there's general agreement that same-sex couples are less likely to divorce in the United States. If PsycINFO is a good measure of research interest, the preponderant connection between loyalty and psychology is in the idea of "brand loyalty": purchasing a product again rather than switching. This is not surprising in a culture in which success is often tied to sales. If one were looking for a clear contrast in loyalty 30 years ago, the comparison of employee loyalty to employers in Japan vs. the United States would have been a standout example. However, the idea of long-term employment, and any associated feelings of loyalty, has eroded significantly in Japan and in several other countries (Lund, 2016).

Exposition, Confrontation, and Simulation

The question of the cross-cultural status of loyalty presents many challenges for study but also many opportunities to engage with essential questions. A start could be made by raising the question of whether loyalty is related to a specific emotion or combination of emotions, as recent research suggests (DeLeersnyder, Koval, Kuppens, & Mesquita, 2017). Discussion might also begin by inventorying and classifying the characteristics that would lead to staying loyal to family, friends, long-term partners, and even political or social leaders (Galak & Crichter, 2023; Zinrelo, n.d.). A survey could be developed that could incorporate these elements. It could then be compared to the scale developed by Lugo Steidel and Contreras (2003) to measure *familismo*, a term used to describe the loyalty to nuclear and extended family in Hispanic culture, and analyzed and discussed in terms of the cultural similarities and contrasts that are revealed. Many sites and research articles in psychology deal with the question of brand loyalty worldwide, and questionnaires from different countries may reveal cultural nuances of the concept.

DOI: 10.4324/9781003300380-38

The demand for loyalty oaths continues to crop up (e.g., Owens, 2015). The question of whether loyalty can be compelled is an important one in intercultural relations in the United States, and a simulation might be based on the 1943 questionnaire presented to interned Japanese American citizens interned in the War Relocation Authority camps in California and other states (Densho Encyclopedia, 2014). Also, searching for stories of loyalty may ultimately lead to an appreciation of the universality of this rare trait. A start could be the story of the shipwreck of the Malaysian cargo ship Selendang Ayu off the Alaska coast in December 2004. The disabled ship's Indian Master assigned 18 of the 26 crewmen deemed nonessential to be airlifted to safety by the US Coast Guard. After the ship ran aground, the Master called for help to evacuate the remaining crew. The rescuing helicopter was swamped by a wave and crashed, and six of the seven just-rescued crew drowned. The survivor was a cadet (apprentice) from either India or the People's Republic of China, who insisted on remaining with the skeleton crew out of "loyalty to the Master" (NTSB, 2006).

References and Suggested Readings

DeLeersnyder, J., Koval, P., Kuppens, P., & Mesquita, B. (2017, June). Emotions and concerns: Situational evidence for their systematic co-occurrence. *Emotion, 17*(6), 895–1045.

Densho Encyclopedia contributors. (2014, May 12). Loyalty questionnaire. *Densho Encyclopedia* (online). Retrieved from https://encyclopedia.densho.org/Loyalty_questionnaire/

Galak, J., & Crichter, C. R. (2023). Who sees political falsehoods as more acceptable and why: A new look at in-group loyalty and trustworthiness. *Journal of Personality and Social Psychology, 124*(3), 563–619. https://doi.org/10.1037/pspi0000264

Lugo Steidel, A. G., & Contreras, J. M. (2003). A new familism scale for use with Latino populations. *Hispanic Journal of Behavioral Sciences*, *25*, 312–330.

Lund, E. (2016, February 16). Study suggests Japanese workers are deeply distrustful of their employers. *Japan Today website* (online). Retrieved from https://japantoday.com/category/features/lifestyle/study-suggests-japanese-workers-are-deeply-distrustful-of-their-employers

NTSB. (2006). *Marine accident brief, Accident No. DCA-05-MM-008 (M/V Selendang Ayu)*. National Transportation Safety Board, Washington, DC (online copy). Retrieved from www.ntsb.gov/investigations/AccidentReports/Reports/MAB0601.pdf

Owens, E. (2015, August 19). ACLU threatens lawsuit over 'McCarthy Era' loyalty oath for Nebraska teachers. *The Daily Caller* (online newspaper, Nebraska). Retrieved from https://dailycaller.com/2015/08/19/aclu-threatens-lawsuit-over-mccarthy-era-loyalty-oath-for-nebraska-teachers/

VIA Institute on Character. (2017). VIA classification of character strengths. *VIA Institute website* (online). Retrieved from www.viacharacter.org/character-strengths

World Population Review. (2023). Divorce rates by country, 2023. *World Population Review Website*. Retrieved from https://worldpopulationreview.com/country-rankings/divorce-rates-by-country

Zinrelo. (n.d.) Rise of influencers in loyalty programs. *Zinrelo (loyalty program platform) website*. Retrieved from www.zinrelo.com/rise-influencers-in-loyalty-programs.html/

The Club (Privilege and Exclusion)

The concepts of privilege and exclusion are central to cultural studies today. They are so essential that they probably need no introduction since they are encountered not only in workshops on racial and gender prejudice but also in humbler settings such as farmer's markets (Rice, 2015). Rather than offering the usual sample of potentially engaging areas for interaction that appear in the other entries, here appears just one, a simple and most compelling enactment of this VICI by my students. (Special thanks to Tyrell Hemingway, the creator of the original "club.")

Exposition, Confrontation, and Simulation

My students created, at 2:30 in the afternoon in an otherwise ordinary classroom in our art building, a posh urban club. The room was darkened; deep violet light and slow strobes replaced the ceiling fluorescents; tables and the projector cart were turned into a DJ stand and a serving center; tables were set in enclaves around a central dance floor. Music boomed, buzzed, and thudded: outside, patrons (members of the class, numbering more than 30) lined up, hemmed in by faux velvet ropes, in front of a class door guarded by a sufficiently brooding bouncer. The club's staff emerged from inside the room and worked the line. Some individuals had special green tickets, received in advance; they were quickly pulled out and let in, free of charge, and then seated at the best tables, designated by flowers and other ornaments. Others in the line shuffled slowly forward, quizzed in depth by the bouncers and grudgingly granted admittance to less desirable locations. Some were, in advance, told to go elsewhere in the building and only much later knew that there was even a club in operation. The students mounting this presentation dressed the part of the managers, with sunglasses and sharp suits, and schmoozed the elite, plying them with perks.

When the lights went up and everyone in the class was reunited, I had to rate this dramatization of wealth inequality (the VICI subject in question) a captivating success. But the wealth hierarchy was not all that was implied. The club's dark and slightly sinister environment conveyed a sense of comfortable separateness from ordinary routine and, by extension, from ordinary law. It exuded the atmosphere of sanctioned illegality, a safe haven for covert dealing—easy enough to link to the idea of corruption and its role in culture (see the Corruption entry in this book). Further connections could easily be made between the situation and the cozy clubbiness of established power networks, embodied in the inspired acting of our "evening's" hosts. (Actually, the acting wasn't anything out of the ordinary and merely suggested subterranean connections to hidden power, but in that environment, little more was needed.) The selective process of

DOI: 10.4324/9781003300380-39

admission and administration of comps, as well as the misdirection of others, perfectly illustrated the concepts of privilege and exclusion (Potapchuk, 2005; Minkov, 2011; Halley, Eshleman, & Vijaya, 2022). I could not *require* that this pop-up club emerge again, but if in the future a student took the hint and recreated it, I'd certainly follow this activity with Davidson (2012) and reading the more extensive background on exclusion and inclusion worldwide available in a fairly recent United Nations report on the world social situation (United Nations, 2016).

References and Suggested Readings

Davidson, A. (2012, March 16). Why are some countries rich and others poor? *NPR Planet Money* (radio broadcast transcript). Retrieved from www.npr.org/sections/money/2012/03/16/148680705/why-are-some-countries-rich-and-others-poor

Halley, J., Eshleman, A., & Vijaya, R. M. (2022). *Seeing white: An introduction to white privilege and race*. Lanham, MD: Rowman & Littlefield.

Minkov, M. (2011). *Cultural differences in a globalizing world*. Bingely: Emerald Publishing Ltd.

Potapchuk, M. (2005). Chapter 6: What is white privilege? In M. Potapchuk, S. Leiderman, D. Bivens & B. Major (Eds.), *Flipping the script: White privilege and community building* (pp. 53–70). Silver Spring, MD: MP Associates.

Rice, J. (2015). Privilege and exclusion at the farmer's market: Findings from a survey of shoppers. *Agriculture and Human Values*, *32*(1), 21–29.

United Nations. (2016). *Leaving no one behind: The imperative of inclusive development*. New York, NY: United Nations. Retrieved from www.un.org/esa/socdev/rwss/2016/full-report.pdf

Respect

Respect is one of the most frequently mentioned VICIs and also one of the cardinal principles in the APA's Ethical Principles of Psychologists and Code of Conduct. Psychological theory (Janoff-Bulman & Werther, 2008) divides respect into categorical and contingent types. Categorical respect is accorded to humans for being human and members of society; contingent respect is established within social subgroups and depends on a complex set of estimations of self and other based on rank, relative power, and degree of equality. Sara Lawrence-Lightfoot (2000) suggests that the extension of respect begins with an attitude of openness and interest and a readiness to communicate. Cross-culturally, respect is closely related with the idea of *face* and its maintenance. The maintenance process, termed *facework* (Ting-Toomey, 2013), involves a similarly complex set of attitudes and behaviors that maintain individuals' standing relative to each other and their group, behaviors that differ depending on whether the culture is primarily individualistic or collectivistic. The relation of respect to power and control becomes clearly visible when its opposite, disrespect, is considered. Relatively powerless groups—for instance, adolescents (Barber, Xia, Olsen, McNeely, & Bose, 2012)—may be especially sensitive to the absence of respect. Groups that have experienced severe social discrimination may perceive the attainment of "respectability" to be a bad bargain involving the loss of autonomy and identity (Young, 2016).

Exposition, Confrontation, and Simulation

Some of my own best experiences in the cross-cultural class have occurred when students have reenacted situations involving disrespect. For a more theoretical approach, consider collecting and taxonomizing instances of disrespect at the hands of VE (Vulgar Euphemism) individuals as described by Howard (2016). There are several sources for facework practice; Domeneci and Littlejohn (2006) provide numerous examples for individual and group practice. Building on the material provided in Leary, Brennan, and Briggs (2005) and Lacosse (2021), a scale with questions specifically focused on respect (vs. esteem) in a Black American context can be created, completed, and discussed.

References and Suggested Readings

Barber, B. K., Xia, M., Olsen, J. A., McNeely, C. A., & Bose, K. (2012). Feeling disrespected by parents: Refining the understanding and measurement of psychological control. *Journal of Adolescence*, *35*(2), 273–287.

DOI: 10.4324/9781003300380-40

Domeneci, K., & Littlejohn, S. W. (2006). *Facework: Bridging theory and practice.* Thousand Oaks, CA: Sage.

Howard, D. J. (2016). The Vulgar Euphemism (VE) Scale: Entitled incivility in social relations. In D. J. Howard (Ed.), *The psychology of consumer and social influence: Theory and research.* Hauppage, NY: Nova Science Publishers.

Janoff-Bulman, R., & Werther, A. (2008). The social psychology of respect: Implications for delegitimization and reconciliation. In A. Nadler, T. Malloy & J. Fisher (Eds.), *The social psychology of intergroup reconciliation* (pp. 145–170). New York, NY: Oxford University Press.

Lacosse, J. (2021, June 7). R-E-S-P-E-C-T: Showing White people what it means to Black people. *SPSP (Society for Social and Personality Psychology) Website.* Retrieved from https://spsp.org/news-center/character-context-blog/r-e-s-p-e-c-t-showing-white-people-what-it-means-black-people

Lawrence-Lightfoot, S. (2000). *Respect: An exploration.* Cambridge, MA: Perseus Books.

Leary, J. D., Brennan, E. M., & Briggs, H. E. (2005). The African American adolescent respect scale: A measure of a prosocial attitude. *Research on Social Work Practice*, *15*(6), 462–469.

Ting-Toomey, S. (2013). Face-negotiation conflict theory. In K. Keith (Ed.), *The encyclopedia of cross-cultural psychology* (pp. 535–539). New York, NY: Wiley-Blackwell.

Young, D. (2016, March 21). The definition, danger, and disease of respectability politics, explained. *The Root* (blog) (online). Retrieved from www.theroot.com/the-definition-danger-and-disease-of-respectability-po-1790854699

Tribalism

Tribalism is among the most ancient formulations of culture study. Tribal life was equated with primitive culture in 19th-century anthropology; then, tribes were viewed politically as enemies (as they were during the aggressions of the United States against its native populations in the 19th century) or, alternately and somewhat later historically, as laboratory case studies of contrast with modern conditions (for instance, Erik Erikson's studies of Hopi culture). Currently, *tribalism* and *tribes* are often used to refer to an exaggerated form of social grouping involving the formation of fragmented clusters centered on particular interests or views, hyper-exclusionary and more aggressively defended. Most definitions of tribalism emphasize the aspect of group loyalty.

Today, discussions of tribalism are also connected with markets and especially with the generation of temporary interest groups via social media. A central founding document for this approach is Cova and Cova (2002), and an interesting contrast between attitudes toward business formation, in which Swedes are said to be tribal and Tanzanians more or less homogenously entrepreneurial, is drawn by Tillmar (2006). Tribalism in a more traditional sense of clannishness has been identified in other secular environments, even in higher education (Daniel & Chew, 2013). The equation of tribalism with the development of consumer communities (Skandalis, Byrom, & Banister, 2016) should not preclude seeing traditional tribalism among Indigenous populations, such as in Kenya and Ghana, or in the connection between traditional family clans and religion, as in Afghanistan and other similar cultures. Nor should religious tribalism be limited to Asian and African environments; the term *tribalism* has emerged as a descriptor of the mix of religious and political value contradictions characterizing current American politics (Reich, 2014). Most recently, the idea of tribalism as socially divisive has been challenged: tribalism may be evidence for group identity and cohesiveness within a cooperative whole (Packer & Van Bavel, 2022).

Exposition, Confrontation, and Simulation

Tribalism offers a naturally contentious area for interaction. While classic demonstrations of group conformity (e.g., Asch) could be done as an introduction to some of the basic psychological processes involved in group cohesion, they would probably not capture the distinguishing features of tribal behavior. For that, something like Sherif's "Robbers' Cave" experiments are a historical precedent but impractical for a time-limited interaction. A sample of tribalism might be induced simply by forming teams for any competition and observing any minor instances of trash talk during the process. Alternatively, search for a film of the London Marathon start described by Kovach (2017) (or

DOI: 10.4324/9781003300380-41

any similar situation involving the merging of two or more groups) to see if similar tribal identification with one of the starting groups occurs while watching. In an attempt to counteract religious tribalism, Ginges, Sheikh, Atran, and Argo (2016) constructed a version of the "trolley problem" in experimental ethics, in which the opportunity to sacrifice either oneself or an in-group member is offered to save the life of an out-group member. In this case, the in-group was practicing Palestinian Muslims and the out-group Israeli Jews. They claimed that adoption of the point of view of Allah by Muslim participants lowered their willingness to sacrifice an out-group member and returned a substantial number of participants to a neutral state on the issue. A simulation or limited replication of their study would be reasonably simple to do and could also introduce discussion of whether the trolley problem itself, widely used in studies of morals and ethics, is the most effective strategy available (Khazan, 2014). In the US sociopolitical context, Hawkins, Yudkin, Juan-Torres, and Dixon (2018) offer an intuitive seven-category description of US political tribalism as a springboard for conceptualizing cultural differences.

References and Suggested Readings

Cova, B., & Cova, V. (2002). Tribal marketing: The tribalisation of society and its impact on the conduct of marketing. *European Journal of Marketing*, *36*(5).

Daniel, D. B., & Chew, S. L. (2013). The tribalism of teaching and learning. *Teaching of Psychology*, *40*(4), 363–367.

Ginges, J., Sheikh, H., Atran, S., & Argo, N. (2016). Thinking from God's perspective decreases biased valuation of the life of a nonbeliever. *Proceedings of the National Academy of Sciences*, *113*, 316–319.

Hawkins, S., Yudkin, D., Juan-Torres, M., & Dixon, T. (2018). *Hidden tribes: A study of America's polarized landscape*. New York, NY: More in Common. Retrieved from https://hiddentribes.us/media/qfpekz4g/hidden_tribes_report.pdf

Khazan, O. (2014, July 24). Is one of the most popular psychology experiments worthless? *The Atlantic* (online magazine). Retrieved from www.theatlantic.com/health/archive/2014/07/what-if-one-of-the-most-popular-experiments-in-psychology-is-worthless/374931/

Kovach, R. (2017, July 26). How tribalism hurts companies, and what to do about it. *Harvard Business Review* (online). Retrieved from https://hbr.org/2017/07/how-tribalism-hurts-companies-and-what-to-do-about-it

Packer, D., & Van Bavel, J. (2022, January 3). The myth of tribalism. *The Atlantic* (online magazine). Retrieved from https://www.theatlantic.com/ideas/archive/2022/01/tribalism-myth-group-solidarity-prejudice-conflict/621008/

Reich, R. (2014, March 25). Robert Reich: Tribalism is tearing America apart. *Salon* (online magazine). Retrieved from www.salon.com/2014/03/25/robert_reich_tribalism_is_tearing_america_apart_partner/

Skandalis, A., Byrom, J., & Banister, E. (2016). Paradox, tribalism, and the transitional consumption experience: In light of post-postmodernism. *European Journal of Marketing*, *50*(7–8), 1308–1325.

Tillmar, M. (2006). Swedish tribalism and Tanzanian entrepreneurship: Preconditions for trust formation. *Entrepreneurship and Regional Development*, *18*(2), 91–107.

Emotion, Motivation, and Health

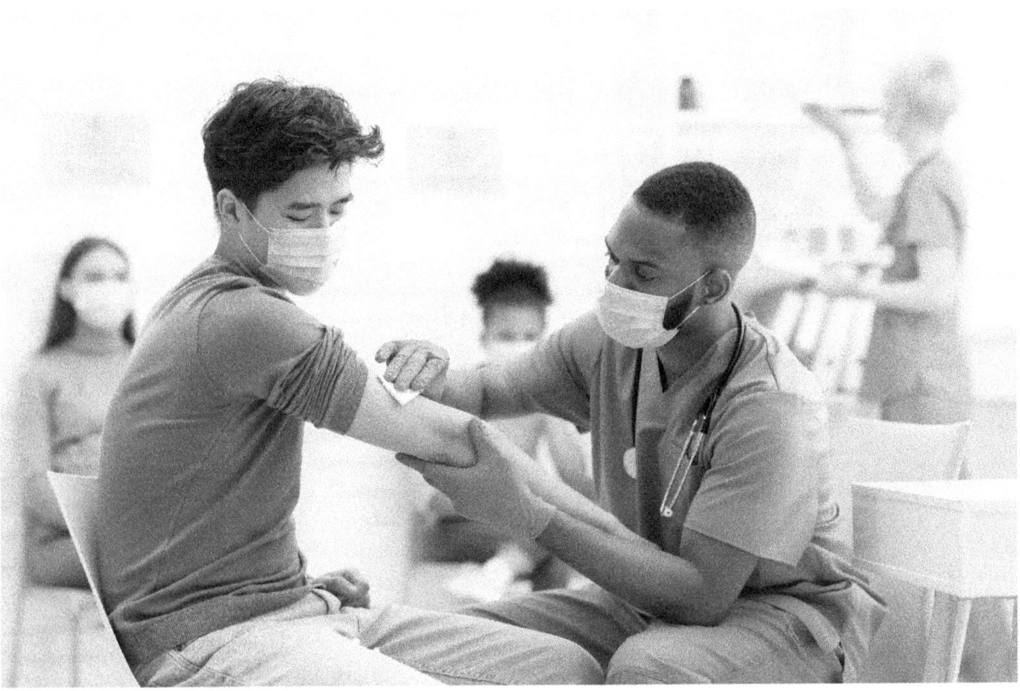

DOI: 10.4324/9781003300380-42

Disabilities

The concept of *disabilities* is fraught and contested; cross-culturally, there are huge gulfs in the acceptance and treatment of disability. In the United States and Canada, blindness and deafness themselves are thought to be cultures themselves (Lutheran Social Service of Minnesota, 2023; Hopfe, 2011). In Africa, stigmatization and isolation still characterize responses to deafness (Fullerton, 2013). Down syndrome, a prime example of intellectual disability, is welcomed in some cultures. In the United States, there are several organizations that encourage acceptance and adoption of children with this condition (e.g., Global Down Syndrome Foundation, n.d.; Reece's Rainbow, n.d.) In other cultures elsewhere in the world, Down syndrome unleashes superstition and intolerance (Bolongaro, 2016). In Europe and the United States, the lifespan of a person with Down syndrome extends due to the wide availability of scientifically based medicine, well past 50 years. In places where medical treatment—for example, for the congenital heart problems that accompany the syndrome in young children—is available only due to donations and charity and almost always takes place out-of-country, most children with Down syndrome die early. Differences also exist in the willingness of cultures and countries to accept European and American medical interpretations of the syndrome and to tolerate abortion in cases of birth defects (Oloyede, 2011). These wide disparities should be the starting point for any simulations or discussions in a cross-cultural format. Disabilities, since they are included in the major psychiatric and psychological diagnostic systems, also stand as proxy for the full spectrum of mental disorders and an entry point for their regional and cultural acceptance and treatment.

Exposition, Confrontation, and Simulation

No practical simulation of the full cultural experience of disability is possible short of actually living with it. Many hearing loss and vision loss simulations are available online, though they are often passive demonstrations of the grades of attenuation of sensation. There are simple interactive activities that have been devised to simulate experiences of blind navigation and recognition (e.g., Willings, 2018); there are fewer similar activities involving hearing loss since simply plugging the ears isn't a good substitute for actual hearing loss. Possibly the closest approach to a demonstration of how hearing loss might affect social interaction and performance would be to set up some form of virtual auditory experience (Shilling & Shinn-Cunningham, 2002) in which sounds were strategically placed around a room to either distort or impede communication. Sign language is eminently teachable and would be another port of entry to understanding deaf culture. Also seek out the very convincing account of the relation of deafness and music (Kolb,

DOI: 10.4324/9781003300380-43

2017) also found in the references to the Silences entry in this book. Stories of individuals who have persevered and emerged victorious over challenging sensory or intellectual conditions have always been attractive and inspiring; search these out (e.g., Gee, 2016). Likewise, blogs of persons actively challenging perceptions of disability—for instance, Carrie Wade (2016)—are essential. Discussion and a simulated ratification of the United Nations Convention on the Rights of Persons with Disabilities (United Nations, n.d.) would provide a full spectrum of the ways in which disabilities integrate with all aspects of culture worldwide. In this context, a search of the range of laws protecting disability worldwide can be undertaken and the results compared.

References and Suggested Readings

Bolongaro, K. (2016, August 15). Living with Down's syndrome in Kinshasa, DRC. *Aljazeera.com* (Online news source). Retrieved from www.aljazeera.com/features/2016/8/15/living-with-downs-syndrome-in-kinshasa-drc

Fullerton, K. (2013, August 6). Deafness in sub-Saharan Africa. *The Borgen Project* (Blog). Retrieved from https://borgenproject.org/deafness-in-sub-saharan-africa/

Gee, A. (2016, September 29). A world without Down's syndrome? *BBC News Magazine* (online). Retrieved from www.bbc.com/news/magazine-37500189

Global Down Syndrome Foundation. (n.d.). Facts and FAQ about Down syndrome. *Global Down Syndrome Foundation website* (online). Retrieved from www.globaldownsyndrome.org/about-down-syndrome/facts-about-down-syndrome/

Hopfe, A. (2011). The culture of blindness. *AEBC (Alliance for Equality of Blind Canadians) website* (online). Retrieved from www.blindcanadians.ca/publications/cbm/14/culture-blindness

Kolb, R. (2017, November 4). Sensations of sound. *The New York Times* (online newspaper). Retrieved from www.nytimes.com/interactive/2017/multimedia/sensations-of-sound-vr-rachel-kolb.html

Lutheran Social Service of Minnesota. (2023). American deaf culture. *Minnesota Hands & Voices Website.* Retrieved from www.lssmn.org/mnhandsandvoices/resources-information/american-deaf-culture

Oloyede, O. A. (2011, August 17). Down Syndrome in Nigerian sub-Saharan Africa. In S. Dey (Ed.), *Prenatal diagnosis and screening for Down Syndrome.* London, England: InTech Open Access. Retrieved from www.intechopen.com/chapters/17996

Reece's Rainbow. (n.d.). Who we are. *Reece's Rainbow* (organizational website). Retrieved from http://reecesrainbow.org/whoweare

Shilling, R. D., & Shinn-Cunningham, B. G. (2002). Chapter 4: Virtual auditory displays. In K. Stanney (Ed.), *Handbook of virtual environments: Design, implementation, and applications* (pp. 65–92). Mahwah, NJ: Lawrence Erlbaum.

United Nations. (n.d.). Convention on the rights of persons with disabilities (CRPD). *Division for Social Policy and Development, United Nations* (website). Retrieved from https://social.desa.un.org/issues/disability/crpd/convention-on-the-rights-of-persons-with-disabilities-crpd

Wade, C. (2016, May 5). A letter to my able-bodied partner. *Upworthy* (online resource). Retrieved from www.upworthy.com/a-letter-to-my-able-bodied-partner

Willings, C. (2018). Simulation activities. *Teaching Students With Visual Impairments* (website). Retrieved from www.teachingvisuallyimpaired.com/simulation-activities.html

Health and Environment: Sanitation

Most audiences for this text will understand health from a personal and individualistic perspective: "my own health" encompassed by the skin and containing both the healthy mind and healthy organs envisioned in the Roman poet Juvenal's phrase *mens sana in corpore sano*. Should this focus be desired, a text in health psychology with a specific cultural flair is recommended, for example that of Regan Gurung (2018). Often, too, health, when considered in a cross-cultural context, becomes a set of contrasts between allopathic medicine (sometimes called "Western" or "scientific" medicine) and other forms of indigenous medicine, or between sets of cultural beliefs (and sometimes superstitions) held by individuals about the causes and cures of disease. In this section, the focus is instead on what René Dubos (1987) said were the real determinants of health: the establishment of equilibrium with pathogens through collective construction of healthy ecosystems. Turning to excrement: while human "wearing out" results in strokes and heart disease worldwide, these are the top causes of death only in highly affluent cultures. Much of the world dies because of problems of sanitation, especially in the early years of life, and billions of people worldwide have no access to sanitary toilets. The Bill and Melinda Gates Foundation has been engaged in "reinventing the toilet" since 2011 and is producing tangible results (Kone, 2021).

Exposition, Confrontation, and Simulation

Regarding individual health and health care, the discussion might start at points at which there appear to be clear cultural differences. There is a fairly sizable literature—locatable via Gurung's text as well as simple googling—on Chinese, Hispanic, and Native American medical traditions. In that context, starting a discussion with the question of what folk remedies are used by class members (and instructors) would lead naturally to a review of the range of folk wisdom. It is worth remembering that medicinal drugging emerged from the collected wisdom of indigenous healers as well as accidental encounters with naturally occurring medicinal plants. A range of cultural locales can be immediately encountered by reviewing any recent issue of the *International Journal of Crude Drug Research* (now *Pharmaceutical Biology*). Nurses and other medical service providers have developed a strong commitment to addressing cultural differences in practice: chief among these over the past several decades has been Larry Purnell, whose system of cultural competences in nursing and health care extends widely beyond that sphere (Purnell, 2014). Clear differences also exist between cultures regarding the social and environmental conditions under which health care is delivered and compensated. Construction of a dramatic simulation of the respect accorded to hospitals in current warfare is recommended (e.g., Human Rights

DOI: 10.4324/9781003300380-44

Watch, 2016; Cole, 2022). Contrast between the state of health care support in the United States and other similarly affluent countries would also be instructive and good preparation for making informed political decisions.

The subject of the hygiene side of this topic pair is selected because of its naturally discomfiting character. Not for nothing did Freud put toilet training at the heart of psychology! For one possible opener, Tyler Oakley's *Binge* contains a breezy account of the physiology of defecation in a hip and polycultural context (Oakley, 2015). For another, read selections from David Waltner-Toews's (2013) *The Origin of Feces*. Julia Scott's (2014) account of her month-long showerless existence is a great introduction to the bacterial context and a stimulant to student construction of surveys of personal hygiene. Questions of how to address the sheer magnitude of the problem of sanitation and waste disposal should lead to innovative speculations and simulations. From a cultural interventionist perspective, how do you convince a person who is used to going wherever and whenever that a toilet is a great idea? From an environmentalist perspective, what is the best way to deal with a river that is choked with fecal foam (Mallonee, 2017; Mogul & Mitra, 2021), next to which people take "smog selfies"? Full discussion of questions of cultural differences in sanitation can lead to other interactive exercises in related areas, for instance trash and garbage disposal and food recycling. If these lead to discussions of environmental activism, well and good.

References and Suggested Readings

Cole, D. (2022, May 24). Russia's 226 attacks on health-care targets in Ukraine are part of a larger pattern. *NPR (National Public Radio) Goats and Soda Website*. Retrieved from www.npr.org/sections/goatsandsoda/2022/03/16/1086982186/russias-strike-on-ukraine-maternity-hospital-is-part-of-a-terrible-wartime-tradi [Accessed March 4, 2023].

Dubos, R. (1987). *Mirage of health: Utopias, progress, and biological change*. New Brunswick, NJ: Rutgers University Press. (Originally published 1959).

Gurung, R. (2018). *Health psychology: Well-being in a diverse world* (4th ed.). Thousand Oaks, CA: Sage.

Human Rights Watch. (2016, August 11). Syria: Government airstrikes closing down hospitals. *Human Rights Watch Website* (online). Retrieved from www.hrw.org/news/2016/08/11/syria-government-airstrikes-closing-down-hospitals [Accessed March 4, 2023].

Kone, D. (2021, July 29). The future of sanitation: 10 years of reinventing the toilet. *The Bill and Melinda Gates Foundation Website*. Retrieved from www.gatesfoundation.org/ideas/articles/sanitation-reinvent-toilet [Accessed March 4, 2023].

Mallonee, L. (2017, April 5). India's most polluted river actually bubbles with toxic foam. *Wired* (online magazine). Retrieved from www.wired.com/2017/04/zacharie-rabehi-toxic-city/ [Accessed March 4, 2023].

Mogul, R., & Mitra, E., (2021, November 11). Toxic foam coats sacred river in India as Hindu devotees bathe in its waters. *CNN (Cable News Network) Website*. Retrieved from www.cnn.com/2021/11/10/india/india-toxic-foam-intl-hnk/index.html#:~:text=The%20white%20froth%2C%20a%20mixture,the%20Himalayas%20through%20several%20states [Accessed March 4, 2023].

Oakley, T. (2015). *Binge*. New York, NY: Gallery Books.

Purnell, L. (2014). *Guide to culturally competent health care* (3rd ed.). Philadelphia, PA: F. A. Davis Co.

Scott, J. (2014, May 25). My no-soap, no-shampoo bacteria-rich hygiene experiment. *The New York Times*. Retrieved from www.nytimes.com/2014/05/25/magazine/my-no-soap-no-shampoo-bacteria-rich-hygiene-experiment.html [Accessed March 4, 2023].

Waltner-Toews, D. (2013). *The origin of feces: What excrement tells us about evolution, ecology, and a sustainable society*. Toronto, ON: ECW Press.

Vaccination, Misinformation, & Masking: COVID-19 Redux

Starting in late 2019, the SARS-COVID-2 virus designated COVID-19 spread rapidly and by mid-2020 had upended ordinary social and cultural practices worldwide. It was particularly deadly and may have resulted, by the end of 2022, in more than 14 million excess deaths (Msemburi et al., 2022). The effects were similar to those of disaster or war; forced isolation, mandated health and safety practices, economic disruption, overwhelming of health care resources, and restriction of movement were all features of the response to the pandemic across countries. The arrival of effective vaccines in early 2021 signaled a turn in the tide; only now can the period be seen as a vast natural experiment in which virtually all social relations were thrust into an unintended position of comparison with previous practices. Consideration of all the aspects of pandemic upheaval will take years (and will probably diminish as normality is restored). Here, singled out as shedding particular light on culture, are the responses to the introduction (or, as some would put it, imposition) of public health measures—vaccination and masking—as well as the upsurge in public misinformation, which contributed directly to increased mortality in areas where it was heavily consumed (Gollwitzer et al., 2020; Picard et al., 2022).

Exposition, Confrontation, and Simulation

To begin with, vaccination offers a springboard to consider inequities in access to health care, and specifically to medications, worldwide. Start with data on inequities in COVID-19 vaccine availability (Pilkington, Keestra, & Hill, 2022), and compare similar inequities in treatment availability (Nolen & Robbins, 2023); is the pattern constant? Vaccination is also an entry point for consideration, if it has not occurred in the context of other instances of medicine in this book, of differing philosophies of medicine; health psychologist Regan Gurung provides a thorough overview of Chinese, Indian, Hispanic, and other Indigenous and traditional systems (Gurung, 2018). Search and examine reports of the ways that Western medicine has intersected with traditional medicine and its cultures. For example, read the appeal for vaccination by the American Lung Association to the Chinese American population, which combines appeals to family and collectivism and evidence for the complementary though secondary effectiveness of traditional Chinese medicine in combating COVID-19 (American Lung Association, 2021). King (2021) provides a nuanced account of all the forces acting to attract or repel Mexican immigrants in the northwestern US from vaccination, including beliefs in the power of *curanderos*.

Widespread dissemination of misinformation revved up an already existing culture of skepticism about and distrust of vaccines. One interactive way of understanding and

DOI: 10.4324/9781003300380-45

appreciating the strength of misinformation is to play the *Bad News* game developed at Cambridge University (UK) (Cambridge University, 2018). Similar to other programs designed to help internet users detect phishing scams and other attacks, this site provides a lifelike simulation of misinformation techniques in a brand-building social media environment. It's unlikely that many who are reading and using this text will be skeptical of vaccines, especially in the COVID context. For them, it might be helpful to develop ways of tripping up vaccine skeptics, if only to confound them. Interview samples of individuals about their COVID vaccination views using a version of the survey about COVID vaccine resistance and misinformation developed by Neely and colleagues (Neely, Eldredge, Ersing, & Remington, 2022), and include a question about tetanus vaccination. (It's likely that most adults, even those who are vaccine-resistant, have received several noncontroversial shots.) This may reveal inconsistency or nuance within the vaccine-skeptic culture.

Vaccination was not the only target of health misinformation; it extended to other public health measures, notably masking. Masks, a subject of enduring anthropological and Jungian interest, became a marker of underlying social tensions, and the introduction of mask mandates, even in tight cultures like Germany, led to episodes of violence (Jordans, 2021). Kemmelmeier and Jami (2021) detail the ways that individualism/collectivism, tight vs. loose cultures, and political identification intersect around the issue in the United States, and they also introduce a new element in the mix, *cultures of honor*, not previously encountered in this book. Honor varies in its worldwide cultural meanings (Shiraev & Levy, 2021). In this instance, the particular view of honor often associated with the southern United States emphasizing an strongly defensive attitude to protecting social status, led to masking being interpreted as weakness and (literally) loss of face. Discussion of masking is a pathway to integrating multiple aspects of culture.

References and Suggested Readings

American Lung Association (2021). Better for it: Unity is strength. *American Lung Association* (medical information website). Retrieved from www.lung.org/getmedia/7b6cd378-e47e-4b8e-995f-5b7eab3e1ec0/Chinese-Toolkit_English_Final.pdf

Cambridge University (UK). (2018). *Bad News* (Interactive online simulation). Retrieved from www.getbadnews.com/books/english/

Conis, E. (2015, August). Vaccine resistance in historical perspective. *The American Historian* (online journal, Organization of American Historians. Retrieved from www.oah.org/tah/issues/2015/august/vaccination-resistance/

Gollwitzer, A., Martel, C., Brady, W. J., Pärnamets, P., Freedman, I. G., Knowles, E. D., & Van Bavel, J. J. (2020). Partisan differences in physical distancing are linked to health outcomes during the COVID-19 pandemic. *Nature Human Behavior*, *4*(11), 1186–1197. Retrieved from www.nature.com/articles/s41562-020-00977-7

Gurung, R. (2018). *Health psychology: Well-being in a diverse world* (4th ed.). Thousand Oaks, CA: Sage.

Jordans, F. (2021, September 21). German officials fear anti-mask radicalization after killing. *Associated Press* (online news source). Retrieved from https://apnews.com/article/europe-arrests-germany-5c853b4e068e1203b890652cc96e8a5c

Kemmelmeier, M., & Jami, W. A. (2021, 21 July). Mask wearing as cultural behavior: An investigation across 45 U.S. States during the COVID-19 pandemic. *Frontiers in Psychology (Section Cultural Psychology)*, *12*. Retrieved from www.frontiersin.org/articles/10.3389/fpsyg.2021.648692/full

King, A. (2021, April 23). It's complicated: Why some Northwest Latinx residents and farmworkers hesitate on COVID vaccine. *NW News Network* (online regional news source). Retrieved from www.nwnewsnetwork.org/health-and-medicine/2021-04-23/its-complicated-why-some-northwest-latinx-residents-and-farmworkers-hesitate-on-covid-vaccine

Msemburi, W., Karlinsky, A., Knutson, V., Aleshin-Guendel, S., Chatterji, S., & Wakefield, J. (2022, December 14). The WHO estimates of excess mortality associated with the COVID-19 pandemic. *Nature, 613*, 130–137. Retrieved from www.nature.com/articles/s41586-022-05522-2

Neely, S. R., Eldredge, C., Ersing, R., & Remington, C. (2022). Vaccine hesitancy and exposure to misinformation: A survey analysis. *Journal of General and Internal Medicine, 37*(1), 179–187. Retrieved from www.ncbi.nlm.nih.gov/pmc/articles/PMC8528483/

Nolen, S., & Robbins, R. (2023, February 7). The drug is a 'miracle' but these families can't get it. *The New York Times* (online news source). Retrieved from www.nytimes.com/2023/02/07/health/cystic-fibrosis-drug-trikafta.html

Picard, L., Pinna, M., & Goessmann, C. (2022, April 15). The impact of Fox News on the US COVID-19 vaccination campaign. *VoxEU* (Online international news source). Retrieved from https://cepr.org/voxeu/columns/impact-fox-news-us-covid-19-vaccination-campaign

Pilkington, V., Keestra, S. M., & Hill, A. (2022, March 7). Global COVID-19 vaccine inequity: Failures in the first year of distribution and potential solutions for the future. *Frontiers in Public Health (Section Public Health Policy), 10*. Retrieved from www.frontiersin.org/articles/10.3389/fpubh.2022.821117/full

Shiraev, E. B., & Levy, D. A. (2021). *Cross-cultural psychology: Critical thinking and contemporary applications* (7th ed.). New York, NY and London, England: Routledge.

Well-being

Well-being has ancient roots; conceptions of the highest good or the good life trace back to the idea of *eudaemonia* in ancient Greece. Even in modern psychology, well-being has a longer history than most social and cultural terms. The current standard definition (in the APA's *Dictionary of Psychology*)—"a state of happiness and contentment, with low levels of distress, overall good physical and mental health and outlook, or good quality of life" (American Psychological Association, 2015)—overlaps with the one found in Howard C. Warren's 1934 *Dictionary of Psychology*: "a condition of general good health and prosperity experienced by an individual, or the conscious state (marked by a pleasant feeling tone) which accompanies this condition" (Warren, 1934). (This latter definition also includes the French and German equivalents, *bien être* and *Wohlsein*, respectively.)

Well-being mirrors the split between individual and social psychology. Some conceptions focus primarily on individual emotional and motivational perceptions (e.g., the five-item World Health Organization Well-Being Index (WHO-5), which asks questions about feelings of cheerfulness, calmness, activity, freshness, and interest) (Bech, 2004). Others conceive of well-being in a broad sociocultural context; for instance, the Global Youth Wellbeing Index of the International Youth Foundation includes the components of gender equality, economic opportunity, education, health, citizen participation, safety and security, and information and communication technology (International Youth Foundation, 2017). It is a variable in explicitly cross-cultural research as well (e.g., Galinha et al., 2016; Brailovska et al., 2022; Choi, Diener, Sim, & Oishi, 2022).

Exposition, Confrontation, and Simulation

There are many scales for measuring well-being. The simplest, though focused only on a collection of individual conscious states, is the aforementioned WHO-5, which is a good example of an appropriately validated measure of the construct cross-culturally (Sischka et al., 2020). The Lee Kum Sheung Center for Health and Happiness at Harvard University points to several scales across multiple dimensions of well-being, including flourishing, meaning in life, life satisfaction, mastery, and optimism (Harvard T. H. Chan, 2022). Searching out and discussing of the contents of these scales should in itself reinforce other ideas across these exercises dealing with cultural aspects of emotional response and happiness. The well-being concept is inherently cross-cutting and can provide a springboard for broaching other related cross-culturally relevant concepts such as mental health (Gopalkrishnan, 2018), success and failure (e.g., the question of whether it's better, in terms of feelings of success, to be a smaller or a bigger frog in the pond, Werber, 2017), and resilience (Skevington et al., 2020).

DOI: 10.4324/9781003300380-46

References

American Psychological Association. (2015). *APA dictionary of psychology* (2nd ed.). Washington, DC: American Psychological Association. Retrieved from https://dictionary.apa.org/well-being

Bech, P. (2004). Measuring the dimensions of psychological general well-being by the WHO-5. *QoL Newsletter*, *32*, 15–16. Retrieved from https://ogg.osu.edu/media/documents/MB%20Stream/who5.pdf

Brailovska, J., Lin, M., Scholten, S., Zhu, M., Fu, Y., Shao, M., Hu, S., Li, X., Guo, W., Cai, D., Lu, S., & Margraf, J. (2022). A qualitative cross-cultural comparison of well-being constructs: The meaning of happiness, life satisfaction, and social support for German and Chinese students. *Journal of Happiness Studies*, *23*, 1379–1402. Retrieved from https://link.springer.com/article/10.1007/s10902-021-00454-6

Choi, H., Diener, E., Sim, J. H., & Oishi, S. (2022). Happiness is associated with successful living across cultures. *Journal of Positive Psychology*. https://doi.org/10.1080/17439760.2022.2155221

Galinha, I. C., Garcia-Martin, M. Á., Oishi, S., Wirtz, D., & Esteves, F. (2016). Cross-cultural comparison of personality traits, attachment security, and satisfaction with relationships as predictors of subjective well-being in India, Sweden, and the United States. *Journal of Cross Cultural Psychology*, *47*(8), 1019–1032.

Gopalkrishnan, N. (2018). Cultural diversity and mental health: Considerations for policy and practice. *Frontiers in Public Health*, *6*, *179*. Retrieved from www.ncbi.nlm.nih.gov/pmc/articles/PMC6018386/

Harvard T. H. Chan School of Public Health. (2022). *Repository of positive psychological well-being scales*. Retrieved from www.hsph.harvard.edu/health-happiness/repository-of-positive-psychological-well-being-scales/

International Youth Foundation. (2017). *The Global Health Wellbeing Index* (online). Retrieved from www.youthindex.org/

Sischka, P. E., Costa, A. P., Steffgen, G., & Schmidt, A. F. (2020). The WHO-5 well-being index: Validation based on item response theory and the analysis of measurement invariance across 35 countries. *Journal of Affective Disorders Reports*, *1*. Retrieved from www.sciencedirect.com/science/article/pii/S2666915320300202

Skevington, S. M., & WHOQOL SRPB Group. (2020, July 30). Is culture important to the relationship between quality of life and resilience? Global implications for preparing communities for environmental and health disasters. *Frontiers in Psychology (Sect. Cultural Psychology)*. Retrieved from www.frontiersin.org/articles/10.3389/fpsyg.2020.01492/full

Warren, H. C. (Ed.). (1934). *Dictionary of psychology*. Boston, MA: Houghton Mifflin Co.

Werber, C. (2017, July 12). East and West have opposite views of personal success, according to psychologists. *Quartz (online magazine)*. Retrieved from https://qz.com/1025291/east-and-west-have-opposite-views-of-personal-success-according-to-psychologists

Hunger

For most of the recent past, hunger in psychology has been either a physiological or a motivational topic. Old-style behaviorism took hunger for granted in order that the animal subjects—cats, dogs, rats, and pigeons—would actively seek solutions to problems that led to relief. One of the signal achievements of mid-20th century neuroscience was the elucidation of brain mechanisms involved in controlling hunger, thirst, and other motivational states.

Students of culture, however, will find only indirect paths if any between the cultural situation of hunger and the lateral hypothalamus. For a cultural view, one can start with the first level of Maslow's motivational system; little is achieved in terms of building higher cultural achievements for the self and for others if basic survival needs are not met. Beyond this truth, several paths of investigation lie open. Across cultures in the United States and worldwide, food insecurity is correlated with cultures of poverty. Grobler (2016), in a South African context, differentiates between food-secure and food-insecure low-income households in terms of the reasons for poverty with those that are food-secure ascribing poverty to a lack of individual effort while those who are food-insecure adopting fatalistic beliefs in environmental or social factors as causes. Similarly, chronic hunger is shown to have negative effects on both physical and mental development across subcultures in the United States (Weinreb et al., 2002; Karpyn, Riser, Tracy, Wang, & Shen, 2019).

Another way in which hunger, mental state, and culture interact outside the area of existential threat is in the process of self-control of hunger states, examples of which are dieting and religious fasting. Trepanowski and Bloomer (2010) compared Islamic Ramadan fasts; Greek Orthodox Nativity, Lenten, and Assumption fasts; and the Christian Daniel fast. This latter ritual is based on a reading of the Biblical book of Daniel (10: 2,3), in which resistance to food is described as both a feature of mourning and a reaction to oppression. They found mostly health-beneficial results of these practices, which, for the most part, lead to healthier food choices as well as restricted intake.

Exposition, Confrontation, and Simulation

A starting point for a discussion of hunger could be to ask whether, and under what circumstances, a day's meals or more were involuntarily missed. Surveys of food accessibility modeled on the USDA short-form food security survey (www.ers.usda.gov/media/8282/short2012.pdf) would augment a discussion along these lines. If students practice fasting, the various reasons for this can also be a starting point for further comparison among subcultures. (For instance, though the practice is never recommended, certain athletic

DOI: 10.4324/9781003300380-47

groups practice forms of enforced fasting for weight management.) Dieting and other methods of controlling appetite psychologically can be introduced as topics as well. Not only are there variations in cultural dietary patterns that are considered healthier choices, but there is also a recent trend to diet less and to become more accepting of variations in normal body shape and size (Aubrey, 2017). Many good examples of the way that hunger and culture reciprocally determine themselves are contained in George Norton's recent book *Hunger and Hope* (Norton, 2014). An engaging account of the interaction of social class, food scarcity, and desire is Adam Rivera's account of his hunger for his food past (Rivera, 2023).

References and Suggested Readings

Aubrey, A. (2017, March 8). Is dieting passe? Study finds fewer overweight people try to lose weight. *NPR Morning Edition: The Salt* (Radio program, 2017). Retrieved from www.npr.org/sections/thesalt/2017/03/08/519080766/is-dieting-passe-study-finds-fewer-overweight-people-try-to-lose-weight

Grobler, W. C. J. (2016). Perceptions of poverty: A study of food secure and food insecure households in an urban area of South Africa. *Procedia Economics and Finance*, *35*, 224–231. Retrieved from www.sciencedirect.com/science/article/pii/S2212567116000289

Karpyn, A. E., Riser, D., Tracy, T., Wang, R., & Shen, Y. (2019). The changing landscape of food deserts. *UNSCN (United Nations Standing Committee on Nutrition) 44*, 46–53. Retrieved from www.ncbi.nlm.nih.gov/pmc/articles/PMC7299236/

Norton, G. W. (2014). *Hunger and hope: Escaping poverty and achieving food security in developing countries*. Long Grove, IL: Waveland Press.

Rivera, A. J. (2023, February 28). I am mourning the loss of something I loved: McNuggets. *The New York Times* (online newspaper). Retrieved from www.nytimes.com/2023/02/28/opinion/processed-food-social-class-america.html

Trepanowski, J. F., & Bloomer, R. J. (2010). The impact of religious fasting on human health. *Nutrition Journal*, *9*, 57. https://doi.org/10.1186/1475-2891-9-57. Retrieved from https://nutritionj.biomedcentral.com/articles/10.1186/1475-2891-9-57

Weinreb, L., Wehler, C., Perloff, J., Scott, R., Hosmer, D., Sagor, L., & Gunderson, C. (2002). Hunger: Its impact on children's health and mental health. *Pediatrics*, *110*(4), e41 (https://doi.org/10.1542/peds.110.4.e41). Retrieved from https://publications.aap.org/pediatrics/article-abstract/110/4/e41/64550/Hunger-Its-Impact-on-Children-s-Health-and-Mental?redirectedFrom=fulltext

Happiness and Sadness

The pairing of happiness and sadness stands as proxy here for the full range of emotions expressed normally and implicated in psychopathology. In this entry, the focus will be on happiness per se and on the particular form of sadness contingent on loss and grief. Each of these has a substantial presence in the cross-cultural psychological literature (Selin & Davey, 2012; Parkes, Laungani, & Young, 2015). Early cross-cultural studies aimed at finding out whether emotional expression is universal across cultures, and, up to now, this has been assumed to be mostly the case. Caution should be exercised, however; a recent study comparing a relatively uncontacted group with US participants revealed that contextual cultural cues may be necessary for the interpretation of supposedly universal facial expressions (Gendron, Roberson, van der Vyver, & Barrett, 2014). Likewise, the concept of happiness, always thought to be complex, is becoming more formally subdivided into distinctly different emotional states (Shiota et al., 2017) or as concurrently containing a negative as well as a positive valence: a mixed emotion (An, Ji, Marks, & Zhang, 2017). Cultures that emphasize balance between emotional states may not attempt to maximize positive emotions (Miyamoto, Ma, & Wilken, 2017). Cultures differ in the regulation of emotional expression and in the consequences of emotional expression or suppression (Krys et al., 2022). Nonetheless, there is support for the idea that emotions are, at their core, culturally universal and measurable (Bieda et al., 2017; Disabato, Goodman, Kashdan, Short, & Jarden, 2016).

Exposition, Confrontation, and Simulation

Emotion is a hub; here is a brief list of directions in which interactives can fly.

1. Examine facial expressions either pictorially or in real time with present company; compare posed emotional selfies with the classic views on Paul Ekman's website (Ekman, n.d.).
2. Find happiness/well-being/positive mental health scales; distribute, complete, and compare results. A cross-culturally validated selection is listed in Bieda et al. (2017).
3. Mine the copious data comparing rated happiness with several other dimensions of experience including gross domestic product and other measures of living standards across cultures on the Our World in Data website (Ortiz-Ospina & Roser, 2023).
4. Discuss which features of psychiatric diagnosis might be universal and which might be culturally conditioned; use any standard text in either cross-cultural psychology, cross-cultural counseling, or cross-cultural health psychology as a guide. Note the subtle interplay between universal features of depression and psychiatrists' culturally

DOI: 10.4324/9781003300380-48

influenced diagnoses (Jeffrey, 2015). Discuss specifically whether mania, the happiness lobe of bipolarity, is perceived differently across cultures and compare to the description in Viswanath and Chaturvedi (2012).

5 Discuss grief and mourning in the context of its measurement: Alves, Oliveira, and Lotufo-Neto (2016) supply the elements of the frequently used TRIG (Texas Revised Inventory of Grief) scale along with cross-cultural validation.
6 Discussion of grief and happiness may lead to considering the rituals and celebrations connected with each emotion and to comparisons of funeral/end-of-life and birth/wedding practices; these are always rich sources of intercultural and interpersonal sharing.
7 Finally—for this list of suggestions, at least—broaden the search to include all of the other emotions, searching for cross-cultural comparisons. For a start, attempt a replication of Skolnick and Dzokoto's (2013) comparison of Ghanian and US perceptions of disgust.

References and Suggested Readings

Alves, T. M., Oliveira, M. C., & Lotufo-Neto, F. (2016). Diagnosis of complicated grief using the Texas Revised Inventory of Grief, Brazilian Portuguese version. *Journal of Psychology and Clinical Psychiatry*, *6*(1), 00316 (https://doi.org/10.15406/jpcpy.2016.06.00316). Retrieved from http://medcraveonline.com/JPCPY/JPCPY-06-00316.pdf

An, S., Ji, L. J., Marks, M., & Zhang, Z. (2017, April 20). Two sides of emotion: Exploring positivity and negativity in six basic emotions across cultures. *Frontiers in Psychology (Sec. Emotion Science)*, *8*. Retrieved from www.frontiersin.org/articles/10.3389/fpsyg.2017.00610/full

Bieda, A., Hirschfeld, G., Schonfeld, P., Brailovskaia, J., Zhang, X. C., & Margraf, J. (2017). Universal happiness? Cross-cultural measurement invariance of scales assessing positive mental health. *Psychological Assessment*, *29*(4), 408–421.

Disabato, D. J., Goodman, F. R., Kashdan, T. B., Short, J. L., & Jarden, A. (2016). Different types of well-being? A cross-cultural examination of hedonic and eudaimonic well-being. *Psychological Assessment*, *28*(5), 471–482.

Ekman, P. (n.d.). Are there universal facial expressions? Find out using this simple test. *PaulEkmanGroup* (website). Retrieved from www.paulekman.com/resources/universal-facial-expressions/

Gendron, M., Roberson, D., van der Vyver, J. M., & Barrett, L. F. (2014). Perceptions of emotion from facial expressions are not culturally universal: Evidence from a remote culture. *Emotion*, *14*(2), 251–262.

Jeffrey, S. (2015, May 26). Cultural differences may affect psychiatric diagnosis. *Medscape Medical News* (online news source). Retrieved from www.medscape.com/viewarticle/845329#vp_2

Krys, K., Yeung, J. C., Capaldi, C. A., Lun, V. M. C., Torres, C., . . . Vignoles, V. L. (2022). Societal emotional environments and cross-cultural differences in life satisfaction: A forty-nine country study. *Journal of Positive Psychology*, *17*(1), 117–130. Retrieved from www.tandfonline.com/doi/full/10.1080/17439760.2020.1858332

Miyamoto, Y., Ma, X., & Wilken, B. (2017). Cultural variation in pro-positive versus balanced systems of emotions. *Current Opinion in Behavioral Sciences, 15*, 27–32. https://doi.org/10.1016/j.cobeha.2017.05.014

Ortiz-Ospina, E., & Roser, M. (2023). Happiness and life satisfaction. *Our World in Data* (online data source). Retrieved from https://ourworldindata.org/happiness-and-life-satisfaction

Parkes, C. M., Laungani, P., & Young, B. (2015). *Death and bereavement across cultures* (2nd ed.). New York, NY: Routledge.

Selin, H., & Davey, G. (Eds.). (2012). *Happiness across cultures: Views of happiness and quality of life in non-Western cultures*. New York, NY: Springer.

Shiota, M. N., Campos, B., Oveis, C., Hertenstein, M. J., Simon-Thomas, E., & Keltner, D. (2017). Beyond happiness: Building a science of discrete positive emotions. *American Psychologist*, *72*(7), 617–643.

Skolnick, A. J., & Dzokoto, V. A. (2013). Disgust and contamination: A cross-national comparison of Ghana and the United States. *Frontiers in Psychology*, *4*, 91 (https://doi.org/10.3389/fpsyg.2013.00091) (online). Retrieved from www.ncbi.nlm.nih.gov/pmc/articles/PMC3583245/

Viswanath, B., & Chaturvedi, S. K. (2012). Cultural aspects of major mental disorders: A critical review from an Indian perspective. *Indian Journal of Psychological Medicine*, *34*(4), 306–312.

Love and Hate

Psychological attempts to quantify love began to emerge in the 1970s. A theory popularized by the Canadian sociologist John Lee (1973), partly based on classical typologies of love and partly original, identified six main types: *eros* (romantic), *ludus* (flirting), *mania* (obsession), *storge* (enduring), *agape* (selfless), and *pragma* (expedient). Robert Sternberg proposed a three-factor theory of love in the 1980s (Sternberg, 1986) that derived a similar typology of love from combinations of measured intimacy, passion, and commitment. Hatfield and Rapson (1996) specifically focused on cross-cultural dimensions of love within a two-variable framework (companionate vs. passionate love). Recent work on love has evolved a more narrative and individualized approach rather than a theoretical-empirical one (e.g. Gleason & Selinger, 2015). Love is so attractive that it leads to forgetting that, historically and culturally, it is locked in an embrace with hate; for Freud, the struggle of Eros against Thanatos was and is the dynamic of all existence. Though not as well-known as his work on love, Sternberg has also published extensively on hate (Sternberg, 2005; Sternberg & Sternberg, 2008). And hate crimes take place worldwide, though they are not always acknowledged as such where they occur (Katsuba, 2023).

Exposition, Confrontation, and Simulation

Love, within a United States psychological context at least, has commonly been contextualized within interpersonal relations, usually sexual or marital at their core. Scales to measure Sternberg triangular factor combinations, for example, can be found in introductory psychology texts as well as on many websites; interpersonal attractiveness likewise offers several entry points in introductory and social psychology. The study of interpersonal dyads does not exhaust the meanings of love, which is as protean a term as pleasure, to which it's semantically and emotionally related. At some level, "love" maps on to "enjoy"; a person visiting a McDonald's and "lovin' it," as the slogan has it, isn't looking for a long-term relationship. Other linguistic traditions can be mined for words and phrases that can extend understanding of love outside of the English language cage. Don't be surprised, however, if things get lost in (back) translation; McDonald's "I'm lovin' it" slogan was translated for China into an idiomatic phrase meaning "I'm lovin' it, no matter what you say" (Sant, 2015). Biblical concordances can be a starting point for extending the concept beyond romance (e.g., John 15:13; "greater love than this hath no man, that he lay down his life for his friends"). Both Louis Armstrong and John Lennon espoused universal love in song. Narratives and analyses of love in understudied cultures, such those of Africa (e.g., Adebayo, 2017; Cole & Thomas, 2009), can be examined and discussed. The extensive anthropological and sociological cross-cultural

DOI: 10.4324/9781003300380-49

literature on love can be engaged as well—for instance, comparing what is known about the near-universality of romantic love (Sorrell, 2005) with the more subsistence-oriented factors that kick in after the honeymoon (McMullin, 2015). Arranged marriages (Emery, 2022) and marriages of convenience provide a contrast to relationships in which love is prominent. And, while it is not currently in fashion as a characterization of love, ambivalence is no less real, and discussion of love can easily lead to discussion of hate, for which there are better heat maps (e.g., Anti-defamation League, 2023).

References and Suggested Readings

Adebayo, A. (2017). *Stay with me*. New York, NY: Knopf.

Anti-defamation League. (2023). ADL H. E. A. T. Map (Hate, Extremism, Antisemitism, Terrorism). *Anti-defamation League Website*. Retrieved from www.adl.org/resources/tools-to-track-hate/heat-map

Cole, J., & Thomas, L. (Eds.). (2009). *Love in Africa*. Chicago, IL: University of Chicago Press.

Emery, L. R. (2022, September 27). What modern arranged marriages really look like. *Brides* (online magazine). Retrieved from www.brides.com/story/modern-arranged-marriages

Gleason, W. A., & Selinger, E. M. (Eds.). (2015). *Romance fiction and American culture: Love as the practice of freedom?* New York, NY: Routledge.

Hatfield, E., & Rapson, R. L. (1996). *Love and sex: Cross-cultural perspectives*. New York, NY: Pearson.

Katsuba, S. (2023, February 6). The decade of violence: A comprehensive analysis of hate crimes against LGBTQ in Russia in the era of the "Gay Propaganda Law" (2010–2020). *Victims & Offenders, 18*. Retrieved from www.tandfonline.com/doi/full/10.1080/15564886.2023.2167142?scroll=top&needAccess=true&role=tab

Lee, J. (1973). *The colors of love: An exploration of the ways of loving*. Toronto, Ontario, Canada: The New Press.

McMullin, Z. (2015, January 21). The married couple's 36 questions for staying in love. *Huffington Post* (online newspaper). Retrieved from www.huffingtonpost.com/zsofi-mcmullin/the-married-couples-36-questions-for-staying-in-love_b_6498012.html

Sant, G. (2015, March 12). McDonalds' self-hating complex: Why its overseas P. R. campaign is the worst of all time. *Salon* (online magazine). Retrieved from www.salon.com/2015/03/12/mcdonalds_self_hating_complex_why_their_overseas_p_r_campaign_is_the_worst_of_all_time/

Sorrell, E. (2005). Romantic love and marriage: An analysis of the functionality of romantic love as a marital stabilizing agent. *Nebraska Anthropologist, 9*, 16–25 (Open access via Digital Commons at). Retrieved from http://digitalcommons.unl.edu/cgi/viewcontent.cgi?article=1008&context=nebanthro

Sternberg, R. J. (1986). A triangular theory of love. *Psychological Review, 93*, 119–135.

Sternberg, R. J. (Ed.). (2005). *The psychology of hate*. Washington, DC: American Psychological Association.

Sternberg, R. J., & Sternberg, K. (2008). *The nature of hate*. New York, NY: Cambridge University Press.

Development

DOI: 10.4324/9781003300380-50

Pregnancy and Childbirth

The perinatal period is the absolute entry point for all cultures. However, while the birth process and the specific physical and psychological needs of the infant are universal, there are differences surrounding the period leading up to and immediately following birth that express cultural differences. A comprehensive reference in this area is the edited volume by Selin (2009). The decision whether or not to conceive and the use of contraception varies between cultures and is influenced by familial, social, and religious factors. Much folk tradition surrounds birth worldwide; an example is the elaborate system of beliefs about the proper foods, temperature, activity level, and spiritual invocations appropriate for a pregnant woman in China (Yeo, 2013). The actual physical setting for birth appears to be conditional, worldwide, on relative affluence and urbanization. For example, a birth in Dakar, Senegal, to an affluent US citizen is accomplished in a private hospital with a five-day postpartum stay; conditions in public health care facilities in Senegal are often vastly different and less serene (Cavallaro & Wong, 2020). In contrast, tradition combined with a lack of trained personnel and extreme resource depletion often lead, in Afghanistan and other remote environments, to high rates of infant and maternal mortality that are the focus of international aid interventions (Naziri et al., 2018). Regional variations based on law embedded in custom and tradition define this area of study.

Exposition, Confrontation, and Simulation

Extending out from the foregoing, discussion of the cultural psychology of pregnancy and birth could continue this dialogue between the universal nature of the process and the extremes of the conditions under which it occurs. For example, the question of how much maternal exercise is helpful or harmful to the developing fetus can be examined in the context of extreme activity such as mountain climbing—elective (and arguably beneficial) for individuals in the United States (Rodden, 2016) and mandatory in Afghanistan. A sheer chasm between the United States and virtually all other countries in the world is reflected in the way in which pregnant women are treated in prison at and after the time of birth. Background for development of the framework for a discussion of this cultural divide can be assembled from the individual country reports contained in the US Library of Congress's document on children in prison worldwide (Library of Congress, 2014) and also Jennifer Warner's comparative study of prison nurseries (Warner, 2015).

DOI: 10.4324/9781003300380-51

References and Suggested Readings

Cavallaro, F., & Wong, K. (2020, March 4). For women giving birth in Senegal, reaching a health facility may be the first hurdle—but it isn't always the last. *MARCH (Maternal, Adolescent, Reproductive, and Child Health) website* (London School of Hygiene and Tropical Medicine). Retrieved from www.lshtm.ac.uk/research/centres/march-centre/news/102566/women-giving-birth-senegal-reaching-health-facility-may-be-first-hurdle-it

Library of Congress. (2014, August). Laws on children residing with parents in prison. *Library of Congress (US) Law Library* (online resource). Retrieved from https://tile.loc.gov/storage-services/service/ll/llglrd/2015296887/2015296887.pdf

Naziri, M., Higgins-Steele, A., Anwari, Z., Yousufi, K., Fossand, K., Amin, S. S., Hipgrave, D. B., & Varkey, S. (2018). Scaling up newborn care in Afghanistan: Opportunities and challenges for the health sector. *Health Policy and Planning*, *33*(2), 271–282. Retrieved from https://academic.oup.com/heapol/article/33/2/271/4668760

Rodden, B. (2016, March 30). Climbing pregnant: Medical study results. *Beth Rodden: Mother-pro climber-writer* (Personal Blog) (online resource). Retrieved from http://bethrodden.com/2016/03/climbing-pregnant-medical-study-results/

Selin, H. (Ed.). (2009). *Childbirth across cultures: Ideas and practices of pregnancy, childbirth, and the postpartum*. Dordrecht: Springer.

Warner, J. (2015). Infants in orange: An international model-based approach to prison nurseries. *Hastings Women's Law Journal*, *26*, 65–147 (online). Retrieved from https://repository.uchastings.edu/cgi/viewcontent.cgi?article=1159&context=hwlj

Yeo, T. R. (2013). Chinese birth rituals. *Singapore Infopedia: National Library Board of Singapore* (online resource). Retrieved from https://eresources.nlb.gov.sg/infopedia/articles/SIP_2013-05-14_113920.html

Abortion

Few US textbooks in any area of psychology index abortion. This is, on one hand, not surprising since, in the United States, it is a volatile political issue and framed as a subject for law. On the other, it is a glaring omission since abortion is obviously psychologically consequential and also has cross-cultural connections and implications. In the United States, abortion has led to confrontation and actual violence with physicians and other clinic staff being assaulted and sometimes killed in workplaces and in churches. It is a prime example of an idea that is fully emotionally charged and on that basis alone is worth psychological scrutiny. Heiphetz, Strohminger, and Young (2017) continue a discussion relating thoughts and decisions about moral issues, with specific reference to abortion, that has roots in the history of moral development research and especially in the conflict between legalistic and interpersonally nurturant roles exemplified by the challenge to Lawrence Kohlberg's theory of moral development raised by Carol Gilligan in the 1980s (Muuss, 1988).

Cross-culturally, abortion reflects the interaction of religion, tradition, and law, and the legal status of abortion varies widely from criminalization in South America, the Middle East, and Africa to constitutionalization in Europe to the recent reversal by the US Supreme Court of a constitutional right to abortion in the United States (Cook, Erdman, & Dickens, 2014; Center for Reproductive Rights, 2023). A comparison of the new landscape of abortion restrictions in the United States, where access to abortion now depends entirely on state laws (Guttmacher Institute, 2023), reflects the same range of variation encountered worldwide. Depending on location, personal and health consequences vary widely. For example, Ville and Mirlesse (2015) contrast outcomes for how medical doctors interact with parents regarding prenatal diagnosis of disability. Abortion based on diagnosis of fetal pathology is legal in France while it is a crime in Brazil, and, consequently, physicians in France are less conflicted about their role in the process than those in Brazil. China's one-child policy, now rescinded (Wee, 2021), socially compelled abortions both to regulate population numbers and to select for males over females (Fong, 2016).

Exposition, Confrontation, and Simulation

Controversy and confrontation may be at a higher pitch in this area than in others, so discussants should proceed with caution. However, proceeding with caution need not equate to avoidance. Objective approaches could include simply listing and discussing all of the cultural dimensions implicated in abortion. What-ifs abound and can be the starting point for thoughtful and critical examination. The question of prenatal diagnosis

DOI: 10.4324/9781003300380-52

and its relation to abortion decisions can be expanded. Examination of the cognitive and emotional dimensions of the decision can be sharpened by situating it in the context of reversing an ongoing chemically induced abortion (Graham, 2017).

References and Suggested Readings

Center for Reproductive Rights. (2023). The world's abortion laws. *Center for Reproductive Rights Website*. Retrieved from https://reproductiverights.org/maps/worlds-abortion-laws/

Cook, R. J., Erdman, J. N., & Dickens, B. M. (Eds.). (2014). *Abortion law in transnational perspective: Cases and controversies*. Philadelphia, PA: University of Pennsylvania Press.

Fong, M. (2016). *One child: The story of China's most radical experiment*. New York, NY: Houghton Mifflin Harcourt.

Graham, R. (2017, July 18). A new front in the war over reproductive rights: "Abortion pill reversal". *New York Times Magazine* (online). Retrieved from www.nytimes.com/2017/07/18/magazine/a-new-front-in-the-war-over-reproductive-rights-abortion-pill-reversal.html?_r=0

Guttmacher Institute. (2023). Interactive map: US abortion policies and access after Roe. *Guttmacher Institute Website*. Retrieved from https://states.guttmacher.org/policies/

Heiphetz, L., Strohminger, N., & Young, L. L. (2017). The role of moral beliefs, memories, and preferences in representations of identity. *Cognitive Science*, *41*(3), 744–767.

Muuss, R. E. (1988). Carol Gilligan's theory of sex differences in the development of moral reasoning during adolescence. *Adolescence*, *23*(8–9), 229–243.

Ville, I., & Mirlesse, V. (2015). Prenatal diagnosis: From policy to practice. Two distinct ways of managing prognostic uncertainty and anticipating disability in Brazil and France. *Social Science and Medicine*, *141*, 19–26.

Wee, S. (2021, September 27). China says it will allow couples to have 3 children, up from 2. *The New York Times* (online newspaper). Retrieved from www.nytimes.com/2021/05/31/world/asia/china-three-child-policy.html#:~:text=China%20said%20on%20Monday%20that,and%20avert%20a%20demographic%20crisis.[Accessed March 5, 2023].

Parenting

Marc Bornstein, who has been writing about cross-cultural issues in child development and parenting for more than 40 years (Bornstein, 2012), quotes an oft-said line that there are only two contributions to children's development: genes and parents. Even further back in the history of psychology, Freud made plain why development should be a focus and why parents in particular were both the bringers of civilization and the most bitter antagonists in the developmental drama. To take up parenting in a cross-cultural class is to engage a subject that, while fascinating, presents ambiguities that will not clear up. Thus, any class on cross-cultural parenting will be founded on the principle of "it depends." The main theories of parenting can serve as a template. Attachment, as Peryl Agishtein and Claudia Brumbaugh observed in a study involving collecting data from more than 50 countries, is highly modulated by culture. For instance, they found that stronger identification with culture overall reduced attachment anxiety and avoidance (Agishtein & Brumbaugh, 2013).

The classic parenting styles—authoritarian, permissive, and authoritative—are likewise affected by culture. For instance, in cultures that emphasize collectivism, a more authoritarian style may be more prevalent. However, the relation between parenting style and culture is highly nuanced; for one example, authoritarian parenting may be understood in Asian cultures as expressive of parental warmth and support, which is not how it is perceived in European and US settings (Kim, 2005). Other variations in parenting emerge from comparative culture study—for instance, the preference in Norway for institutionalized daycare starting at one year of age, a practice that emerges haphazardly in the United States based on the same economic pressures but without the foundation of substantial state-supported parental leave (Choi, 2014).

Exposition, Confrontation, and Simulation

With such a great amount of individual variation and interaction between parenting styles and culture, restrained exploration with tentative conclusions should especially be sought in this area. Lansford, Rothenberg, and Bornstein (2021) contrast parenting across nine countries and also offer insight into variations among ethnic groups in the United States. Any course in cross-cultural parenting should view the film *Babies* (Balm'es & Chabat, 2010; visit the film's website at http://focusfeatures.com/babies), which conveys both the nuances and the universal experience of parenting across several cultures (Namibia, Mongolia, Japan, and California), filmed on site, and which can be the platform for discussion leading in several directions. For instance, the practice of accelerated childhood education in Japan and the United States is contrasted with more informal and quotidian

DOI: 10.4324/9781003300380-53

practices in Namibia and Mongolia. Excellent insight into the environmental and social frameworks for development are likewise visible and can serve as openings for discussion not only of parenting but also of lifestyle. Classes can serve as their own laboratories as well. The thorough (322 pages long) and well-designed training manual of the Calgary (Canada) Cross Cultural Parenting Program of the Calgary Immigrant Women's Association (2005) contains many simple prompts for response and discussion that draw out personal experiences and can be interpreted from the perspectives of monocultural, multicultural, and immigrant individuals. Finally, the focus on parenting is typically on early to middle childhood. Classes in cross-cultural psychology can forge new research paths by concentrating on the stages of development from adolescence (Kapetanovic et al., 2020) and beyond, on single parenting across cultures (Stavrova & Fetchenhauer, 2014), and especially on grandparenting (Gardiner, 2020) and other forms of extended family parental assistance.

References and Suggested Readings

Agishtein, P., & Brumbaugh, C. (2013). Cultural variation in adult attachment: The impact of ethnicity, collectivism, and country of origin. *Journal of Social, Evolutionary, and Cultural Psychology*, 7(4), 384–405.

Balmès, T. (director) & Chabat, A. (Producer). (2010). *Babies (Bébés) Documentary film*. Universal City, CA: Focus Features.

Bornstein, M. H. (2012). Cultural approaches to parenting. *Parenting Science and Practice*, *12*(2–3), 212–221.

Calgary Immigrant Women's Association. (2005). *Cross cultural parenting program: Facilitator's guide and participants' notes* (2nd ed.). Calgary, Alberta, Canada: CIWA. Retrieved from https://ciwa-online.com/uploads/pdf/CCPP%20Resource%20Manual%202011.pdf

Choi, A. (2014). How cultures around the world think about parenting. *Ted Online* (online informational talk). Retrieved from https://ideas.ted.com/how-cultures-around-the-world-think-about-parenting/

Gardiner, H. W. (2020). Grandparenting across cultures. In B. K. Ashdown & A. N. Faherty (Eds.), *Parents and caregivers across cultures* (pp. 273–281). Cham, Switzerland: Springer.

Kapetanovic, S., Rothenberg, W. A., Lansford, J. E., Bornstein, M. H., Chang, L., . . . Bacchini, D. (2020). Cross-cultural examination of links between parent-adolescent communication and adolescent psychological problems in 12 cultural groups. *Journal of Youth and Adolescence*, *49*(6), 1225–1244. Retrieved from www.ncbi.nlm.nih.gov/pmc/articles/PMC7237396/

Kim, E. (2005). Korean American parental control: Acceptance or rejection? *Ethos*, *33*(3), 347–366.

Lansford, J. E., Rothenberg, W. A., & Bornstein, M. H. (Eds.). (2021). *Parenting across cultures from childhood to adolescence: Development in nine countries*. New York, NY: Routledge.

Stavrova, O., & Fetchenhauer, D. (2014). Single parents, unhappy parents? Parenthood, partnership, and the cultural normative context. *Journal of Cross Cultural Psychology*, *46*(1), 134–149.

Family

Although sexuality gets more press, family is probably the most important aspect of interpersonal relations within culture. Freudian psychology is entirely a psychology of family relations and looks backward to conceptions of primal social groups headed by powerful fathers as well as to a body of imaginative literature that sees family conflict as eternal and inevitable. However much this anthropological conceit might be modified, the success of psychoanalysis as a means of interpreting human life rests mainly on its ability to present family dynamics dramatically as reflections of an eternal human process of enculturation. Many religions conceive of God as a father; Catholicism organizes itself around the concept of a one-child family. Until recently, and still in many cultures and many parts of the world, legal and governmental power rested with powerful families and was legally heritable rather than transferrable by popular consent. Moving from the iconography of the Madonna or the monarch to more secular current social-scientific approaches, Ko et al. (2020) place family bonds and kin care at the center of human motivation. What follows is a partial sample of the possibilities of a discussion of family within a cross-cultural framework. Leaving aside the anthropological literatures on kinship and family structure and also the equally vast sociological literature on the family as a primary socializing agent and focusing on psychology alone, there is ample interest in and impetus for discussion and further study among at least the following areas.

Exposition, Confrontation, and Simulation

1 **Family size:** Though family size has attracted attention from population theorists and economists rather than from psychologists, most individuals have an opinion about optimal family size, and a survey of these opinions is a good starting point for discussion. The optimal size is usually greater than the replacement fertility rate of two children per woman; usually, lively discussion can be instigated by raising the possibility of rationing of children, such as was officially attempted by China until recently (Hall, 2017, Cheng, 2021; Stevenson & Wang, 2023). Family size varies world- and culture-wide due to several factors (easily accessible by cursory googling) including poverty and access to education, though the results of studies are often ambivalent in their results. Though historically poorer cultures have higher fertility rates and larger families (Central Intelligence Agency, 2023), grinding poverty sometimes results in poverty Malthusianism—that is, reducing the number of children in the family because of lack of resources or opportunities to escape. A basic decision tree incorporating factors that are influential in determining reproductive decisions can be used to simulate the way in which demographers and economists predict family size (Lawson & Mace, 2010).

DOI: 10.4324/9781003300380-54

2 **Paid family leave:** Discussion can always be sparked by presenting data showing the United States compared to other countries in terms of how much paid parental leave is available after childbirth. However, though there isn't an official US national policy for paid leave, the situation is more nuanced with several states and municipalities offering paid leave as well as a number of corporations, which results in a patchwork of leave policies (Isaacs, Healy, & Peters, 2017; Miller, 2021; Williamson, 2023). Further tempering of the sometimes rancorous reaction to the lack of paid leave might result from considering the results of studies that have attempted to measure psychological benefits of paid leave. A recent largescale study comparing paid leave across countries, fraught with methodological problems including a small number of studies and substantial confounds, suggests that the outcomes of family leave may not always confirm the positive sentiment that the practice arouses (Aitken et al., 2015). Most studies, too, focus on mothers rather than fathers; attention should be given to this information gap as there appear to be some psychological benefits for paternal leave as well (Coltrane, 2013).

3 **Familismo:** The generic cultural trait of familism, in which family predominates in individual choices and behaviors, is especially prominent in Latinx cultures, where it is called familismo. There are several scales for measuring it that have the virtue of simplicity; one is only five items long (the Pan-Hispanic Familism Scale, Villareal et al., 2005). This scale includes "I am proud of my family," "My family is always there for me in times of need," "I cherish the time I spend with my family," "I know my family has my best interests in mind," and "My family members and I share similar values and beliefs." Villatoro, Morales, and Mays (2014) relate familismo to the use of informal or religious forms of psychotherapy rather than specialized psychotherapeutic or general medical services. A study of largely undocumented Latino day laborers in the United States identified familismo, along with perceptions of good general health and work satisfaction, as contributing to both life satisfaction and resistance to the bad effects of discrimination (Ojeda & Piña-Watson, 2013). Completion of the Pan-Hispanic Familism Scale and discussion of the results can open further conversations about the elements of familismo that are common to all humans in families.

4 **Family violence:** This topic has been studied cross-culturally for several years (e.g., Levinson, 1988); its impact differentially targets women (Caralis, 2022). Recently, Leyaro, Selaya, and Trifkovic (2017) performed a field experiment investigating whether environmental and economic conditions, including apportionment of domestic responsibilities, might affect the amount of justification for violence against women in intimate or family relationships. Because of a prior observation that lower levels of altruism may be related to increased acceptance of violence, they used a version of a dictator game to gauge relative altruism between men employed in marine fishing vs. lake fishing in Tanzania, economies that differ in the relative equality of women in domestic relationships. While their results did not support a relation between altruism and violence, they did show increases in perceived acceptability of violence in areas where women's roles were more unequal. Demonstration or replication of parts of this study could be a starting point for examination of a creative way of researching an otherwise difficult-to-view problem. It can also serve as a starting point for hypothesizing the social factors that might lead to more or less violence in families—substance abuse, for instance, or membership in subcultures such as law enforcement (Blumenstein, Fridell, & Jones, 2012).

5 **Foster, adoptive, and rescue families:** Probably the best proof of the preeminent importance placed on the family as the source of developmental support is the worldwide effort to provide care for children who have lost their families, either temporarily or permanently. Examination of Kenya's Guidelines for the Alternative Family Care of Children in Kenya (Republic of Kenya, 2014), linked to the tenets of the United Nations Convention on the Rights of the Child, provides insight into the centrality and complexity of the system for assuring continuity of support for children. The problem of alternative family care is particularly acute there. As of 2014, Kenya, a country with a population of 40 million out of which about 40 percent are below the age of 14, counted 2.4 million orphans—mainly because of parental deaths from AIDS. The document asserts at the outset that "the family is a nurturing and caring environment and is the ideal place in which to raise a child" (p. 4) and goes on to describe in detail systems for providing care similar to those in place everywhere else in the world yet, at the same time, culturally specific. For instance, primary emphasis is on kinship care and the Muslim practice of contract adoption, kafaalah, followed by foster care, temporary shelter, guardianship, and adoption. Special provision is made for child-headed households. Options for discussion of issues in this area could include comparison of the Kenyan fostering system with any local system; simulating a situation in which a child from the Democratic Republic of the Congo, orphaned during ethnoreligious conflict there, finds her way to Kenya and needs placement; or tracing the path of a refugee child arriving in Italy from Africa. The Better Care Network (https://bettercarenetwork.org/), a consortium of international organizations focused on providing alternative family care to children who have lost their families, is a resource for information for problems such as these.

References and Suggested Readings

Aitken, Z., Garrett, C. C., Hewitt, B., Keogh, L., Hocking, J. S., & Kavanagh, A. M. (2015). The maternal health outcomes of paid maternity leave: A systematic review. *Social Science and Medicine*, *130*, 32–41.

Blumenstein, L., Fridell, L., & Jones, S. (2012). The link between traditional police sub-culture and police intimate partner violence. *Policing: An International Journal of Police Strategies and Management*, *35*(1), 147–164.

Caralis, P. (2022, May 31). In this culture of violence, we are all to blame. *Women's eNews Website*. Retrieved from https://womensenews.org/2022/05/in-this-culture-of-violence-we-are-all-to-blame/

Central Intelligence Agency. (2023). Country comparison: Total fertility rate. *CIA World Factbook* (US Government official website). Retrieved from www.cia.gov/the-world-factbook/field/total-fertility-rate/

Cheng, E. (2021, July 21). China scraps fines, will let families have as many children as they'd like. *CNBC Website* (online news source). Retrieved from www.cnbc.com/2021/07/21/china-scraps-fines-for-families-violating-childbirth-limits.html

Coltrane, S. (2013, December 29). The risky business of paternity leave. *The Atlantic* (online magazine). Retrieved from www.theatlantic.com/business/archive/2013/12/the-risky-business-of-paternity-leave/282688/

Hall, C. (2017, February 2). How has the end of its one-child policy affected China? *Aljazeera* (online news source). Retrieved from www.aljazeera.com/features/2017/2/2/how-has-the-end-of-its-one-child-policy-affected-china

Isaacs, J., Healy, O., & Peters, H. E. (2017, May). Paid family leave in the United States: Time for a new national policy. *Urban Institute* (non-profit organization website). Retrieved from www.urban.org/sites/default/files/publication/90201/paid_family_leave.pdf

Ko, A., Pick, C. M., Kwon, J. Y., Barley, M., Krems, J. A., . . . Kendrick, D. T. (2020). Family matters: Rethinking the psychology of human social motivation. *Perspectives on Psychological Science*, *15*, 173–201. Retrieved from https://journals.sagepub.com/doi/full/10.1177/1745691619872986

Lawson, D. W., & Mace, R. (2010). Optimizing modern family size: Trade-offs between fertility and the economic costs of reproduction. *Human Nature*, *21*(1), 39–61.

Levinson, D. (1988). Family violence in cross-cultural perspective. In V. B. Van Hasselt, R. L. Morrison, A. S. Bellack, & M. Hersen (Eds.), *Handbook of family violence* (pp. 435–445). New York, NY: Springer.

Leyaro, V., Selaya, P., & Trifkovic, N. (2017). Fishermen's wives: On the cultural origins of violence against women. *United Nations University UNU-WIDER* (online). Retrieved from www.wider.unu.edu/sites/default/files/Publications/Working-paper/PDF/wp2017-205.pdf

Miller, C. C. (2021, October 25). The world 'has found a way to do this': The U. S. lags on paid leave. *The New York Times* (online newspaper). Retrieved from www.nytimes.com/2021/10/25/upshot/paid-leave-democrats.html

Ojeda, L., & Piña-Watson, B. (2013). Day laborers' life satisfaction: The role of familismo, spirituality, work, health, and discrimination. *Cultural Diversity and Ethnic Minority Psychology*, *19*(3), 270–278.

Republic of Kenya. (2014, October). *Guidelines for the alternative family care of children in Kenya.* (Official publication of the Government of Kenya in conjunction with Sweden and UNICEF) (online). Retrieved from https://bettercarenetwork.org/sites/default/files/Guidelines%20for%20the%20Alternative%20Family%20Care%20of%20Children%20in%20Kenya.pdf

Stevenson, A., & Wang, Z. (2023, January 16). China's population falls, heralding a demographic crisis. *The New York Times* (online newspaper). Retrieved from www.nytimes.com/2023/01/16/business/china-birth-rate.html

Villareal, R., Blozis, S. A., & Widaman, K. F. (2005). Factorial invariance of a pan-Hispanic familism scale. *Hispanic Journal of Behavioral Sciences*, *27*, 409–425.

Villatoro, A. P., Morales, E. S., & Mays, V. M. (2014). Family culture in mental health help-seeking and utilization in a nationally representative sample of Latinos in the United States: The NLAAS. *American Journal of Orthopsychiatry*, *84*(4), 353–363.

Williamson, M. W. (2023, January 5). The state of paid family and medical leave in the U. S. in 2023. *American Progress Website*. Retrieved from www.americanprogress.org/article/the-state-of-paid-family-and-medical-leave-in-the-u-s-in-2023/

Young and Old

The young and the old are themselves distinct cultures, and distinctly different laws and regulations govern each of these groups within all societies. Most cross-cultural studies focus on individuals in the spectrum from late adolescence through middle adulthood. But while, across the world, there is no shortage of children (some countries, such as Ghana, have more than 40 percent under 14), the aged, due to medical and environmental advances and also to changes in national birth rates, are the most rapidly growing part of the human population worldwide. China's elderly population, for example, is projected to triple by 2050. The elderly are especially viewed as subjects for medical or psychotherapeutic intervention rather than a group of vibrant and autonomous individuals. Though the elderly, as a group, are perceived positively cross-culturally as wise and deserving of respect, this positive estimation is balanced by equivalent weights of negative impressions of unattractiveness and incompetence (Löckenhoff et al., 2009). This is true despite the average age of elected political representatives worldwide, which, in the US Congress, is nearly 60 (The British House of Lords' average age is 69 while its House of Commons is about 50)—not to mention the median age of business chief executives worldwide, which is also nearly 60 (Romei, 2015). But the prejudicial street runs both ways; age asserts restrictive legislative dominance over youth (Blazina & Desilver, 2021).

Exposition, Confrontation, and Simulation

There are voluminous sources for developmental psychological issues across cultures; consult the most current culturally oriented textbooks (e.g., Arnett & Jensen, 2021) for these. A little further digging will uncover articles containing materials that can be adapted to illustrate the sorts of cognitive tasks—for instance, judging relatedness in pictorial images—that are used to probe cross-cultural cognitive developmental differences (Kuwabara & Smith, 2012). For contrast with the research literature, which often focuses on children in relatively safe and affluent environments, directly examine lives of children on the edge (e.g., street children; Street Child United, 2023). Jose Solís's (2017) account of his experience seeing the Disney film *Anastasia* in Tegucigalpa, Honduras, as an 11-year-old already conscious of his divergent gender identity, touches on immigration, discrimination, and sexuality. But it also illustrates, and can be a departure point for discussion of, the way that adult thought coalesces just at that age, and the Disney film will be easily available as well.

Regarding age, Skinner and Margaret Vaughan (1997) suggested—possibly with tongue slightly in cheek—that, to simulate old age, you should smear your glasses with butter and wear oven mitts. In fact, their highly regarded book offers an optimistic view

DOI: 10.4324/9781003300380-55

of the aging process and numerous practical suggestions (as would be expected from one of the great practical psychologists) to cope successfully with the inevitable outcomes of aging. Positive and stereotype-mitigating discussion might turn on these; it might also be an outcome of addressing the design of products that can make older life more livable. An exercise might be designed around adaptive technology, for instance, for driving (Brody, 2017), and the relative availability of such assistive devices worldwide could be explored. The relative comfort of retirement might also be vicariously experienced via interactive websites that compare retirement conditions worldwide—for instance, via the interactive map of retirement ages around the globe (Aperion, 2017) or the detailed data on social security programs worldwide provided by the US Social Security Administration (Social Security Administration (US), 2017). Finally, discussion and possible simulation/enaction with roleplaying could be designed around the intercultural patterns of socialization of elder Koreans in a Queens (New York City) McDonald's, a more complicated and continuing story than this account provides (Kimmelman, 2014).

References and Suggested Readings

Aperion. (2017). Retirement age around the globe (interactive map). *Aperion Care* (Corporate website) (online). Retrieved from https://aperioncare.com/blog/retirement-age-around-world/

Arnett, J. J., & Jensen, L. A. (2021). *Child development: A cultural approach* (3rd ed.). New York, NY: Pearson.

Blazina, C., & Desilver, D. (2021, February 12). Boomers, Silents still have most seats in Congress, though number of Millennials, GenXers is up slightly. *Pew Research Center Website*. Retrieved from www.pewresearch.org/fact-tank/2021/02/12/boomers-silents-still-have-most-seats-in-congress-though-number-of-millennials-gen-xers-is-up-slightly/

Brody, J. (2017, August 28). Safer cars keep older drivers on the road. *The New York Times* (online newspaper). Retrieved from www.nytimes.com/2017/08/28/well/safer-cars-help-keep-older-drivers-on-the-road.html?mcubz=3

Kimmelman, M. (2014, January 28). The urban home away from home: Lessons from McDonald's clash with older Koreans. *The New York Times* (online newspaper). Retrieved from www.nytimes.com/2014/01/29/arts/design/lessons-from-mcdonalds-clash-with-older-koreans.html?mcubz=3

Kuwabara, M., & Smith, L. B. (2012). Cross-cultural differences in cognitive development: Attention to relations and objects. *Journal of Experimental Child Psychology*, *113*(1), 20–35.

Löckenhoff, C., De Fruyt, F., Terracciano, A., McCrae, R., De Bolle, M., Costa, P. T., Aguilar-Vafaie, M. E., . . . Yik, M. (2009). Perceptions of aging across 26 cultures and their culture-level associates. *Psychology of Aging*, *24*(4), 941–954. Retrieved from www.ncbi.nlm.nih.gov/pmc/articles/PMC2933107/

Romei, V. (2015, September 11). Half of global CEOs are in their 50s. *Financial Times* (online newspaper). Retrieved from www.ft.com/content/226fbb53-1c36-32f0-ba15-414d8a807761

Skinner, B. F., & Vaughan, M. E. (1997). *Enjoy old age*. New York, NY: Norton.

Social Security Administration (US). (2019). Social security programs throughout the world. *United States Social Security Administration website* (official government website). Retrieved from www.ssa.gov/policy/docs/progdesc/ssptw/

Solís, J. (2017, September 13). I saw myself in "Anastasia" and I knew I had to leave Honduras. *The New York Times* (online newspaper). Retrieved from www.nytimes.com/2017/09/13/theater/anastasia-broadway-honduras.html?mcubz=3&_r=0

Street Child United. (2023). *Street Child United* (charity website) (online). Retrieved from https://streetchildunited.org/

Government

DOI: 10.4324/9781003300380-56

Tight vs. Loose

The construct of tightness-looseness was advanced in 2006 by cross-cultural organizational psychologist Michele Gelfand and colleagues (Gelfand, Nishii, & Raver, 2006). It has since been buttressed by many research studies, especially a frequently cited *Science* study comparing 33 national cultures on the concept (Gelfand et al., 2011), and a book (Gelfand, 2018). This intuitive formulation parallels similar dichotomous dimensional conceptions—for example, Hofstede's cultural dimensions. Where Hofstede emphasizes inherent cognitive structures such as risk tolerance, Gelfand's approach focuses on social norms and rules and their enforcement.

Briefly, tight cultures strictly monitor deviance and enforce compliance with social norms. Violations garner little tolerance and are punished, often severely. In contrast, loose cultures afford more latitude regarding social norms and mores and are generally more tolerant and less punitive of deviance. It's surmised that tight cultures evolve under pressure of threat and the need for social solidarity for survival in the face of aggression, disease, or other invasive factors; loose cultures benefit from relatively few ecological and social stressors. Advantages of tight cultures are order and predictability while loose cultures are more open to variation and innovation. However, as Gelfand notes, mixtures of both *flexible tightness* and *structured looseness* are expected and preferable (Nussbaum, 2019).

Exposition, Confrontation, and Simulation

A starting point for discussion would be to take the brief (20-question) quiz, located on Gelfand's website (Gelfand, 2021), that delivers a rating on a 100-point scale of personal looseness or tightness. (Note at the beginning that the quiz cannot be taken repeatedly although one's personal score can be accessed along with some advice on managing tight and loose mindset.) Tightness-looseness has captured the popular imagination, so there are currently many sites with different takes on the theory—often from a business or management point of view. Likewise, Gelfand herself is a prolific popularizer and can be found on several podcasts.

The tightness-looseness construct is not limited to between-nation comparisons; graphic maps of the relative prevalence of tightness or looseness within countries have been constructed for the United States (Harrington & Gelfand, 2014) and also for the 31 Chinese provinces (Gelfand, 2019). Compare the map of tightness vs. looseness within the United States to the results of national elections or to the pattern of votes on socially divisive questions (e.g., gay marriage) and also to the level of tolerance of diversity (Lopez, Devos, & Somo, 2022). The tight-loose dichotomy appears to relate to and can

DOI: 10.4324/9781003300380-57

lead to discussion of the relation of political and social authoritarianism to cultural differences (Altemeyer, 2006).

Another question to raise: since the tightness-looseness dichotomy is often found discussed in connection with business or school administration, is tightness-looseness within organizations, schools, or even individual families (Cook, 2018) the same as that which produces these distinct national and regional patterns of tightness-looseness? Lastly (for now), tightness-looseness offers a point of entry to the discussion of creativity within a cultural framework. Is a tight culture a hindrance to creative thinking across cultures, or does the convergent thinking associated with cultural tightness focus and sharpen creativity? Chua, Roth, and Lemoine (2015) suggest that both outcomes are possible. Similarly, the question of whether tight or loose cultures are more conducive to nonconformity, often posited as a precursor to or prerequisite for creativity, can be addressed.

References and Suggested Readings

Altemeyer, B. (2006). *The authoritarians. Free online book*. Retrieved from https://theauthoritarians.org/

Chua, R. Y. J., Roth, Y., & Lemoine, J. F. (2015). The impact of culture on creativity: How cultural tightness and cultural distance affect global innovation crowdsourcing work. *Administrative Science Quarterly, 60*(2), 189–227. https://doi.org/10.1177/0001839214563595

Cook, G. (2018, September 11). A powerful force that shapes all of our decisions. *Scientific American* (Mind Matters section). Retrieved from www.scientificamerican.com/article/a-powerful-force-that-shapes-all-of-our-decisions/

Gelfand, M. (2018). *Rule makers, rule breakers: How tight and loose cultures wire our world*. New York, NY: Scribner.

Gelfand, M. (2019, April 2). Universal and culture-specific patterns of tightness-looseness across the 31 Chinese provinces. *PNAS, 116*(14), 6522–6524. Retrieved from www.ncbi.nlm.nih.gov/pmc/articles/PMC6452652/

Gelfand, M. (2021). Mindset quiz: How tight or loose are you? *Michele Gelfand Website*. Retrieved from www.michelegelfand.com/tl-quiz

Gelfand, M., Nishii, L. H., & Raver, J. (2006). On the nature and importance of cultural tightness-looseness. *Journal of Applied Psychology, 91*(6), 1225–1244. https://doi.org/10.1037/0021-9010.91.6.1225

Gelfand, M. J., Raver, J. L., Nishii, L., Leslie, L. M., Lun, J., . . . Yamaguchi. S. (2011). Differences between tight and loose cultures: A 33-nation study. *Science, 332*(6033), 1100–1104. https://doi.org/10.1126/science.1197754

Harrington, J. R., & Gelfand, M. J. (2014, June 3). Tightness-looseness across the 50 United States. *PNAS, 111*(22), 7990–7995. Retrieved from www.pnas.org/doi/pdf/10.1073/pnas.1317937111

Lopez, H., Devos, T., & Somo, A. (2022). State-level cultural tightness-looseness accounts for implicit associations between American and White identities. *Current Research in Ecological and Social Psychology, 3*, 100033. Retrieved from www.sciencedirect.com/science/article/pii/S2666622721000265

Nussbaum, D. (2019, January 17). Tight and loose cultures: A conversation with Michele Gelfand. *Behavioral Scientist*. Retrieved from https://behavioralscientist.org/tight-and-loose-cultures-a-conversation-with-michele-gelfand/

Freedom and Slavery

A core value of the primary reference culture for these exercises, the United States, is freedom. The defining historical events in the United States have questions of freedom at their core: freedom from colonization at the founding and freedom from enslavement, the purpose and ostensible outcome of the US Civil War. President Franklin D. Roosevelt, while addressing the US Congress on January 6, 1941, declared that there were four essential freedoms the United States would fight to maintain everywhere in the world: freedom of speech, freedom of worship, freedom from want, and freedom from fear (Roosevelt, 1941). Today, the US Department of State maintains an Office of International Religious Freedom headed by the Ambassador-at-Large for International Religious Freedom. This person is tasked to, among other things, "promote freedom of religion and conscience throughout the world as a fundamental human right and as a source of stability for all countries" and also to "assist religious and human rights NGOs in promoting religious freedom" (US Department of State, 2023).

The greatest contrast to freedom is slavery. The Global Estimates of Modern Slavery reported by the United Nations International Labour Organization for 2022 estimated that, at that time, 50 million people worldwide were enslaved in some form (International Labor Organization, 2022). Both freedom and slavery are implicit in psychology, and yet they are addressed only obliquely. For instance, the term *freedom* does not have a standalone entry in the recent *APA Dictionary of Psychology* (VandenBos, 2015) while *freedom* is indexed only in conjunction with psychological reactance—resistance to authority or contrariness—in *The Encyclopedia of Cross-Cultural Psychology* (Keith, 2013). A collection of essays on freedom and autonomy from the perspective of self-determination theory addresses various aspects of the relation of freedom and culture (Chirkov, Ryan, & Sheldon, 2011).

Exposition, Confrontation, and Simulation

Although psychology has mostly compressed questions about freedom into the "freedom vs. determinism" mold derived from the philosophy of science, there have been great advocates for freedom within the field. Readings could be drawn from classic sources, such as Carl Rogers's *Freedom to Learn* (Rogers, 1969), which encourage principles of discussion and speculation essential to learning in classrooms and also between cultures. Ranking cultures within and outside of the United States in terms of Rogers's supposed opponent B. F. Skinner's definition of freedom as the relative absence of aversive control might lead to mapping coerciveness, military rule, and other aspects of punitive government to the distribution of slavery. The International Labour Organization estimates,

DOI: 10.4324/9781003300380-58

along with the Global Peace Index (Vision of Humanity, 2023), can provide insights into the distributions of elements promoting freedom or repression worldwide. Theoretical analyses of slavery are in short supply; Hu (2003) provides an intuitive game-theoretic approach to the difference between conditions of control that lead to either slavery (absolute dominance of one player over another) or power sharing. Possibly a video game featuring slavery could be procured, played, and discussed. Mukherjee (2016) provides some leads in this direction. Discussion could also extend to considerations of the history of slavery and proposals for current redress and restitution (Blazina & Cox, 2022).

References and Suggested Readings

Blazina, C., & Cox, K. (2022, November 28). Black and White Americans are far apart in their views of reparations for slavery. *Pew Research Center Website*. Retrieved from www.pewresearch.org/fact-tank/2022/11/28/black-and-white-americans-are-far-apart-in-their-views-of-reparations-for-slavery/

Chirkov, V., Ryan, R., & Sheldon, K. (Eds.). (2011). *Human autonomy in cross-cultural context: Perspectives on the psychology of agency, freedom, and well-being*. Berlin, Germany: Springer Science + Business Media.

Hu, X. (2003). On authority distributions in organizations: Controls. *Games and Economic Behavior*, *45*(1), 153–170.

International Labor Organization. (2022). Global estimates of modern slavery: Forced labor and forced marriage. *ILO (International Labor Organization, United Nations) Website*. Retrieved from www.ilo.org/wcmsp5/groups/public/---ed_norm/---ipec/documents/publication/wcms_854733.pdf

Keith, K. (Ed.). (2013). *The encyclopedia of cross-cultural psychology* (Vol. 3). New York, NY: Wiley-Blackwell.

Mukherjee, S. (2016). Video games and slavery. *Transactions of the Digital Games Research Association*, 2(3), 243–260. Retrieved from http://todigra.org/index.php/todigra/article/view/60

Rogers, C. (1969). *Freedom to learn*. Columbus, OH: C. E. Merrill Co.

Roosevelt, F. D. (1941). The four freedoms (Speech delivered to the US Congress, January 6, 1941). *American Rhetoric website: Top 100 Speeches* (online). Retrieved from www.americanrhetoric.com/speeches/fdrthefourfreedoms.htm

US Department of State. (2023). Religious freedom (homepage of the Office of International Religious Freedom). *US Department of State website* (online). Retrieved from www.state.gov/bureaus-offices/under-secretary-for-civilian-security-democracy-and-human-rights/office-of-international-religious-freedom/

VandenBos, G. R. (Ed.). (2015). *APA dictionary of psychology* (2nd ed.). Washington, DC: American Psychological Association.

Vision of Humanity. (2023). 2022 Global Peace Index (interactive map). *Vision of Humanity Website*. Retrieved from www.visionofhumanity.org/maps/#/

Rights, Citizenship, and Voting

A conundrum: which comes first, citizenship or rights? On one hand, rights are often understood, especially in countries where rights have been elemental in their creation, as primary and sometimes even "God-given." On the other hand, throughout human history, rights have been granted only at the pleasure of elders or rulers, and it is just as fair to say that rights depend, even today, on citizenship. Citizenship, whether acquired through birth or naturalization, awards a package of rights all at once; awarding citizenship is a serious matter and a closely guarded process. Citizenship tests function not only as part of the ritual of naturalization but also as potential barriers and immigration controls (Etzioni, 2007). In a democratic environment, rights and citizenship are two legs of a tripod, the last of which is free choice of political and social options by voting. Few if any countries have no form of voting at all, although it is only a recent arrival in some. For instance, elections in Saudi Arabia have been rare, and women's right to vote in them was conferred by the country's king only a few years ago (NPR Staff, 2015). The degree to which rights are enumerated and extended, the levels of citizenship, and the prevalence and practice of voting determine to a large extent the framework in which all Indigenous cultures exist worldwide. Rights are fragile; decades of progress for women's rights in Afghanistan were reversed by the Taliban's retaking the country in 2021 (Fitzgerald, 2023). Psychologists have taken an interest in voting as both a cognitive process and a social practice. Among the most prominent and accessible currently is Jon Krosnick of Stanford University (Martin, 2016; American Psychological Association, 2020).

Exposition, Confrontation, and Simulation

Taking rights, citizenship, and voting in order, a first and very typical activity is to personally enumerate rights, either as a list of known or expected rights or as a theoretical exercise. Generate lists of rights, collate them, and then compare the generated lists with the *Universal Declaration of Human Rights* first published by the United Nations in 1948 (United Nations, 2023). This comparison can be carried out further with local constitutions, starting with the US Bill of Rights, which is widely available. There are also several sources available to support the important collateral discussion of rights vs. privileges that usually evolves from doing this, both independent (e.g., Tokarev, 2012) and quasi-official (for instance, the various publications of the American Civil Liberties Union dealing with rights and privileges). The concept of privileges comes sharply into view when rights are curtailed; explore the degree of right vs. privilege through the lens of imprisonment (ACLU, 2023). For citizenship, review the requirements for immigration as suggested in the Immigration and Refugees entry in this book. Observe especially

DOI: 10.4324/9781003300380-59

the length of time and the costs involved in attempting to change one's citizenship. For voting, set up a simulated election, utilize a variety of voting methods, and compare and discuss both the results and the perception of fairness of each (an overview source is Pacuit, 2017). The psychosocial arguments for voting, even in the face of its apparent futility, were made eloquently by Paul Meehl (1977) and ought to be introduced into any discussion as well.

References and Suggested Readings

ACLU. (2023). Know your rights: In prison—privileged and non-privileged mail. *ACLU (American Civil Liberties Union) website*. Retrieved from www.aclu.org/know-your-rights/prisoners-rights#i-want-to-send-and-receive-mail-in-prison

American Psychological Association. (2020, October). What drives voter behavior? (podcast and transcript). *American Psychological Association Website*. Retrieved from www.apa.org/news/podcasts/speaking-of-psychology/voter-behavior

Etzioni, A. (2007). Citizenship tests: A comparative, communitarian perspective. *The Political Quarterly*, *78*(3), 353–363.

Fitzgerald, M. (2023, January 4). A timeline of women's rights in Afghanistan. *US News and World Report Website*. Retrieved from www.usnews.com/news/best-countries/slideshows/womens-rights-in-afghanistan-a-timeline

Martin, S. (2016, October). Conversation: Five questions for Jon Krosnick. *APA Monitor (American Psychological Association News Journal)*, *47*(9), 27. Retrieved from www.apa.org/monitor/2016/10/conversation-krosnick

Meehl, P. (1977). The selfish voter paradox and the thrown-away vote argument. *American Political Science Review*, *71*(1), 11–30.

NPR Staff. (2015, December 19). After historic elections in Saudi Arabia, what's the future for women? *NPR (National Public Radio)* (online website feature). Retrieved from www.npr.org/2015/12/19/459491653/after-historic-elections-in-saudi-arabia-whats-the-future-for-women

Pacuit, Eric. (2017, Fall). Voting methods. In E. N. Zalta (Ed.), *The Stanford encyclopedia of philosophy* (online). Palo Alto, CA: Stanford University. Retrieved from https://plato.stanford.edu/archives/fall2017/entries/voting-methods/

Tokarev, S. (2012, February 28). Right vs. privilege distinction. *USCivilliberties.org* (Blog). Retrieved from https://uscivilliberties.org/4398-right-v-privilege-distinction.html

United Nations. (2023). Universal declaration of human rights. *United Nations website*. Retrieved from www.un.org/en/about-us/universal-declaration-of-human-rights

Ownership, Property, and Possession

Possession, it is said, is nine tenths of the law, at least in societies with a heritage in English common law. Ownership, the psychological state of feeling in possession of either goods or abilities, flows from rights and also confers rights, which allow people to function unimpeded in their culture. The withering of enforced collectivism in recent political history has affirmed the strength of the private ownership concept worldwide, as has the globalization of capitalist enterprises. Owning something legally allows claims against others for theft, both of things and of services; laws protect both real and intellectual property as well as chattel goods. This is truly a cross-cutting area of study in psychology and culture.

Philippe Rochat's *Origins of Possession* (Rochat, 2014) provides a developmental perspective on ownership. Rudmin (1996), from a combined psychological, anthropological, and historical perspective, details the cross-cultural commonalities that underlie private ownership, which include aspects of agricultural production, work specialization, family membership, patriarchy and matriarchy, and commercial principles. A free recall study of property conceptions conducted with adult Canadians (Rudmin & Berry, 1987) revealed that, while the meaning of *property* is distributed across four semantic categories (control or possession, attachment, purchase or legal ownership, and crafting or gifting), the strongest argument for ownership was means of acquisition (purchase or gifting, for example). Cross-cultural variations in ownership are often quite striking, for instance, the comparative rates of home ownership between the United States and China.

Exposition, Confrontation, and Simulation

Several opportunities are available for simple simulation of empirical studies in the area of cross-cultural ownership and possession. If you are lucky enough to have access to young children, numerous developmental tasks may be tried out on them to illustrate the developmental aspects of research in this area. For instance, children are sensitive to the concept of *first possession*, the idea that the first person to hold an item is its owner, and adopt a heuristic for determining ownership that embodies this (Friedman & Neary, 2008). It might be interesting to see if comparisons could be carried out between children and older persons in this regard. A study by Rochat et al. (2014) on children's decisions about third-party ownership involved two identical dolls fighting over possession of a single but divisible object. Replication of this study and possible comparison with adult behaviors could affirm the study's findings of the variability in solutions to this problem across several cultures as well as illustrating experimental procedure in this area.

DOI: 10.4324/9781003300380-60

(Apparently, Chinese children were more apt to decide like Solomon, splitting the object in two, than were children from several other cultures.)

Turning toward specifically adult ideas about ownership and property and considering experimental approaches to these, simulation of the endowment effect is uncomplicated (World of Work Project, 2019). In the endowment effect, a monetary value is assigned to an object to represent (a) what a person would pay to acquire it and (b) how a person would price it if they owned it and were selling it. Should the difference between the selling and buying prices be positive, it is a complicated indicator of both value and avarice. Gobel et al. (2014) demonstrated experimentally that persons from collective cultures in Asia achieved a substantially higher endowment effect when they visualized the priced object being used in a private setting vs. a public one.

A starting point for raising the question about the emotional and interpersonal aspects of ownership could be artist David Hockney's observation, in the context of deciding to remain in a non-marital partnership, that marriage is about property and that divorce certainly proves it (Solomon, 2017). Examination of variances in divorce and estate planning, comparing local experiences and settlements with the results of cross-cultural research (Greenstein & Davis, 2006; Marrs, 2009; Islamic Wills, 2023), can be instructive beyond the boundaries of cross-cultural psychology. Intellectual property is subject to piracy, an interesting psychological subject that cuts across the boundaries of property and ethics. Possible replications might involve the construction of vignettes involving opportunities for piracy and the introduction of specific moral information into the decision process, an intervention that has been shown to be effective in Arabic Muslim cultures (Brown, 2013).

The study of the value of things in themselves has a moderate research history in psychology; a local replication of the study of Watson, Lysonski, Gillan, and Raymo (2002) on the cross-cultural valuation of possessions can be attempted. Look into the cost of moving valued household and personal goods to, say, France; just doing the inventory and reviewing the rules for importing goods will be instructive. Good luck finding a price! Another way of looking at ownership is to break out of the individualistic framework and investigate de-ownership orientation, a form of collaborative consumption (or possibly backyard communism?) practiced by individuals who are younger, poorer, and more affected by economic downturns (Lindblom & Lindblom, 2017). Collect stories or other evidence of these informal means of adult sharing of possessions. Finally, ownership is sometimes equated with personal mastery. Scales such as the Ryff Scales of Psychological Well-Being (Seifert, 2018), which incorporate a specific environmental mastery component, can be administered and the correlation between mastery scores and number of possessions or other evidence of ownership calculated and discussed.

References and Suggested Readings

Brown, S. (2013). Digital piracy and the moral compass. *The Psychologist* (British Psychological Society), *26*, 528–539.

Friedman, O., & Neary, K. (2008). Determining who owns what: Do children infer ownership from first possession? *Cognition*, *107*, 829–849.

Gobel, M. S., Ong, T., & Harris, A. (2014). A culture-by-context analysis of endowment effects. In P. Bello, M. Guarini, M. McShane & B. Scassellati (Eds.), *Proceedings of the 36th annual conference of the cognitive science society* (pp. 2269–2274). Austin, TX: Cognitive Science Society. Retrieved from www.ucl.ac.uk/lagnado-lab/publications/harris/GobelEtAlCogSci2014.pdf

Greenstein, T. N., & Davis, S. (2006). Cross-national divorce: Effects of women's power, prestige, and dependence. *Journal of Comparative Family Studies*, *37*(3), 253–273.

Islamic Wills. (2023). *Islamic Wills Website*. Retrieved from www.islamicwillsusa.com/

Lindblom, A., & Lindblom, T. (2017). De-ownership orientation and collaborative consumption during turbulent economic times. *International Journal of Consumer Studies*, *41*(4), 431–438.

Marrs, T. (2009, February 5). Money in misery. *The Economist* (online magazine). Retrieved from www.economist.com/briefing/2009/02/05/money-in-misery

Rochat, P. (2014). *Origins of possession: Owning and sharing in development*. Cambridge: Cambridge University Press.

Rochat, P., Robbins, E., Passos-Ferreira, C., Donato Oliva, A., Dias, M. D. G., & Guo, L. (2014). Ownership reasoning in children across cultures. *Cognition*, *132*, 471–484.

Rudmin, F. W. (1996). Cross-cultural correlates of the ownership of private property: Zelman's gender data revisited. *Cross-Cultural Research*, *30*(2), 171–188.

Rudmin, F. W., & Berry, J. W. (1987). Semantics of ownership: A free-recall study of property. *The Psychological Record*, *37*(2), 257–268.

Seifert, T. (2018, April). The Ryff scales of psychological well-being. *Wabash College (Crawfordsville, IN) Center for Inquiry*. Retrieved from https://centerofinquiry.org/wp-content/uploads/2018/04/Ryff_Scales.pdf

Solomon, D. (2017, September 5). David Hockney, contrarian, shifts perspectives. *The New York Times* (online newspaper). Retrieved from www.nytimes.com/2017/09/05/arts/design/david-hockney-los-angeles-metropolitan-museum-of-art-reverse-perspective.html?mcubz=3&_r=0

Watson, J., Lysonski, S., Gillan, T., & Raymore, L. (2002). Cultural values and important possessions: A cross-cultural analysis. *Journal of Business Research*, *55*(11), 923–931.

World of Work Project. (2019). The endowment effect: A cognitive bias. *World of Work Project Website*. Retrieved from https://worldofwork.io/2019/08/the-endowment-effect/

Corruption

Corruption in an earlier, historical sense refers to the dissolution of the body after death: spoilage. It has evolved to signify a pervasive social malaise that might be an underculture or even an anticulture. Corruption subverts laws and customs and ensures beneficial returns to its lawless practitioners. From the perspective of the pervasive law-based culture inside which cultural studies in the United States are premised, corruption distorts the institutions and practices that are the basis for comparisons with other cultures. Zephyr Teachout's (2016) book *Corruption in America: From Benjamin Franklin's Snuffbox to Citizens United* suggests that the US constitutional government was intentionally designed to frustrate corruption, thus making outbreaks of corruption appear like virulent diseases. In other cultures, corruption is more widespread and endemic; bribery and other extra-legal workarounds are expected and even encouraged, socially if not officially. The technical theoretical literature on corruption extends widely over the social sciences, encompassing cognitive (Dupuy & Neset, 2018) as well as political and economic views, and converges on corruption viewed as a cultural phenomenon. Rotondi and Stanca (2015), in the *Journal of Economic Psychology*, integrate several strands of evidence that suggest that particularism creates a framework in which individual bribery or malinfluence may occur. Kravtsova, Oshchepkov, and Welzel (2016) assert that holding *postmaterialist* values—described by Ronald Inglehart (1977) as valuing individual self-expression over economic security and widely discussed since that time—may predispose one toward accepting corrupt behavior. Recent political events in the United States have expanded the range and definition of what might count as corruption (Goldstein & Drybread, 2023).

Exposition, Confrontation, and Simulation

There is probably good reason to not try to uncover evidence and information about corruption directly within either the classroom or the immediate environs, although an approach could be made in a standard academic setting by asking questions about grade inflation, television revenues for athletics, or legacy admissions. The subject of corruption leads to considerations of other pervasive ways in which societies or cultures may be metaphorically said by some to be perverted or sickened—for instance, by lessening emphasis on self-reliance or on military preparedness. At the least, surveys could be conducted about the relative use of bribery and other dodgy techniques and also about the approval of those techniques. This would lead naturally to the exploration of the database used by Kravtsova et al., the 250-plus-question World Values Survey (World Values Survey, 2023). Question 202 in the 2010–2014 version specifically addresses acceptance of bribery as necessary for living.

DOI: 10.4324/9781003300380-61

An excellent though grisly case study would be the Grenfell Tower fire in London in June 2017 (Erlanger, 2017). Though this may be a case of simple cost-cutting rather than outright illegality, many points of possible corruptibility exist in this situation and could be identified and discussed. Also, the contrast between different levels of legal regulation and oversight in societies puts in higher relief the underlying mechanisms that kick in when regulation and law are illegally evaded.

References and Suggested Readings

Dupuy, K., & Neset, S. (2018). The cognitive psychology of corruption. *U4 (Chr. Michelsen Institute, Norway)*, 2. Retrieved from www.u4.no/publications/the-cognitive-psychology-of-corruption

Erlanger, S. (2017, June 28). After Grenfell Tower fire, U.K. asks: Has deregulation gone too far? *The New York Times* (online resource). Retrieved from www.nytimes.com/2017/06/28/world/europe/uk-grenfell-tower-fire-deregulation.html?_r=0

Goldstein, D. M., & Drybread, K. (Eds.). (2023). *Corruption and illiberal politics in the Trump era*. New York, NY: Routledge.

Inglehart, R. (1977). *The silent revolution: Changing values and political styles among Western publics*. Princeton, NJ: Princeton University Press.

Kravtsova, M., Oshchepkov, A., & Welzel, C. (2016). Values and corruption: Do postmaterialists justify bribery? *Journal of Cross-Cultural Psychology*, *48*(1).

Rotondi, V., & Stanca, L. (2015). The effect of particularism on corruption: Theory and empirical evidence. *Journal of Economic Psychology*, *51*, 219–235.

Teachout, Z. (2016). *Corruption in America: From Benjamin Franklin's snuffbox to Citizens United*. Cambridge, MA: Harvard University Press.

World Values Survey. (2023). *World Values Survey Website*. Retrieved from www.worldvalues-survey.org/WVSOnline.jsp

Conscription and Volunteerism

Underlying conscription and volunteerism is a basic conception of shared community obligations and national service. This splits into two streams: a military and a civilian one. Compulsory military service, with or without conscription (a forced draft), is more intermittent worldwide than in the past. It is hard to predict based on national cultural characteristics whether or not compulsory service will be required. Conscription, by its nature, is perceived as intrusive and, especially in the hyper-individualistic United States, has often been resisted. In the United States, forced conscription for an unpopular war in the 1960s resulted, ultimately, in the institution of a volunteer force in 1973.

But conscription and compulsory service are contingent on world conditions, and what goes away may soon return. For example, Sweden, which ended a long tradition of enforced military service in 2010, reinstated that requirement in 2018 due to fears about Russian aggression (Stanglin, 2017). The eruption of war between Russia and Ukraine has resulted in increased pressure to expand conscription in Russia, which might sweep up non-Russian nationals in the country due to the perceived urgency of the situation (Debusmann, 2023). The requirement for mandatory nonmilitary service is less prevalent at present worldwide. Several studies suggest that the motives for civilian volunteering in different countries are influenced by cultural values (Aydinli, Bender, & Chasiot, 2013; Gronlund, Holmes, Kang, & Zrinščak, 2011); presumably, these differences determine different rates of volunteering within nations as well.

Exposition, Confrontation, and Simulation

Investigate the variability in requirements for both military and civilian service worldwide using the CIA World Factbook (US Central Intelligence Agency, 2023). Direct debates about military conscription cannot reasonably succeed at present because there is no way to comprehend involuntary conscription in current US society and no passion for the subject; probe the concept in several indirect ways, however. Simulate a draft lottery and come up with all the excuses that would exempt a person from military service. (This is pretty instinctive!) Since this is dead history at present, introduce the history of the passionate opposition to the Vietnam War and especially to the draft; Phil Ochs's song from the middle 1960s, "Draft Dodger Rag" (Ochs, 1964), could serve as a musical theme.

Address the question of whether public service or personal gain is the goal of study and life. The merits of William James's suggestion in *The Moral Equivalent of War* (James, 1910) of a conscripted army for public service and its historic offshoots, the Peace Corps and AmeriCorps, can be evaluated; would it be possible, in the United States at present, to require public service in charitable causes as is done in other regions of

DOI: 10.4324/9781003300380-62

the world? Consider arguments pro and con (see e.g., Friedersdorf, 2013). Inevitably, though, the question of conscription is grounded in military service, historically and culturally, and the question of which values are worth dying for—whether in combat or in arduous national service—is the one to which those considering the subject will, and should, always return.

A more upbeat approach would evaluate the opportunities for civilian volunteer service in the immediate area. In conjunction with this, use the resources provided in the Charity entry in this book. Using a list of potential volunteer activities (e.g., Center for Community Health and Development, n.d.), examine the differences between passive and active volunteering. A survey comparing the number and kind of charitable activities already done or ongoing can provide the impetus for more.

References and Suggested Readings

Aydinli, A., Bender, M., & Chasiotis, A. (2013). Helping and volunteering across cultures: Determinants of prosocial behavior. *Online Readings in Psychology and Culture*, *5*(3). Retrieved from https://scholarworks.gvsu.edu/orpc/vol5/iss3/6/

Center for Community Health and Development. (n.d.). Community tool box (Chapter 28: Spirituality and community building). *Community Tool Box website of the KU CCHD* (University of Kansas, online). Retrieved from https://ctb.ku.edu/en/table-of-contents/spirituality-and-community-building/being-charitable-towards-others/main

Debussmann, B. (2023, February 13). US warns that dual citizens face Russian conscription. *BBC News Website*. Retrieved from www.bbc.com/news/world-us-canada-64629156

Friedersdorf, C. (2013, June 26). The case against universal national service. *The Atlantic* (online magazine). Retrieved from www.theatlantic.com/politics/archive/2013/06/the-case-against-universal-national-service/277230/

Gronlund, H., Holmes, K., Kang, C. H., & Zrinščak, S. (2011). Cultural values and volunteering: A cross-cultural comparison of students' motivation to volunteer in 13 countries. *Journal of Academic Ethics*, *9*(2), 87–106.

James, W. (1910). The moral equivalent of war. *Popular Science Monthly*, *77*, 400–410 (Online at several sources, for example). Retrieved from https://en.wikisource.org/wiki/Popular_Science_Monthly/Volume_77/October_1910/The_Moral_Equivalent_of_War

Ochs, P. (1964). *Draft Dodger's Rag. (Musical composition.) Online version, recording from 1968.* Retrieved from www.youtube.com/watch?v=tFFOUkipI4U

Stanglin, D. (2017, March 2). Sweden reinstates military draft over concerns about Russian aggression. *USA Today* (online newspaper). Retrieved from www.usatoday.com/story/news/2017/03/02/sweden-reinstates-draft-over-concerns-russia/98641010/

US Central Intelligence Agency. (2023). Military service age and obligation. *The World Factbook* (US Central Intelligence Agency online resource). Retrieved from www.cia.gov/the-world-factbook/field/military-service-age-and-obligation

Disaster, War, and Culture War

Natural disasters and war provide opportunities to confront several paradoxes of culture. Culture is pervasive and strong, and yet it is fragile, at the mercy of the violence of both the natural environment and other humans, singly or in groups (not to mention the threats of other species and diseases). A scene of natural disaster reveals humanity at its most vulnerable and defenseless points. At the same time, disasters are arenas in which the highest heroism and physical endurance are encountered. Extreme individualism—hoarding and stealing without regard for the community—is matched by extreme communalism—for instance, the outpouring of shared sympathy and resources that occurs worldwide after earthquake, flood, or storm. Over time, utter devastation gives way to rebuilding, a tribute to human resilience. Oishi and Komiya (2017) observe that the relative risk of natural disaster is positively associated with some measures of collectivism. However, this relationship is not a primary determinant of the relative individualism or collectivism present in a culture. All cultures evince adaptive collective responses to disaster. Cultures that frequently experience natural disasters get better at this situationally induced collectivism through frequent practice.

Like natural disasters, war is a recurring source of devastation across the world. In some regions, war is endemic; in others, it is a theoretical possibility but mainly a historical memory with all the distortions and inaccuracies that attend to distant memories. Whether it is a natural phenomenon like bad weather or something more intimately psychological, psychologists, especially analytic psychologists, have attested to its power and its uncanny attractiveness to the human species (Freud, 1915/1957; Hillman, 2004). Like disaster, war is a proving ground for extremes of cowardice and cruelty and also for bravery, courage, and heroism. It is deeply woven into virtually all cultures' systems of values and collective memory. War provides a potent stimulus for changing established cultural traditions. For example, women's entry into the US workforce out of necessity during the Second World War had major and lasting social and cultural repercussions (Devonis, 2014). Tributes to the fruits of peace in the form of institutions for learning and art are matched by monuments to war. War also allows death, the ultimate natural disaster, to be publicly acknowledged and commemorated; cemeteries and monuments spread across the fields of Arlington, Virginia, and northern France as well as in North Korea and Tehran. Sometimes—for instance, in Hiroshima and Nagasaki, Japan—monuments to destruction counsel peace; in other places, they suggest vigilance and preparation for future conflict.

DOI: 10.4324/9781003300380-63

Exposition, Confrontation, and Simulation

War and natural disasters are the focus of attention for simulators; search and find examples of each. For background on war simulation, consult Michel Chossudovsky (2018) while listening to Nobel Prize winner Bob Dylan's "Talkin' World War III Blues." Of actual war games and simulations there seems to be no end; find a local expert or online group of experts. Participation in a war game may be as engaging a way to begin the conversation about the paradoxes of war as any, especially if there isn't any real war to speak of. However, don't forget that, in the United States, Canada, and other countries, there are refugees attending classes who can provide first-hand accounts; utilize these for instruction. If possible, institutional investment in a disaster-simulation program would be great; however, plans for simulation are available at no cost from the Pan American Health Organization, the regional affiliate of the World Health Organization, via its online publication *Guidelines for Developing Emergency Simulations and Drills* (PAHO, 2011).

Examination of the role played by international medical aid organizations, such as Doctors Without Borders, in providing psychological counseling can aid in designing a role for counselors and other psychological specialists in the direct response to disasters. Disasters and wars result in displacement of people and the creation of refugees. There are several suggestions regarding refugee mental health services in the APA refugee mental health resources material mentioned in the Immigration and Refugees entry in this book. Likewise, discussion can include reference to the specific environmental and health consequences of physical destruction. Discussion of war can lead directly to considering military organizations themselves as cultures; the APA provides psychologists with a primer on military culture (American Psychological Association, 2016). Search also for specific methods in use for preparing for lifesaving operations within military organizations worldwide and compare the role of service personnel in specific disaster situations. Region-specific news accounts of the coordination between military and civilian responders can assist.

The question of what to rebuild after a war is not without controversy. The rebuilding of Germany after the Second World War is well documented (e.g., Leick, Schreiber, & Stoldt, 2010), and, in that context, a discussion of priorities for rebuilding—either in an established context such as post-WWII Germany, in the aftermath of a recent conflict such as that which devastated Syria (Humanity & Inclusion, 2023), or a speculative simulation based on the degree of expected destruction in the local culture—can illustrate cultural traditions and values. The question can also be asked as to whether rebuilding the physical environment alters the pattern of the society and the culture as well. Finally, questions can be raised about whether, in light of its engagement with core human values, all war is "culture war" (Malka, 2014; Stanton, 2021).

References and Suggested Readings

American Psychological Association. (2016). Understanding military culture. *American Psychological Association Practice Organization Website*. Retrieved from www.apaservices.org/practice/good-practice/military-culture.pdf

Chossudovsky, M. (2018, May 26). When war games go live? "Simulating World War III". *Global Research. Montreal, Canada: Organization website* (online). Retrieved from www.globalresearch.ca/when-war-games-go-live-preparing-to-attack-iran-simulating-world-war-iii/28542

Devonis, D. C. (2014). *History of psychology 101*. New York, NY: Springer Publishing Co.

Freud, S. (1957). Thoughts for the times on war and death. In J. Strachey (Ed.), *The standard edition of the complete psychological works of Sigmund Freud* (Vol. 14, pp. 275–300). London, England: The Hogarth Press (Original work published by 1915).

Hillman, J. (2004). *A terrible love of war*. New York, NY: Penguin Books.

Humanity & Inclusion. (2023). "It will take at least two generations to rebuild". *Humanity and Inclusion (charity) Website*. Retrieved from www.hi-us.org/news_syria_crisis_10year_two_generations_rebuild_after_conflict

Leick, R., Schreiber, M., & Stoldt, H. U. (2010, August 10). A new look at Germany's postwar reconstruction. *Spiegel Online* (online news source). Retrieved from www.spiegel.de/international/germany/out-of-the-ashes-a-new-look-at-germany-s-postwar-reconstruction-a-702856.html

Malka, A. (2014). Political culture and democracy. In A. B. Cohen (Ed.), *Culture reexamined: Broadening our understanding of social and evolutionary influences*. Washington, DC: American Psychological Association.

Oishi, S., & Komiya, A. (2017). Natural disaster risk and collectivism. *Journal of Cross-Cultural Psychology*, *48*(8), 1263–1270.

PAHO. (2011). Guide for developing emergency situations and drills. *Department of Health Emergencies, Pan American Health Organization (WHO)* (online). Retrieved from www.paho.org/disasters/dmdocuments/SimulationsGuide.pdf

Stanton, Z. (2021, May 20). How the 'culture war' could break democracy. *Politico* (online political news source) *Website*. Retrieved from www.politico.com/news/magazine/2021/05/20/culture-war-politics-2021-democracy-analysis-489900

Separateness and Secession

National culture usually implies togetherness of some sort, either a collective mass or a unity of individualists as in the United States. Likewise, cross-cultural psychology tends to favor impulses toward social cohesiveness and intercultural awareness and inclusion rather than centrifugal separatist ones. Separateness fits on a continuum from individual introversion as a personality dimension to group secession. In between these poles fit exiles, hermits, or isolates by choice, to intentional communities formed based on religious, lifestyle, or political principles (e.g., Green, 2017), to secession, which itself ranges from individual withdrawal from an organized system (for instance, divorce) to group secession, either small or national in scope. Isolates and hermits as well as secessionist movements provide a contrast to ordinary views of culture similar to how dystopias project a negative image of the ideals of social life. In many ways, too, they reflect the ways that cultures are oppressive and how individuals and groups can, by their actions, increase separation, engender cultural unity, or resist perceived oppression. For instance, in 2017, the US president called, in the wake of a lone shooter's violent acts, for a renewal of unity around shared cultural values (Landler & Sullivan, 2017). Movements for national independence, either by regions or colonies separating from parent nations or by established nations wishing to discontinue membership in political alliances or unions (for example, the movement in Great Britain to exit the European Union—"Brexit") share some features of secession (Frantziou, 2022). Nascent secessionist movements within targeted territories may also provide leverage for aggressor nations bent on conquest (Minakov, 2022).

Exposition, Confrontation, and Simulation

Following the pattern set out in the introduction to this entry, the psychology of the introvert can be considered; suggested paths are reading drawn from the recent popular book *Quiet* (Cain, 2013) and examination of the personality variable introversion via many available assessment instruments. This may also be a starting point for consideration of personality within and between cultures, taking cues from the procedures for cross-cultural comparison via personality measures described by Afshan, Askari, and Manickam (2015). Biographies of productive (Emily Dickinson) and destructive (Ted Kaczynski) loners can be read and discussed in relation to the ways that these individuals reflected as well as remained separated from the culture of their times. Start the process of becoming a hermit monk; there are many sites that give instructions and advice for this (e.g., Anonymous, 2012). Look into other religious communities as well (e.g., Amish Christians) and compare their rules and expectations for joining with those expected for

DOI: 10.4324/9781003300380-64

citizenship or immigration. Likewise, sketch out a plan for an intentional community, and then compare with the brochures, websites, and manuals available from the many intentional communities worldwide with web presences (e.g., Milagro Cohousing near Tucson, Arizona, United States; Milagro Housing, 2023).

At the macrosocial, national level, successful secession is venerated as the achievement of independence. Independence histories and myths are food for discussion. In contrast, consider the negative of secession; the attempt to preserve independence or separateness in the face of attack; and the tragedies that result when colonizers or invaders destroy communities, peoples, or cultures—for instance, the genocide of the Ovaherero by Germany in Africa in 1904 (Steinmetz, 2005), the persistent revengeful memory of the Conquistadores in New Mexico (Romero, 2017), or the 2022 invasion of Ukraine by Russia (Farago, Kerr, Tiefenthäler, & Willis, 2022). For those who desire a more limited and simplified secession episode, consider one that occurred in Oregon in 2016. A group of individuals intending to resist what they perceived as federal government oppression of their rights as independent rural ranchers maintained an occupation in force of the Malheur National Wildlife Refuge in eastern Oregon (Oregonian Staff, 2017). Their siege was broken by local, state, and federal law enforcement after 41 days; a subsequent trial found the leaders of the occupation not guilty of conspiracy (Bernton, 2016). The ambiguous ending to this episode adds complexity to a story; the occupiers bore hallmarks not only of independent libertarians but also of a family clan. The verdict suggests some level of official tolerance for the action and illustrates well the tension between the universalism of the law and the individual liberty that it is designed to protect, a good entry point for a discussion of the polarity universalism-particularism (Culver, 2023).

References and Suggested Readings

Afshan, A., Askari, I., & Manickam, L. S. S. (2015, April–June). Shyness, self-construal, extraversion-introversion, neuroticism, & psychoticism: A cross-cultural comparison across college students. *Sage Open* (online open-source journal), 1–8. Retrieved from https://journals.sagepub.com/doi/pdf/10.1177/2158244015587559

Anonymous. (2012). How I became a medieval-style anchorite. *Catholic Herald* (online newspaper). Retrieved from https://catholicherald.co.uk/how-i-became-a-medieval-style-anchorite/

Bernton, H. (2016, October 27). Jury acquits leaders of Malheur wildlife-refuge standoff. *The Seattle Times* (online newspaper). Retrieved from www.seattletimes.com/seattle-news/law-justice/verdict-near-in-malheur-wildlife-refuge-standoff-trial/

Cain, S. (2013). *Quiet: The power of introverts in a world that can't stop talking*. New York, NY: Broadway Books.

Culver, J. (2023). Intercultural training: Universalism, particularism, and the road to Kumasi. *Target Training Website*. Retrieved from www.targettraining.eu/intercultural-training/

Farago, J., Kerr, S., Tiefenthäler, A., & Willis, H. (2022, December 19). A culture in the crosshairs. *The New York Times* (online newspaper website). Retrieved from www.nytimes.com/interactive/2022/12/19/arts/design/ukraine-cultural-heritage-war-impacts.html

Frantziou, E. (2022, April 29). Was Brexit a form of secession? *Global Policy*, *13*, 69–78. Retrieved from https://onlinelibrary.wiley.com/doi/full/10.1111/1758-5899.13062

Green, E. (2017, January 15). Seeking an escape from Trump's America. *The Atlantic* (online magazine). Retrieved from www.theatlantic.com/politics/archive/2017/01/anarchism-intentional-communities-trump/513086/

Landler, M., & Sullivan, E. (2017, October 2). Trump, after Las Vegas shooting: "Our unity cannot be shattered by evil." *The New York Times* (online newspaper). Retrieved from www.nytimes.com/2017/10/02/us/politics/trump-las-vegas-mass-shooting.html?action=click&contentCollection=US&module=RelatedCoverage&region=Marginalia&pgtype=article

Milagro Housing. (2023). *Milagro Housing Website*. Retrieved from https://milagrocohousing.org/

Minakov, M. (2022, April 19). Ukrainian statehood at risk: The Kremlin's secessionist plans. *Wilson Center Website*. Retrieved from www.wilsoncenter.org/blog-post/ukrainian-statehood-risk-kremlins-secessionist-plans

Oregonian Staff. (2017, February 15). Oregon standoff timeline: 41 days of the Malheur refuge occupation and the aftermath. *The Oregonian/OregonLive* (online newspaper). Retrieved from www.oregonlive.com/portland/2017/02/oregon_standoff_timeline_41_da.html

Romero, S. (2017, September 30). Statue's stolen foot reflects divisions over symbols of conquest. *The New York Times* (online newspaper). Retrieved from www.nytimes.com/2017/09/30/us/statue-foot-new-mexico.html?mcubz=3&_r=0

Steinmetz, G. (2005). The first genocide of the 20th century and its postcolonial aftermath: Germany and the Namibian Ovaherero. *The Journal of the International Institute (University of Michigan)* (online institutional journal). Retrieved from https://quod.lib.umich.edu/j/jii/4750978.0012.201/-first-genocide-of-the-20th-century-and-its-postcolonial?rgn=main;view=fulltext

Law

DOI: 10.4324/9781003300380-65

Firearms

Firearms have a long history. For now, the focus will be on the current US prototype concept of firearms: a portable weapon firing a projectile. Included in this would be pistols, shotguns, and rifles, automatic or not; heavy weaponry such as artillery and rocketry is usually not included in the concept of a firearm. The *APA Dictionary of Psychology* (American Psychological Association, 2015) doesn't have an entry for firearms nor one for guns, but it does have one for the weapon-focus effect (the tendency of eyewitnesses to attend more to weapons than to other elements of the environment). Research in this area has focused more on gender and race than other cultural variables (e.g., Pickel & Sneyd, 2018). Moving from this forensic psychological focus toward a cultural one, the idea of culture as a weapon that can be deployed alongside actual firearms emerges from an analysis of the way that the US Army homogenized and distorted the diversity in Iraqi culture (and Middle Eastern culture generally) in its training manuals (Davis, 2010). A focus on stylized aspects of individuals' appearance or dress may become analogous to "weapon focus" among soldiers equipped with firearms.

In the United States, gun ownership and especially the degree to which the right to possess, use, and display a gun can be granted are the basis of what Lemieux (2014) is termed *gun culture*. Within gun culture, subcultures of gun enthusiasts support fewer limitations while gun-control advocates support tighter restrictions. This polarity contributes to political conflict and differentials in the enactment and enforcement of gun law based on the prevalent local or regional attitude toward guns. As might be expected, gun enthusiasm is associated with increases in firearm-caused deaths and gun control with decreases.

US gun culture projects a romantic frontier image with a long historical lineage (Russell, 1980), and this along with its relatively less restrictive firearms policies makes the United States a destination for gun tourism—for example, from highly gun-restrictive China (Gardner, 2017). Internationally, guns are regulated more stringently elsewhere than in the United States, which stimulates booming illegal gun markets. For example, in India, although a person is only one-twelfth as likely to be killed by a firearm there than in the United States, more than 90 percent of those deaths are due to illegal guns (FirstPost, 2016). At present—as through all of modern history—arms manufactured in the United States as well as Europe, Russia, and Asia are supplied to areas of live conflict (Hartung, 2022) and leak into the channels of illegal supply.

Exposition, Confrontation, and Simulation

US gun culture can be debated within and outside the United States; a comprehensive background source is Utter (2015). Simulating the process of applying for a permit to

DOI: 10.4324/9781003300380-66

purchase a gun will graphically illustrate the baseline characteristics of responsible citizenship in the United States and in any other culture for which the process can be initiated online; view Person (2013) or Knight (2022) for examples of stringent gun laws outside of the United States. Examination of cases where even very strict gun laws do not deter criminal firearm use can underscore the seeming irrepressibility of guns across cultures (Schuetze & Eddy, 2023). Discussion of whether guns are part of the core value structure of US culture or not can be initiated by consulting Jouet (2019) and Estwick (2022).

References and Suggested Readings

American Psychological Association. (2015). *APA dictionary of psychology* (2nd ed.). Washington, DC: American Psychological Association.

Davis, R. (2010). Culture as a weapon. *Middle East Research and Information Project*, *40*(255) (online). Retrieved from https://merip.org/2010/05/culture-as-a-weapon/

Estwick, T. (2022, April 25). Why is gun culture so prominent in the U.S.? *Scripps News Website*. Retrieved from https://scrippsnews.com/stories/why-is-gun-culture-so-prominent-in-the-u-s/

FirstPost. (2016, June 14). Americans 12 times vulnerable to gun violence than Indians: UP, Bihar lead in illegal arms: Report. *FirstPost* (online news source). Retrieved from www.firstpost.com/world/americans-12-times-vulnerable-to-gun-violence-than-indians-up-bihar-lead-in-illegal-arms-report-2834730.html

Gardner, H. (2017, April 29). In gun-taboo China, tourism to U.S. Firing ranges grows. *USA Today* (online newspaper). Retrieved from www.usatoday.com/story/news/world/2017/04/09/beijing-china-guns-united-states-tourism/99121058/

Hartung, W. (2022, October 20). Promoting stability or fueling conflict? The impact of US arms sales on national and global security. *Quincy Paper No. 9* (Quincy Institute for Responsible Statecraft Website). Retrieved from https://quincyinst.org/report/promoting-stability-or-fueling-conflict-the-impact-of-u-s-arms-sales-on-national-and-global-security/

Jouet, M. (2019, November 5). Guns, identity, and nationhood. *Palgrave Communications*, *5* (138). Retrieved from www.nature.com/articles/s41599-019-0349-z

Knight, B. (2022, December 12). Gun control and firearms possession in Germany. *Deutsche Welle Website*. Retrieved from www.dw.com/en/gun-control-and-firearms-possession-in-germany/a-52450664

Lemieux, F. (2014). Gun violence and mass shootings in the United States: A multi-level quantitative analysis. *International Journal of Criminal Justice Sciences*, *9*, 74–93.

Person, C. (2013, December 10). Legally owning a gun in Japan is really, really hard. *Kotaku* (online magazine). Retrieved from https://kotaku.com/legally-owning-a-gun-in-japan-is-really-really-hard-1479865283

Pickel, K. L., & Sneyd, D. E. (2018). The weapon focus effect is weaker with Black versus White perpetrators. *Memory*, *26*(1), 29–41. Retrieved from https://pubmed.ncbi.nlm.nih.gov/28436249/

Russell, C. P. (1980). *Guns on the early frontiers: A history of firearms from Colonial times through the years of the Western fur trade*. Lincoln, NE: University of Nebraska Press.

Schuetze, C. F., & Eddy, M. (2023, March 10). German police had spoken to man who opened fire at Jehovah's Witness hall. *The New York Times* (online newspaper) Website. Retrieved from www.nytimes.com/2023/03/10/world/europe/germany-shooting-jehovahs-witnesses.html/

Utter, G. (2015). *Guns in contemporary society: The past, present, and future of firearms and firearm policy* (Vol. 3). New York, NY: Praeger/ABC-Clio

Law Enforcement

To the extent that culture is a creation of law, it owes its survival to some form of law enforcement. We hardly think of the punishments and sanctions for rule breaking carried out by families and schools as law enforcement, though these are the first line of this cultural defense. In current societies, worldwide, beyond this locally intimate level, law enforcement is a function of policing by force of arms, carried out by either an officially sanctioned governmental institution (for example, a state police force) or, during an emergency, an arm of a national military force. Enforcement can also be carried out by armed enforcers operating outside the law for the benefit of opposition forces within a state (e.g., a militia connected to a radical opposition group) or, sometimes, for its own benefit (e.g., a group of pirates). Consideration of the rules of engagement for organizations at an international level (e.g. a United Nations Peacekeeping Unit in Africa) or for lawless enforcers (e.g., a criminal mob) may be interesting and appropriate, but for most individuals studying cross-cultural psychology, the face of law enforcement meeting culture in the United States is embodied in the patrol officer in a municipal police force.

Police, like the military, are a culture unto themselves, and discussion of policing can be an entry point to a discussion of military culture as well. In the United States, Ellen Kirschman's book *I Love a Cop* (Kirschman, 2006) is a requisite introduction to the insular and defensive world of enforcers. Recently, consideration has expanded to the specific concerns and stresses on members of other national or social cultures in policing. Police in interaction with other cultures function as either occupying forces or negotiators; episodes differ in their relative crudity and cruelty of approach. Looking at the situation from the perspective of those who are on the receiving end of law-enforcement techniques, policing is a flashpoint revealing the cultural tensions that smolder in US society. Highly publicized cases—made more so by the introduction of car and body cameras—have rendered a picture of a volcanically active edge between several cultures in the United States and the gunfire of enforcers (Fines and Fees Justice Center, 2020). Background reading on the conditions of arbitrary punishment and inflexible enforcement leading to this could start with Victor Rios's *Punished: Policing the Lives of Black and Latino Boys* (Rios, 2011).

Exposition, Confrontation, and Simulation

It's not typical for many students of culture in the United States to have had experiences with law enforcement in other cultures or countries, but that does not mean that there will be no place to start with basic discussion and information gathering. At the outset, sharing of experiences about encounters with law enforcement can set a context.

DOI: 10.4324/9781003300380-67

Simulation of the perception of danger from an officer's point of view can be helpful in gaining perspective. In my classes, we have had success with simply role-playing a traffic stop, an activity that is common in secondary schools; this can work well even if it is seriously done by members of similar cultures, but in the context of cross-cultural learning, it works even better if the person being stopped has the features and language of *otherness*. Collect and compare descriptions of policing/law enforcement in contrasting countries and cultures (e.g., police counter-reform in autocratic states such as Venezuela or Russia, Tremaria, 2022; policing in multicultural Nordic countries, Mulinari & Keskinen, 2020; criminalization of behavior of Indigenous populations in the United States, Wang, 2021). Much of the interface of culture and policing is potentially or actively violent; discussion of alternatives to violence such as nonviolent resistance could be introduced in this context (e. g. Bloch, 2016).

References and Suggested Readings

Bloch, N. (2016, October). Education and training in nonviolent resistance. *United States Institute of Peace Special Report (USIP Website)*. Retrieved from www.usip.org/sites/default/files/SR394-Education-and-Training-in-Nonviolent-Resistance.pdf

Fines and Fees Justice Center. (2020, June 3). George Floyd, police violence, and our work. *Fines and Fees Justice Center Website*. Retrieved from https://finesandfeesjusticecenter.org/2020/06/03/george-floyd-police-violence-and-our-work/

Kirschmann, E. (2006). *I love a cop: What police families need to know* (2nd rev. ed.). New York, NY: Guilford Press.

Mulinari, L. S., & Keskinen, S. (2020, April 23). Racial profiling in the racial welfare state: Examining the order of policing in the Nordic region. *Theoretical Criminology*, *26*(3) (Online open access). Retrieved from https://journals.sagepub.com/doi/10.1177/1362480620914914

Rios, V. (2011). *Punished: Policing the lives of Black and Latino boys*. New York, NY: New York University Press.

Tremaria, S. (2022). Policing and autocratisation in Bolivarian Venezuela. *Bulletin of Latin American Research*, *41*(1), 159–174, Retrieved from https://onlinelibrary.wiley.com/doi/full/10.1111/blar.13298

Wang, L. (2021, October 8). The U. S. criminal justice system disproportionately hurts Native people: The data, visualized. *Prison Policy Initiative Website*. Retrieved from www.prisonpolicy.org/blog/2021/10/08/indigenouspeoplesday/

Petty Crime

The focus in most studies of criminology is typically on highly visible and violent crime. Murder and its prohibition are probably culturally universal (Rachels, 1999). But what of pickpocketing, shoplifting, and other more common but less glamorous crimes? In the case of pickpocketing in the United States, the increased use of debit and credit cards, heightened surveillance, more severe penalties, dismantling of the previously existing system of apprenticeship in the pickpocketing trade, and also the increased availability of firearms and the consequent increase in armed robberies led to pickpocketing dropping from sight between 1970 and 2010 (NPR Staff, 2011). However, worldwide, pickpocketing is viewed—at least by online travel advisors—as ubiquitous (Potter, 2016).

The question of whether a crime is "petty" depends on the society in which it happens. For instance, petty theft might draw a fine (Denmark) or, in Indonesia, a severe beating before a prison sentence (Wockner & Erviani, 2016). In some parts of the world, petty thievery is less a crime than a part of the informal economy.

Exposition, Confrontation, and Simulation

Discussion could start by trying to establish at least a local norm for petty crime. What behaviors constitute petty crime, and when does "unauthorized use of a vehicle" become "grand theft auto"? After this, the variation of consequences for petty crimes should be researched and compared within and across nations. At the very least, this could be an exercise in beginning comparative legal scholarship and would dovetail with discussion of law and penalties in other exercises in this book. Also, it would reveal divergences of opinion about whether any crimes at all are petty or insignificant. In some cultures, severe punishment for minor offenses is common while, in others, some forms of petty crime are essentially tolerated. This could be a good springboard for examination of informal, off-the-books economies as well as the texture of criminality worldwide. Some attention could be given to the correlation of petty crime with economic deprivation. Examination of the ways that neighborhoods change from crime-ridden to relatively crime-free could be undertaken, using the process of gentrification as an example to tie together many strands of economic and social factors determining the petty crime rate (Rotondaro & Ewing, 2013).

Developmental research indicates a relation between parental monitoring of behavior and the development of self-control, leading to lower tendency to commit crimes (Vazsonyi, Ksinan, & Javakhishvili, 2021). Conversation about the extent to which parents tolerated or did not tolerate petty offenses could corroborate these findings. To promote empathy, role-playing the situation of an impoverished 16-year-old with a 1-year-old

DOI: 10.4324/9781003300380-68

child in Indonesia engaging in petty stealing, as in the example mentioned earlier (Wockner & Erviani, 2016), could involve the calculation of risk and benefit for snatching a cellphone. There are many YouTube videos providing demonstrations of defenses against pickpockets and snatchers; simulation of such situations could be a possibility with proper safeguards and spotters.

References and Suggested Readings

NPR Staff. (2011, March 6). Pickpocketing: An art that's stealing away. *NPR (National Public Radio), All Things Considered (transcript of radio broadcast)* (online). Retrieved from www.npr.org/2011/03/06/134298101/pickpocketing-an-art-thats-stealing-away

Potter, E. (2016, May 11). Five myths about pickpockets. *USA Today* (online newspaper). Retrieved from www.usatoday.com/story/travel/advice/2016/05/11/pickpockets/84179812/

Rachels, J. (1999). *The challenge of cultural relativism* (online). Retrieved from https://faculty.uca.edu/rnovy/Rachels--Cultural%20Relativism.htm (Adapted from Rachels, J. (1986). *Chapter 2: The elements of moral philosophy*. New York, NY: McGraw-Hill).

Rotondaro, V., & Ewing, M. (2013, January 15). The ins and outs. *Narratively* (online literary magazine). Retrieved from https://narratively.com/the-ins-and-the-outs/

Vazsonyi, A. T., Ksinan, A. J., & Javakhishvili, M. (2021). Problems of cross-cultural criminology no more! Testing two central tenets of self-control theory across 28 nations. *Journal of Criminal Justice*, *75*. Retrieved from www.sciencedirect.com/science/article/abs/pii/S0047235221000477

Wockner, C., & Erviani, K. (2016, November 30). Bali teen accused of stealing mobile from Australian woman 'beaten' by security. *News.com.au* (online newspaper). Retrieved from www.news.com.au/world/asia/bali-teen-accused-of-stealing-mobile-from-australian-woman-beaten-by-security/news-story/ecc135bf846f93477c7027aa247b675b

Punishment and Prisons

Prisons evolved along with law and have existed since at least the time of ancient Athens (Allen, 2002). In the United States, which currently has one of the highest incarceration rates in the world, psychology—though its most famous 20th-century experiments involved simulations of punishment delivery and imprisonment—has not evolved a consistent or subtle theory of punishment. And regarding prisons, psychologists interested in reform have fought a continual uphill battle. Perhaps psychology's single most glaring ethical problem of the past two decades has been the involvement of psychologists in the design and implementation of overt torture in the US military prison maintained as a military-colonial enclave in Cuba (Risen, 2015).

Extreme variations exist between regions and cultures in the style and frequency of prison punishment. A recent study compared three European or European-derived cultures (the United States, Canada, and Germany) with widely different incarceration rates (currently—2023—US, 505/100,000; Canada, 85/100,000; and Germany, 67/100,000). The results suggest that, even though there are some individual-level cultural differences in punitiveness in these societies, they are not the main driver of differential incarceration rates. However, these statistics probably reflect more the social endorsement of the status quo established by lawmakers' choices of punishment strategies (Kugler, Funk, Braun, Gollwitzer, & Kay, 2013).

Exposition, Confrontation, and Simulation

No credible simulation of prisons that captures the full cruelty of the experience can be done either in a classroom or in a laboratory. Consideration of prison issues must rely on the testimony of past and current prisoners, family members, prison staff members and administrators, and other interested individuals. Begin by examining the data available for prisons worldwide on the *World Prison Brief* website (World Prison Brief, 2023). This resource not only ranks basic prison statistics (total number of prisoners; rate per 100,000 population; percentage under 18, female, etc.) but also hosts a series of international prison reports including downloadable *Guidance Notes on Prison Reform* with chapters on demilitarization of prisons, overcrowding, and pretrial detention, a nagging worldwide problem. After this, search for comparisons between cultural attitudes toward prisoners, especially toward prisoners returning to society. One such comparison could be between Miriam (pseudonym), an illiterate woman incarcerated in Sierra Leone because of her ignorance of the meaning of her plea, who was glad to have learned to write during her time in prison, and Michelle Jones, incarcerated in the United States for 20 years for killing her child and released. Jones's rehabilitation was complete, and

DOI: 10.4324/9781003300380-69

her academic work in prison qualified her for admission to Harvard University, which rejected her, demonstrating the US cultural belief in crime as a permanent moral stain (Hager, 2017).

References and Suggested Readings

Allen, D. S. (2002). *The world of Prometheus: The politics of punishing in democratic Athens*. Princeton, NJ: Princeton University Press.

BBC. (2017, September 14). 100 Women: I didn't mean to plead guilty. *BBC News Magazine* (online magazine). Retrieved from www.bbc.com/news/magazine-40881469

Hager, E. (2017, September 13). From prison to Ph. D: The redemption and rejection of Michelle Jones. *The New York Times* (online newspaper). Retrieved from www.nytimes.com/2017/09/13/us/harvard-nyu-prison-michelle-jones.html?mcubz=3

Kugler, M. B., Funk, F., Braun, J., Gollwitzer, M., & Kay, A. C. (2013). Differences in punitiveness across three cultures: A test of American exceptionalism in justice attitudes. *The Journal of Criminal Law and Criminology*, *103*(4), 1071–1114.

Risen, J. (2015, April 30). American Psychological Association bolstered torture program, report says. *The New York Times* (online newspaper). Retrieved from www.nytimes.com/2015/05/01/us/report-says-american-psychological-association-collaborated-on-torture-justification.html?mcubz=3

World Prison Brief. (2023). *World Prison Brief Website* (Data). Retrieved from www.prisonstudies.org/world-prison-brief-data

Religion and Law

Neither religion nor law can be treated in any degree of detail in a cross-cultural psychology course. Like marriage, money, or privilege, religion and law are part of the context in which any such course will take place. Presumably both law and religion stem from a primordial source of the evolution of human social behavior; both Freud (in his rarely read *Group Psychology and the Analysis of the Ego* as well as in his frankly anthropological *Totem and Taboo*) and more recent commentators (e.g., Facchini, 1991) offer insights on this. From a cultural psychological point of view, it is where law intersects with religion that offers the best starting point for discussion. It is a highly contested area and a primary source for culture war and would be ideal for a course that treats culture as evolving from conflict but less so for other less warlike approaches. Beaman (2020) provides case examples of the translation of religion into law and culture in Canada, France, and the United States.

Exposition, Confrontation, and Simulation

First, achieve some basic familiarity with law's incorporation of religion. Sharia is a good starting point since many essential legal issues in Muslim cultures are influenced by religious principles, including marriage and divorce, inheritance, finance, and insurance. There are several reasonably accurate and simple summaries available of the ways in which Muslim legal practice depends on religious tenets (e.g., Rashid, 2011). There are similar intersections between traditional Jewish religious law and current secular law, and sources detailing aspects of these (e.g., Greenberg-Kobrin, 2014) can be mined for discussable examples, for instance, the *get*. In the same spirit as the suggestions for approaching rights and citizenship, students should be encouraged to draft codes of laws de novo and then to compare these with the structure of secular and religious codes. Beyond this, case studies can be developed for examination.

The following two US cases have a good deal of documentation, so a convincing interactive exercise can be developed from the evidence, either simulation of some stage of the legal proceedings or posing of the ethical problems involved. These are the Nickel Mines school shooting that occurred in 2006 (Kocieniewski & Gately, 2006) and the controversy over a display of a Ten Commandments stele in front of an Alabama courthouse in 2001. The Nickel Mines case, one of many well-publicized terroristic events involving shootings at schools over the past 20 years, is notable because its targets forgave the shooter (Shapiro, 2007). The judge in the Ten Commandments case, Roy Moore of Alabama, was ordered to remove the large monument displaying the Decalogue, refused, and was ultimately removed from office over the issue (CNN, 2003). Comparison of

DOI: 10.4324/9781003300380-70

current events with these somewhat distant ones may reveal fluctuations of the law/religion boundary.

References and Suggested Readings

Beaman, L. (2020). *The transition of religion to culture and law in public discourse*. New York, NY: Routledge.

CNN. (2003, November 14). Ten Commandments judge removed from office. *CNN (Cable News Network)* (online news source). Retrieved from www.cnn.com/2003/LAW/11/13/moore.tencommandments/

Facchini, F. (1991). The roots of ethics: An anthropological approach. *Human Evolution*, *6*(5–6), 461–469.

Greenberg-Kobrin, M. (2014). Religious tribunals and secular courts: Navigating power and powerlessness. *Pepperdine Law Review*, *41*, 997–1012.

Kocieniewski, D., & Gately, G. (2006, October 3). Man shoots 11, killing 5 girls, in Amish school. *The New York Times* (online newspaper). Retrieved from www.nytimes.com/2006/10/03/us/03amish.html?mcubz=3

Rashid, Q. (2011, November 4). Shariah law: The five things every non-Muslim (and Muslim) should know. *Huffington Post* (The Blog) (online news source). Retrieved from www.huffpost.com/entry/shariah-law-the-five-things-every-non-muslim_b_1068569

Shapiro, J. (2007, October 2). Amish forgive school shooter, struggle with grief. *NPR (National Public Radio) All Things Considered* (online broadcast transcript). Retrieved from www.npr.org/2007/10/02/14900930/amish-forgive-school-shooter-struggle-with-grief

Economics and Work

DOI: 10.4324/9781003300380-71

Corporate and Work Culture

The idea of corporate culture emerges from organizational sociology, which itself is an outgrowth of the main historical roots of that field in the work of Emile Durkheim and Max Weber (Lincoln & Guillot, 2006). The idea that corporations shape character has circulated in social science since the 1950s, when the concept of the *organization man* was current (Whyte, 1956). It has persisted through the update of Arlie Russell Hochschild's *The Managed Heart* (Hochschild, 2012), which portrays the ways that corporations can compel conformity to not only corporate policies but also regulations that ultimately define, and may deform, human interaction. Organizational culture extends across cultures (Gelfand, 2007), and distinct national differences in corporate styles emerge in interaction with regional and national cultural characteristics.

At the level of work itself rather than its larger social organization, the individual again emerges. Individuals bear the marks of their professions, as Sherlock Holmes often astutely observed. They are shaped not only by their home culture but also by the universal demands of their jobs (driving and plumbing are the same wherever they are practiced, subject only to specific environmental constraints) and by their interactions with apprentice masters, coworkers, and customers.

Exposition, Confrontation, and Simulation

During a visit to the Iowa State Fair, Mitt Romney, a candidate for president of the United States in 2011, said that corporations are people. He probably meant only that corporations are a convenient way of collectively referring to groups of people. However, he was vilified in the press and by the opposing party for what seemed to be an endorsement of extending legal rights that properly belong to free human individuals to abstract legal fictions ramifying soulless corporate behemoths (Rucker, 2011). Romney's statement could introduce the concept of *corporate personhood* as a discussion topic, which could be amplified by a replication of the findings of Mentovich, Huq, and Cerf (2014) that individuals are unlikely to grant this status to corporations, especially large, profit-making ones.

Older generations may still remember when a job in the United States promised support for a long time, often a lifetime. However, today, even in some cultures where the idea of long-term employment was bolstered by collective pressure to stay in place, job security has been replaced by transience and uncertainty. One place where this uncertainty becomes visible is during corporate mergers and acquisitions, whose pace has increased over the past few decades. M&As, as these are called, are observed to be active sites of culture clashes that can render mergers unworkable (Stafford & Miles, 2013).

DOI: 10.4324/9781003300380-72

Most students of culture, at least in college, will not have much experience with employment or corporate culture, and most graduates will tend to stay in their home culture rather than becoming involved with a multinational enterprise, although this is becoming more likely as globalization progresses. As it stands, M&As are probably the best place to observe the power of organizational culture, but for persons without experience and outside of the corporate environment, it might be difficult to imagine why a job transition might be traumatic. Probably the best advice would be to structure discussion around situations in which the rules have changed with the takeover. A corporate case in point could be the unsuccessful merger of automakers Daimler and Chrysler in the first decade of this century, a widely documented episode (Watkins, 2007); a more recent example is the takeover of Twitter by Elon Musk (Chowdhury, 2023). Other ways to conceptualize the psychological effects of a bad merger are to compare it to a bad divorce or a bad remarriage in terms of the rancor involved, viewed from the perspective of any of the parties involved. Many of the same events—arbitrary changes of roles and rules, introduction of new and possibly foreign values, and changes in organizational aim—can be easily analogized to the elements that cause mergers to founder (Jacobsen, 2018).

To get at the culture of individual professions, choose one that is accessible and concrete: plumbing, for example. Water doesn't run uphill in Nigeria, nor does it behave under pressure there any differently than it does in Britain. And plumbing, from the standpoint of public health at least, is a universal need, although plumbing with pipes and running water is itself not universal, not even in the United States (Ingraham, 2014; Jones, 2022). Investigate how plumbing can cross borders and cultures by following the stories of Anselm Okoukoni, who parlayed training he received as an illegal immigrant in Britain into professionally bringing competent plumbing to Nigeria, where it is in short supply (Nwaubani, 2015); Edy Cartagena, a refugee from Honduras working as a plumber in San Diego, California (Cartagena, 2023); and Safa'a, a Syrian refugee starting a new life as a plumber in Jordan (Rescue.org, 2016).

References and Suggested Readings

Cartagena, E. (2023, February 24). Opinion: I am a Honduran immigrant living the American dream. I want to help others succeed. *San Diego Union-Tribune* (online newspaper). Retrieved from www.sandiegouniontribune.com/opinion/commentary/story/2023-02-03/opinion-many-people-have-been-forced-to-seek-asylum

Chowdhury, R. (2023, February 17). I watched Elon Musk kill Twitter's culture from the inside. *The Atlantic* (online magazine). Retrieved from www.theatlantic.com/technology/archive/2023/02/elon-musk-twitter-ethics-algorithm-biases/673110/

Gelfand, M. J. (2007). Cross-cultural organizational behavior. *Annual Review of Psychology*, *58*, 479–514.

Hochschild, A. R. (2012). *The managed heart: The commercialization of human feeling* (Update with a new preface). Berkeley, CA: University of California Press (Originally work published by 1983).

Ingraham, C. (2014, April 23). 1.6 million Americans don't have indoor plumbing. Here's where they live. *The Washington Post* (online newspaper). Retrieved from www.washingtonpost.com/news/wonk/wp/2014/04/23/1-6-million-americans-dont-have-indoor-plumbing-heres-where-they-live/

Jacobsen, D. (2018, March 15). 6 big mergers that were killed by culture (and how to stop it from killing yours). *WorkHuman* (online blog). Retrieved from www.workhuman.com/blog/6-big-mergers-that-were-killed-by-culture-and-how-to-stop-it-from-killing-yours/

Jones, J. (2022, August 11). U. S. Cities where most residents lack running water in 2021. *Construction Coverage Website*. Retrieved from https://constructioncoverage.com/research/cities-where-most-residents-lack-running-water-2021

Lincoln, J. A., & Guillot, D. (2006). A Durkheimian view of organizational culture. In M. Korczynski, R. Hodson, & P. Edwar (Eds.), *Social theory at work* (pp. 88–120). Oxford: Oxford University Press.

Mentovich, A., Huq, A., & Cerf, M. (2014). *The psychology of corporate rights* (University of Chicago Public Law & Legal Theory Working Paper No. 497) (Online). Retrieved from http://chicagounbound.uchicago.edu/cgi/viewcontent.cgi?article=1956&context=public_law_and_legal_theory

Nwaubani, A. T. (2015, December 21). Illegal migrant makes good as plumber in Nigeria. *BBC News* (online news magazine, British Broadcasting Corporation). Retrieved from www.bbc.com/news/world-africa-35131170

Rescue.org. (2016, September 28). The plumber: An unexpected path. *Rescue.org* (nonprofit organization website). Retrieved from www.rescue.org/article/plumber-unexpected-path

Rucker, P. (2011, August 11). Mitt Romney says 'corporations are people'. *The Washington Post* (online newspaper). www.washingtonpost.com/politics/mitt-romney-says-corporations-are-people/2011/08/11/gIQABwZ38I_story.html?utm_term=.fbf899758c6e. Retrieved from

Stafford, D., & Miles, L. (2013, December 11). Integrating cultures after a merger. *Bain Brief* (Bain & Company Corporate website). Retrieved from www.bain.com/insights/integrating-cultures-after-a-merger

Watkins, M. D. (2007, May 18). Why DaimlerChrysler never got into gear. *Harvard Business Review* (online). Retrieved from https://hbr.org/2007/05/why-the-daimlerchrysler-merger

Whyte, W. H. (1956). *The organization man*. New York, NY: Simon & Schuster.

Work: Hiring and Firing

Work defines the self at its most basic motivational levels. Yet it is unusual to encounter many of the actual practices of work in cross-cultural course settings, especially at the level of non-management employees needing to fit into a culture's economic system to survive. This unintentional blindness to the cultural pervasiveness of work and its importance to basic life systems (e.g., the linkage of health insurance to employment in the United States) makes this a provocative area for attention. From a perspective of US industrial/organizational psychology, most treatments of work focus on hiring and evaluation, less on termination and job loss, and are pitched to stable employment situations in corporate settings. The realities of the growing temporariness and unpredictability of work, gender inequality in work, and the replacement by automation of the traditional conceptions of jobs, not only in manufacturing but in almost every other aspect of employment (for instance, the projected near-total automation of banking and the replacement of the department store by e-commerce), signal seismic cultural shifts.

Over the past quarter century, many corporations worldwide have taken seriously the need to expand operations into other countries and have taken a lead in making at least their own internal corporate cultures plain. An excellent example of this is the *culture deck* generated by Netflix (Netflix Corporation, 2009). The explicit statement of Netflix's value system—which emphasizes directness, speed, efficiency, self-direction, and public criticism and evaluation—allows it to be easily contrasted with the values implicit in other cultures. For instance, Netflix encountered resistance to its conception of rapidly terminating B-level performers—albeit with generous severance pay—in Japan, where employment, especially in a corporate setting, is often for life. Other cultures—for example, Islamic culture—place at least as strong an emphasis on morality and social solidarity as on trade (Ali & Al-Owaihan, 2008) and may place more emphasis on maintaining personal relationships rather than adopting the attitude that "being let go from an Olympic team makes one no less great," a prevalent attitude in Netflix's corporate culture toward termination (Fairchild, 2016, n.p.).

Exposition, Confrontation, and Simulation

Employment law is complex no matter what the culture. One approach to understanding this highly regulated area of human behavior is to review employment law (and laws protecting employees from unfair dismissal) across cultures—many examples worldwide are available online by googling "termination law" along with the country of interest (e.g., Kenya: IkiGai, 2022). Likewise, all other aspects of the employment process—from the search through the interview and from apprenticeship to promotion to dismissal—are

DOI: 10.4324/9781003300380-73

treated extensively online, providing fruitful sources for comparative analysis of at least the explicit legal aspects of culture. Another approach would be to take the perspective of an immigrant to a new culture needing to find work—for instance, a US citizen wishing to work in Portugal (Visa Guide, 2023). Confrontation and simulation can be blended here and, for purposes of starting discussion, can focus on the immediate cultural environment rather than comparing across cultures. For example, try simulation or role-playing of termination scenarios across several types of organization, such as an informal, very small business setting, such as a lawn and landscaping business with five employees compared with a fast-food restaurant with explicit and strict policies (publicly available on the net) compared with an advanced corporate setting. Attention can be given not only to the interaction of explicit rules with unstated underlying family or personal dynamics between the persons involved but also to the emotions that may be expressed when personal values conflict with corporate ones.

References and Suggested Readings

Ali, A. J., & Al-Owaihan, A. (2008). Islamic work ethic: A critical review. *Cross-cultural Management*, *15*(1), 5–19.

Fairchild, C. (2016, June 20). Netflix redefined American company culture: Will it do the same abroad? *CNBC MakeIt* (online resource). Retrieved from www.cnbc.com/2016/06/20/netflix-redefined-american-company-culture-will-it-do-the-same-abroad.html

IkiGai (2022, May 17). What happens when the employment relationship turns sour: Termination and summary dismissal in Kenya. *IkiGai Nairobi Website*. Retrieved from https://ikigai.co.ke/2022/05/17/what-happens-when-the-employment-relationship-turns-sour-termination-and-summary-dismissal-in-kenya/

Netflix Corporation. (2009). *Culture deck* (online power point presentation). Retrieved from www.slideshare.net/reed2001/culture-1798664

VisaGuide (2023). Portugal work visa. *VisaGuide.world Website*. Retrieved from https://visaguide.world/europe/portugal-visa/work-visa/

Insurance: Risk and Time

Insurance maintains continuity of financial and material resources over time under conditions of variable risk. Though it is not typically considered in cross-cultural contexts, insurance offers a launching point for discussion of some factors related to insurance that have cross-cultural relevance. Relative perception of risk has been shown to vary across cultures. For instance, Li (2017) cites data showing that risks are rated differently by Japanese and US student participants with Japanese rating more risks as uncontrollable, dreaded, and catastrophic. Another plausible theoretical variable related to insurance is Hofstede's long-term orientation, which includes a focus on future rewards as well as on maintaining long-lasting and noncontingent relationships (Hofstede, Hofstede, & Minkov, 2010). Logically, purchasing insurance implies a degree of foresight and commitment, and there appears to be a relation between long-term orientation and life insurance purchase (Park & Lemaire, 2011). Related to the implicit future focus in long-term orientation is the idea of a future time perspective (Zimbardo & Boyd, 2008), in which coming events can be anticipated and, to some extent, planned for. Though not a great deal of research on future time perspective has accumulated, there has been some indication that cultural differences in the relative orientation to past, present, and future time exist (Sobol-Kwapińska, Jankowski, Przepiorka, Oinyshi, Sorokowski, & Zimbardo, 2018).

Exposition, Confrontation, and Simulation

Measurement scales for risk—for instance, the DOSPERT scale (Blais & Weber, 2008)—could be a framework for discussion of cross-cultural comparisons (Breuer, Kollath, Salzmann, & von Nitzsch, 2013). The following comparison between the United States and Pakistan can be a prompt for discussion about risk and time. Automobile liability insurance has been compulsory in most countries for generations; few if any countries in the world do not have an official policy mandating at least third-party coverage. Even so, extreme variations exist in the numbers of individuals who avoid obtaining coverage, regionally as well as cross-nationally. For example, in the United States, the percentage of uninsured drivers ranges from a low of 3.1 percent in New Jersey to more than 25 percent in Michigan and Mississippi (Insurance Information Institute, 2023). In contrast, Pakistan, where third-party insurance is also mandatory, reportedly has a rate as high as 75 percent of drivers without insurance (Daily Times, 2016). Why, although insurance is mandatory in each country, is there such a discrepancy in compliance between Pakistan and the United States? Some reasons are traceable to the structure of law; in Pakistan, many cars are obtained used (Ansari, 2015), and transactions outside of the scrutiny of

DOI: 10.4324/9781003300380-74

dealerships and official registration procedures allow avoidance of the insurance mandate. Pakistan's relative poverty compared to the United States may also be a factor influencing the decision to purchase automobile insurance. But Pakistan also rates higher on long-term orientation than the United States, which is contrary to making a decision not to prepare for future costs. How could this apparent contradiction be explained? Turning to the regional differences in the United States, could they be explained by a future time factor, possibly related to age?

Discussion of future time perception may be extended to other situations involving risk and future time concerns—for example, obtaining contraceptives (Baum et al., 2016) or immunization or traveling during a pandemic (Fong, Sun, Chan, & Law, 2023). Sometimes, insurance becomes a defining feature of national culture. The lack of universal health insurance in the United States renders its outlier status among high-income countries (Commonwealth Fund, 2023; Taber, Leyva, & Peroskie, 2015) a glaring cultural trait. The conflict about US health insurance coverage is often framed in terms of individualist repugnance toward socialism; in what ways could perceptions of risk and time enter into that debate, along with the cultural heritage of racial discrimination (Interlandi, 2019)?

References and Suggested Readings

Ansari, N. (2015, September 7). Need a ride? Here's the ultimate guide to buying used cars in Karachi. *Dawn* (online news source). Retrieved from www.dawn.com/news/1204648/

Baum, S., Burns, B., Davis, L., Yeung, M., Scott, C., Grindlay, K., & Grossman, D. (2016). Perspectives among a diverse sample of women on the possibility of obtaining oral contraceptives over the counter. *Women's Health Issues*, *26*(2), 147–152.

Blais, A. R., & Weber, E. U. (2008). A domain- specific risk-taking (DOSPERT) scale for adult populations. *Judgment and Decision Making*, *1*(1), 33–47. Retrieved from https://journal.sjdm.org/jdm06005.pdf

Breuer, W., Kollath, J., Salzmann, A. J., & von Nitzsch, R. (2013, January). The assessment of risk behavior: A cross-cultural analysis using the DOSPERT scale. In I. Venezia (Ed.), *Behavioral finance: Sophistication, gender, attention, media, and culture effects on investor decisions* (pp. 159–180). Singapore: World Scientific Publishing Co (Online open access). Retrieved from https://papers.ssrn.com/sol3/papers.cfm?abstract_id=2292364

Commonwealth Fund. (2023). U.S. health care from a global perspective, 2022: Accelerating spending, worsening outcomes. *The Commonwealth Fund Website*. Retrieved from www.commonwealthfund.org/publications/issue-briefs/2023/jan/us-health-care-global-perspective-2022

Daily Times (2016, August 20). 75% of cars uninsured in Pakistan, survey reveals. *Daily Times* (online newspaper, Pakistan). Retrieved from https://dailytimes.com.pk/62384/75-of-cars-uninsured-in-pakistan-survey-reveals/

Fong, L. H. N., Sun, S., Chan, I. C. C., & Law, R. (2023, January 16). The influence of time orientation on infection risk evaluation: Moderating role of public health crisis. *Journal of Hospitality and Tourism Research*. Retrieved from https://journals.sagepub.com/doi/10.1177/10963480221147437?icid=int.sj-full-text.citing-articles.34

Hofstede, G., Hofstede, G. J., & Minkov, M. (2010). *Cultures and organizations: Software of the mind* (3rd ed.). New York, NY: McGraw-Hill.

Insurance Information Institute. (2023). Facts + statistics: Uninsured motorists. *Insurance Information Institute Website*. Retrieved from www.iii.org/fact-statistic/facts-statistics-uninsured-motorists

Interlandi, J. (2019, August 14). Why doesn't the United States have universal health care? The answer has everything to do with race. *The New York Times Magazine*. Retrieved from www.nytimes.com/interactive/2019/08/14/magazine/universal-health-care-racism.html

Li, E. P. H. (2017). Cognitive styles and personality in risk perception. In G. Emilien, R. Weitkunat & F. Ludicke (Eds.), *Consumer perception of product risks and benefits* (pp. 267–282). Basle, CH: Springer International Publishing AG.

Park, S., & Lemaire, J. (2011, July 28). Culture matters: Long-term orientation and the demand for life insurance. *Asia-Pacific Journal of Risk and Insurance*, *5*(2). Retrieved from www.degruyter.com/document/doi/10.2202/2153-3792.1105/html?lang=en

Sobol-Kwapińska, M., Jankowski, T., Przepiorka, A., Oinyshi, I., Sorokowski, P., & Zimbardo, P. (2018, November 1). What is the structure of time? A study on time perspective in the United States, Poland, and Nigeria. *Frontiers in Psychology (Sec. Quantitative Psychology and Measurement)*, *9*. Retrieved from www.frontiersin.org/articles/10.3389/fpsyg.2018.02078/full

Taber, J., Leyva, B., & Peroskie, A. (2015). Why do people avoid medical care? A qualitative study using national data. *Journal of General Internal Medicine*, *30*(3), 290–297.

Zimbardo, P., & Boyd, J. (2008). *The time paradox: The new psychology of time that will change your life*. New York, NY: Atria Books.

Materialism and Consumer Culture

Materialism can take a couple of paths into philosophical deep water. It can lead to contrasts with idealism or spiritualism, or it can lead to consideration of the ethical and moral proposition that the best life is the one that is most well-equipped with physical comforts and goods. For the purposes of this brief introduction, the latter will be followed. The extreme form of goods-based materialism is the cargo cult, which has a more complicated history than the usual account of the veneration of the litter of war by credulous Pacific Islanders as gifts sent directly from heaven and obtainable again by invocation (Worsley, 2009; Dunning, 2010; Raffaele, 2006). Less extreme forms of materialism connected to ordinary consumer economics have been measured, and those measurements are prominent in the consumer behavior and marketing literature. Cross-cultural comparisons have proved difficult to make on psychometric grounds, although the effort continues to establish differences (Masoom, Sarker, & Liu, 2017; Watchravesringkan, 2012; Ohno, Lee, & Maeno, 2022).

Consumer culture as a specific term can be found in use in several contexts. It can be understood as a force that differentiates groups within a society. For instance, art historian Pamela Karini locates the tension between traditional religion and modern secularization in Iran specifically in the ways that ordinary Iranian citizens made choices about household design and household equipment (Karimi, 2013). Consumerism can also be understood as one of the core elements of a whole society; a pervasive ideology (Schmitt, Brakus, & Biraglia, 2022).

Searching on "mental health" crossed with "consumer culture" in PsycINFO leads to hundreds of hits leading to critiques varying in emphases from the commodification of health care services and those who consume them (Sturgeon, 2014) to the promotion in popular music lyrics of overconsumption of intoxicants (Holody, Anderson, Craig, & Flynn, 2016) to the interpretation of seduction by product advertising as a form of classic Freudian hysteria (Castro, 2016).

Exposition, Confrontation, and Simulation

Most psychological studies of consumer materialism refer to the scale developed in the early 1990s by Marsha Richins and Scott Dawson, the Material Values Scale (MVS; see Richins & Dawson, 1992; Richins, 2004). The contents of the MVS can be deduced from these published materials, and discussion of individual questions from the MVS and/or examination of the results of its group administration can provide a baseline for materialistic value orientation in the immediate environment. The connection of materialism and consumerism with psychological well-being has been meta-analyzed (Dittmar, Bond, Hurst, & Kasser, 2014), and the scales used in that analysis can be tracked down, examined, and

DOI: 10.4324/9781003300380-75

discussed as well; among them, along with the MVS, are the Money Ethic Scale, the Money Over Mind Questionnaire, the Spending Tendency Scale, and the Compulsive Buying Scale. Further discussion of the consumer concept can be engendered by following up on Sturgeon (2014) and asking, in the context of psychology becoming more and more closely aligned with the health care system worldwide, whether health care is best considered a commodity and persons seeking contact with therapists consumers.

Turning to more mundane and material matters, examination of the provenance of the clothing worn by members of any classroom group will certainly locate the world centers of apparel production. Consider also the question of luxury consumption vs. subsistence. Seek where the largest markets for luxury German auto brands are (hint: China) and how luxury consumption might square with typical characterizations of that society as collectivistic. For a lighter touch, visit the IKEA website (www.ikea.com/), which contains catalogs specialized for each of its many countries of operation and production. Access them and compare the iconography, product descriptions, and relative availability of products. Also examine the distribution, worldwide, of Costco outlets.

References and Suggested Readings

Castro, J. C. L. (2016). The discourse of hysteria as the logic of mass consumption. *Psychoanalysis, Culture, and Society*, *21*(4), 403–421.

Dittmar, H., Bond, R., Hurst, M., & Kasser, T. (2014). The relationship between materialism and well-being: A meta-analysis. *Journal of Personality and Social Psychology*, *107*(5), 879–924.

Dunning, B. (2010, March 30). Cargo cults. *Skeptoid Podcast. Skeptoid Media* (online source). Retrieved from http://skeptoid.com/episodes/4199

Holody, K. J., Anderson, C., Craig, C., & Flynn, M. (2016). 'Drunk in love': The portrayal of risk behavior in music lyrics. *Journal of Health Communication*, *21*(10), 1098–1106.

Karimi, P. (2013). *Domesticity and consumer culture in Iran: Interior revolutions of the modern era*. New York, NY: Routledge.

Masoom, M. R., Sarker, M. M., & Liu, G. (2017). Rising materialism in the developing economy: Assessing materialistic value orientation in contemporary Bangladesh. *Cogent Business and Management*, *4*(1) (Published online 7/5/2017). Retrieved from www.tandfonline.com/doi/full/10.1080/23311975.2017.1345049

Ohno, H., Lee, K. T., & Maeno, T. (2022, August 13). The Japanese version of the Material Values Scale: Construct assessment and relationship with age, personality, and subjective well-being. *BMC Psychology*. Retrieved from https://bmcpsychology.biomedcentral.com/articles/10.1186/s40359-022-00889-3#Sec1

Raffaele, P. (2006, February). In John they trust. *Smithsonian Magazine* (online). Retrieved from www.smithsonianmag.com/history/in-john-they-trust-109294882/

Richins, M. L. (2004). The material values scale: Measurement properties and development of a short form. *Journal of Consumer Research*, *31*(1), 209–219.

Richins, M. L., & Dawson, S. (1992). A consumer values orientation for materialism and its measurement: Scale development and validation. *Journal of Consumer Research*, *19*(3), 303–316.

Schmitt, B., Brakus, J. J., & Biraglia, A. (2022). Consumption ideology. *Journal of Consumer Research*, *49*(1), 74–95. Retrieved from https://academic.oup.com/jcr/article/49/1/74/6358727

Sturgeon, D. (2014). The business of the NHS: The rise and rise of consumer culture and commodification in the provision of healthcare services. *Critical Social Policy*, *34*(3), 405–416.

Watchravesringkan, K. (2012). Cross-cultural equivalence of Materialistic Values Scale (MVS): An exploratory study between the United States and Thailand. *Journal of Targeting, Measurement, and Analysis for Marketing*, *20*(3–4), 235–253.

Worsley, P. (2009, May 1). 50 years ago: Cargo cults on Melanesia. *Scientific American* (online magazine). Retrieved from www.scientificamerican.com/article/1959-cargo-cults-melanesia/

Money and Exchange

No culture is without some means of exchange, and the presence or absence of money is a prime conditioner of cultural differences. Typical readers and users of this set of exercises will usually be familiar with systems of money and credit similar to those in the United States as well as investing and saving. Also, many will have experienced money as a constant background fuel supply for cultural life and may not have had too much experience in not having it. Housel (2020) provides an overview of typical attitudes and behaviors relating to the acquisition and uses of money in relatively affluent cultures. Cohen, Shin, and Liu (2019), drawing on behavioral economics, introduce a wider variety of money perceptions and uses across different classes and cultures. In many cultures, scarcity of both resources and money is the rule, and, in those situations, mutual aid, barter, and other forms of adaptation to the challenge of obtaining basic goods emerge. Also, religious prohibitions against lending at interest that exist in strictly Muslim cultures, for example, change fundamental perceptions of the availability of money and the means for its repayment (Alexander, 2011). Relative levels of wealth within and between cultures can determine the view that insiders have of outsiders' personalities (Chan et al., 2011). Informal economies outside of the ordinary channels of exchange develop under poverty conditions, in the United States as well as elsewhere (Bonnet & Venkatesh, 2016; Glinton, 2017). Economic sociology reveals many other ways in which the perception of money and wealth is conditioned by culture, including gender factors (e.g., Zelizer, 2005, 2011).

Exposition, Confrontation, and Simulation

Depending on the experience of the group, some basic familiarization with money economies compared with barter economies might be advised at the start. There are elementary simulations of barter contrasted with money (e.g., Carolina K-12, 2012). For a more ambitious project, imagine a culture in which forms of microfinance, interest-free credit, illegal trade, and barter are the main ways in which goods are obtained by persons outside of the elite. Local accounts from cultures with extreme wealth differentials (for example, Ghana, Dadzie, 2015) can assist in setting a context. Simulate a susu collective money pool (Peachey & Darko, 2020); use play money or chips, and set up a market with desirable goods to buy at local prices depending on the culture or region. Throw in a few medical supplies and automotive repairs or transportation as desirable goods, and set up both barter and black market systems on the side. Assign players to be possessors of goods and others to be seekers, a few with no ready cash and a few others with some cash or other resources. Operate this set of simulated markets for a short while, and take

DOI: 10.4324/9781003300380-76

specific note not only of the relative amounts gained by individuals but also of any sign of coalition or alliance building, development and utilization of bargaining techniques, and skill in detecting which form of exchange is desired by each possessor. If poverty is the focus, then starting with a questionnaire about poverty experiences could start the conversation about wealth differentials in the immediate environment; section VII of the somewhat dated but still applicable NPR-Kaiser Family Foundation-Kennedy School of Government Poverty Study (NPR, 2001) is a short and efficient path toward revealing histories and attitudes.

References and Suggested Readings

Alexander, D. (2011, May 16). Understanding how money works in different cultures. *The Chronicle of Philanthropy* (online magazine). Retrieved from www.philanthropy.com/article/understanding-how-money-works-in-different-cultures/

Bonnet, F., & Venkatesh, S. (2016). Poverty and informal economies. In D. Brady & L. M. Burton (Eds.), *Oxford handbook of the social science of poverty* (pp. 637–659). Oxford: Oxford University Press.

Carolina K-12. (2012). Barter and money. *Carolina Public Humanities* (online educational resource). Retrieved from https://k12database.unc.edu/wp-content/uploads/sites/31/2012/05/Money10.pdf

Chan, W., McCrae, R. R., Rogers, D. L., Weimer, A. A., Greenberg, D. M., & Terracciano, A. (2011). Rater wealth predicts perceptions of outgroup competence. *Journal of Research in Personality*, *45*(6), 597–603.

Cohen, D., Shin, F., & Liu, X. (2019). Meanings and functions of money in different cultural milieus. *Annual Review of Psychology*, *70*, 475—497. Retrieved from www.annualreviews.org/doi/10.1146/annurev-psych-010418-103221

Dadzie, E. (2015, January 19). Working for poor wages: Ghana's example stinks. *GhanaWeb* (online newspaper). Retrieved from www.ghanaweb.com/GhanaHomePage/NewsArchive/Working-for-poor-wages-Ghana-s-example-stinks-343593

Glinton, S. (2017, October 27). Some black Americans turn to informal economy in the face of discrimination. *NPR (National Public Radio) All Things Considered* (Broadcast transcript). Retrieved from www.npr.org/2017/10/27/560239264/some-black-americans-turn-to-informal-economy-in-the-face-of-discrimination?utm_source=facebook.com&utm_medium=social&utm_campaign=npr&utm_term=nprnews&utm_content=2054

Housel, M. (2020). *The psychology of money: Timeless lessons on wealth, greed, and happiness.* Petersfield, UK and Hampshire, UK: Harriman House.

NPR (National Public Radio). (2001). *The NPR-Kaiser family foundation-Kennedy school of government poverty study* (online). Retrieved from https://news.npr.org/programs/specials/poll/poverty/poll.html

Peachey S., & Darko, A. D. (2020). Preserving liquidity in Ghana's susu collection system during the COVID-19 crisis. *Oxford Policy Management Website.* Retrieved from www.opml.co.uk/blog/preserving-liquidit-ghan-susu-collection-system-during-covid-19

Zelizer, V. (2005). *The purchase of intimacy.* Princeton, NJ: Princeton University Press.

Zelizer, V. (2011). *Economic lives: How culture shapes the economy.* Princeton, NJ: Princeton University Press.

Environment

DOI: 10.4324/9781003300380-77

Fuel

Fuel is a ubiquitous necessity and a potent force both in structuring and maintaining cultures and in hastening their change. Any fuel will serve as a starting point; here are some examples of how coal connects with culture. Coal is the most prevalent fuel worldwide at present (Kottasova, 2022). Coal mining in the United States, a physically demanding and dangerous trade, is associated with a set of cultural values that result in a fatalistic and traditionalist mindset (Law, 2012) that is resistant to the introduction of new fuel technologies and new ways of thinking about energy in a larger framework than that of the immediate region. In an entirely different region, as a perceptive essay by Derks (2015) demonstrates, coal in Vietnam has served as a way out of economic privation by preserving forests, which were in danger of destruction because of overuse of wood for fuel. But, at the same time, coal is devalued as a survival of an older, dirtier past that is being replaced, symbolically and actually, by the use of gas as a fuel for cooking. Architects and planners are determining that coal, which needs to be burned outside because of the threat of carbon monoxide poisoning, will not be prominent as a fuel in the future since new apartments are being built that incorporate indoor kitchens integrated with the living space, each equipped with gas and electric appliances. In this case, within a couple of generations, an older way of life centered on fire-tending and slow cooking has been replaced with a lifestyle incorporating elements of European and American speed, efficiency, and relative cleanliness in both household and environmental terms. Also, in rural areas, biogas produced from waste from pig farming is supplanting wood (Hunt, 2018).

Exposition, Confrontation, and Simulation

Most US and West European readers won't have much experience with fuel famine. A start could be made by simulating a power outage, a common occurrence in Iraq (cut the lights and, if possible, the A/C—but beforehand, let people know that a power outage might be imminent and that the use of open flames is not permitted during the outage). Observe closely and note the reactions, emotional, cognitive, and behavioral. Fuel use is a habit, so a thought experiment could be done imagining what might happen if oil, for instance, or natural gas were restricted in supply. What strategies would come into play that would be different under those changed conditions? An actual demonstration of learning new fuel use habits can be done (outdoors!) with a Coleman stove equipped with the baking oven attachment. My own experience with baking soda bread when using this device for the first time resulted in a loaf that was exactly 1/2 raw and 1/2 charred. Keep a stock of edible versions of whatever is attempted on hand to alleviate any disappointment with the experimental product.

DOI: 10.4324/9781003300380-78

Alternatively, discussion could center on what happens when a new energy source is introduced into a culture. Sketch a vignette in which electricity is delivered for the first time to a Muslim village in East Africa; list as many consequences of this event as possible, and also place the consequences in order of their occurrence, immediate to delayed. After this, compare the list with the consequences described by Tanja Winther (2013), especially noting whether anyone mentioned the specific consequences described on pages 167 and 168. The entire edited volume from which Winther's essay is drawn (Strauss, Rupp, & Love, 2013) provides a rich variety of examples of how cultural traditions are being modified by worldwide energy needs and extractive practices, which can be drawn on and modified for discussion as well.

References and Suggested Readings

Derks, A. (2015). Fueling change: A biography of the beehive coal briquette in post Đổi Mới Vietnam. *Journal of Material Culture*, *20*(3), 331–349.

Hunt, K. (2018, May 31). Vietnam is turning pig waste into biofuel to cut down on carbon emissions. *GreenMatters.com Website*. Retrieved from www.greenmatters.com/renewables/2018/08/01/ZYkAE5/vietnam-pig-biogas-carbon-emissions

Kottasova, I. (2022, December 16). The world is burning more coal than ever before, new report shows. *CNN.com Website*. Retrieved from www.cnn.com/2022/12/16/world/coal-use-record-high-climate-intl/index.html

Law, B. M. (2012). Coal miners' dilemma: In West Virginia, the demise of rehab programs for coal miners means a reduced likelihood of psychological treatment. *APA Monitor on Psychology*, *43*(4), 40. Retrieved from www.apa.org/monitor/2012/04/coal-miners

Strauss, S., Rupp, S., & Love, T. (Eds.). (2013). *Cultures of energy: Power, practices, technologies*. Walnut Creek, CA: Left Coast Press.

Winther, T. (2013). Space, time, and sociomaterial relationships: Moral aspects of the arrival of electricity in rural Zanzibar. In S. Strauss, S. Rupp & T. Love (Eds.), *Cultures of energy: Power, practices, technologies*. Walnut Creek, CA: Left Coast Press.

Water and Air

Water and air are symbolically central in culture (two of the four elements) as well as in psychology. Freud intuited, though he did not himself experience it, an "oceanic" feeling connected to religion; Jung understood water as symbolic of the unconscious and air as related to the soul or spirit, as did the ancient Greeks. *Pneumatoliberalism* has been advanced as a way of air-centered thinking, dissolving cultural boundaries and conceiving all things as simultaneously co-present and co-interactive (Su & Beiser, 2018).

Descending from these heights to more practical cultural psychology, the way that water is used may convey messages about the user and be a factor in cultural solidarity. For example, homeowners in the southwestern United States may feel pressure to use water-intensive landscaping to be positively evaluated by peers rather than using more environmentally sound water-conserving plantings (Neel, Sadalla, Berlin, Ledlow, & Neufeld, 2014). As the climate changes, drought along with rising temperatures becomes a more frequent environmental event. A recent study by Pachter et al. (2016) surveyed three Latinx populations in Guatemala, Mexico, and the United States (Texas) about their folk beliefs regarding sunken fontanel, a depression of the skull in infants that is due to dehydration. While the individuals surveyed related sunken fontanel to illness, they rarely assigned the correct cause or treatment for it (rehydration), a demonstration of the interaction of environmental change and folk medicine. Their beliefs did not extend to thinking in terms of environmental cause and effect.

Another example of the interaction of culture, environment, and psychology is dehydration related to climatic change in El Salvador. The ingrained ethos of hard work leads farm workers accustomed to long hours and stoic persistence to either not notice or override any signals from ambient temperatures now dangerously elevated due to climate change. This then leads to epidemic kidney failure (Palmer, 2019). Air, as well, is under assault from climate change interacting with the emissions of modern culture worldwide (Ramirez, 2023).

Exposition, Confrontation, and Simulation

A starting point for discussing the role of water in culture could be a comparison of individual and group water use in the immediate environment. There are several sites available that detail the amount of water consumed in everyday activities (e.g., Water Footprint, 2023). Put these totals against lists of water consumption in other regions worldwide (e.g., The Water Information Program, 2023). Trace the history of air-destructive products, tetraethyl lead and chlorofluorocarbons (Johnson, 2023), and the positive effects on all cultures

DOI: 10.4324/9781003300380-79

by banning them worldwide (Domonoske, 2021; Johnson, 2023). Demonstrations and simulations involving chemically compromised air would be too dangerous to attempt; the study of Berry et al. (2017) comparing the relative rate of delay discounting for air vs. money could be simply done, and also add water to the mix.

Another interesting and simple replication would be to follow up the experiments of Mony et al. (2013). They note that European and Asian people prefer room-temperature water or hot beverages (tea) with meals and that the temperature of water accompanying various foods (including chocolate!) affects several sensory and affective dimensions of the consumption experience. Since iced water, preferred by North Americans, reduces the perception of sweetness, this may be one variable explaining the desire for more highly sweetened foods in the United States.

References and Suggested Readings

Berry, M. S., Friedel, J. E., DeHart, W. B., Mahamane, S., Jordan, K. E., & Odum, A. L. (2017). The value of clean air: Comparing discounting of delayed air quality and money across magnitudes. *The Psychological Record*, *67*(2), 137–148.

Domonoske, C. (2021, August 30). The world has finally stopped using leaded gasoline. Algeria used the last stockpile. *NPR (National Public Radio) Website*. Retrieved from www.npr.org/2021/08/30/1031429212/the-world-has-finally-stopped-using-leaded-gasoline-algeria-used-the-last-stockp

Johnson, S. (2023, March 17). The brilliant inventor who made two of history's biggest mistakes. *The New York Times* (online newspaper). Retrieved from www.nytimes.com/2023/03/15/magazine/cfcs-inventor.html.

Mony, P., Tokar, T., Pang, P., Fiegel, A., Meullenet, J. F., & Seo, H. S. (2013). Temperature of served water can modulate sensory perception and acceptance of food. *Food Quality and Preference*, *28*(2), 449–455.

Neel, R., Sadalla, E., Berlin, A., Ledlow, S., & Neufeld, S. (2014). The social symbolism of water-conserving landscaping. *Journal of Environmental Psychology*, *40*, 49–56.

Pachter, L. M., Weller, S. C., Baer, R. D., Garcia de Alba Garcia, J. E., Glazer, M., . . . Gonzalez, E. (2016). Culture and dehydration: A comparative study of Caída de la Mollera (Fallen Fontanel) in three Latino populations. *Journal of Immigrant and Minority Health*, *18*(5), 1066–1075.

Palmer, J. (2019, September 20). Climate change is turning dehydration into a deadly epidemic. *BBC Science Focus Website*. Retrieved from www.sciencefocus.com/planet-earth/climate-change-is-turning-dehydration-into-a-deadly-epidemic/

Ramirez, R. (2023, March 14). Only 13 countries and territories had 'healthy' air quality in 2022. *CNN Website*. Retrieved from www.cnn.com/2023/03/14/world/air-pollution-report-2022-climate/index.html

Su, A., & Beiser, B. (2018). Pneumatoliberalism: A conversation with Maria José de Abreu. *Columbia Journal of Literary Criticism*, *XVI*, 76–87. Retrieved from http://c-j-l-c.org/wp-content/uploads/2018/05/CJLC-2018–1 - 1.pdf

The Water Information Program. (2023). Water facts. *The Water Information Program: Providing Water Information to the Communities of Southwest Colorado* (Informational website, online). Retrieved from https://waterinfo.org/#:~:text=The%20Water%20Information%20Program%20is,topics%20and%20water%20related%20issues

Water Footprint (2023). What's your water footprint? *Water Footprint Calculator Website*. Retrieved from www.watercalculator.org/wfc2/q/household/

Housing, Personal Space, and Segregation

Housing is part of the universal set of human environmental needs. Historically, cultures have developed unique ways of solving the shelter problem utilizing locally available materials and creating distinct cultural architectural styles. However, as population expands and technology globalizes, traditional ways of dealing with the universal problem of shelter are giving way to modularization. Even so, the utilization of standardized architectural spaces, for example the modernist apartment block (Lara & Kim, 2010) or the stylized public space that remains after apartments are erected (Qian, 2014), are conditional on culture. In the same way, space, whether for housing (Marquardt, 2016) or just for ordinary living, has an emotional dimension, and deprivation of it, or violation of it, provokes a visceral response. The combination of housing and space can lead in several productive directions, as follows.

Exposition, Confrontation, and Simulation

For demonstrating personal space, an ancient sociological concept, consult any of the numerous sources detailing cross-cultural comparisons of standing distance and touching rules (e.g., IIMN, n.d.). For a striking visual rendition of personal space, attach flexible strips of tubing or heavy cardboard to caps in an umbrella-like arrangement such that the circumference of the outer edge approximates the personal space radius for various cultures. Regarding housing itself, search comparatively across regions for typical housing, condition, and prices. Compare, for example, the factors leading to housing crises in Botswana (Ngowi, 2015) with those operating on the Pine Ridge Reservation in South Dakota (Strickland, 2016). Regarding housing combined with space, consult any of the numerous sources offering comparative data on average square area and costs for living worldwide (e.g., Christie's, 2016; Wilson, 2023). It is effective, if in a space that is large enough, to take a 25-foot or 10-meter tape measure and lay out a typical living room in a high vs. low space environment, marking the limits with painter's tape. If there are sufficient people to simulate a party, put them in the largest space and gradually compress them. It could be more amusing if furniture could be brought in as well: utilize the IKEA catalog for creative ideas on how to equip a living room space of 100 square feet or 9 square meters (this would be comparatively large in some regions). Switching from the micro to the macrosocial level, investigate the relative willingness of individuals to live outside the boundaries of their cultures by consulting recent maps detailing the relative cultural or ethnic segregation of US cities (e.g., Bloch, Cox, & Giratikanon, 2015; Menendian, Gambhir, & Gailes, 2021). Print (or arrange to project) the individual maps

DOI: 10.4324/9781003300380-80

and set up a matching task for identifying the cities or regions most to least segregated by proximity.

References and Suggested Readings

Bloch, M., Cox, A., & Giratikanon, T. (2015, July 8). Mapping segregation (online interactive map). *The New York Times (online newspaper)*. Retrieved from https://www.nytimes.com/interactive/2015/07/08/us/census-race-map.html?mcubz=3&_r=0 [March 18, 2023].

Christie's. (2016, November 15). The price of luxury: A global comparison of square foot prices. *Christie's International Real Estate Website (luxurydefined) (online)*. Retrieved from https://www.christiesrealestate.com/blog/the-price-of-luxury-a-global-comparison-of-square-foot-prices/ [Accessed March 18, 2023].

IIMN. (n.d.). Body language and personal space. *International Institute of Minnesota Website (Culture at Work: Finding Common Understanding) (online organizational website)*. Retrieved from https://iimn.org/publication/finding-common-ground/culture-at-work/body-language-personal-space/ [Accessed March 18, 2023].

Lara, F., & Kim, Y. (2010). Built global, lived local: A study of how two diametrically opposed cultures reacted to similar modern housing solutions. *Journal of Architectural and Planning Research*, *27*(2), 91–106.

Marquardt, N. (2016). Learning to feel at home. Governing homelessness and the politics of affect. *Emotion, Space, and Society*, *19*, 29–36.

Menendian, S., Gambhir, S., & Gailes, A. (2021, June 21). The roots of structural racism project: Twenty-first century racial residential segregation in the United States (project website). Retrieved from https://belonging.berkeley.edu/roots-structural-racism. [Accessed March 18, 2023].

Ngowi, K. (2015, April 27). There's no place like home: Botswana's housing problem. *UrbanAfrica.net (online news source)*. Retrieved from https://www.urbanafrica.com/news/theres-no-place-like-home/ [Accessed March 18, 2023].

Qian, J. (2014). Performing the public man: Cultures and identities in China's grassroots leisure class. *City and Community*, *13*(1), 26–48.

Strickland, P. (2016, November 2). Life on the pine ridge native American reservation. *AlJazeera (online news source)*. Retrieved from https://www.aljazeera.com/features/2016/11/2/life-on-the-pine-ridge-native-american-reservation. [Accessed March 18, 2023].

Wilson, L. (2023). How big is a house? Average house size by country-2023. *Shrink That Footprint Website*. Retrieved from https://shrinkthatfootprint.com/how-big-is-a-house/. [Accessed March 18, 2023].

Home and Homelessness

"Home is the place where, when you have to go there, they have to take you in." Thus the poet Robert Frost, in the poem "The Death of the Hired Man" (Frost, 1915), expressed the dual nature of home—both place and people. The word "home" can encompass a whole region or culture, yearned for in the Czech national song "Kde domov můj (Where is my home?)." This evocative multilayered concept is culturally universal. Psychologists have examined its physical and social dimensions, yes, but especially its emotional ones. Environmental psychologist Susan Clayton observes that home is essential to identity (Beck, 2011); the transition to independent living and concomitant homeownership is a durable marker of the transition to adulthood (Cepa & Furstenberg, 2021), although its timing and even its availability are contingent on economics and social factors such as persistent discrimination.

Homelessness, the polar opposite of home, has an entry in the *APA Dictionary of Psychology* (American Psychological Association, 2015). That definition underscores scholarly consensus that homelessness is a condition with determinants that sort out in two broad classes: problems with socialization, personal responsibility, or mental capacity on one hand and economic, environmental, and social pressures on the other. It may appear that homelessness is overlaid on individuals' cultures due to illness or ill luck, but a good case can be made for it being a culture itself (Ravenhill, 2008). Homelessness is encountered worldwide across a spectrum of cultures. Rapid urbanization, driven by economics and underlying climate change issues, for instance, results in some regions in a homelessness rate of over 10% (ref). (For comparison, the approximately 580,000 homeless individuals in the United States make up about 0.16% of the population.)

Homelessness differentially impacts the poor, young, and powerless.

Exposition, Confrontation, and Simulation

Regarding the meaning of home as domicile, Andersson and colleagues (Andersson et al., 2020) provide sufficient information in their published report on an application of the MOH (Meaning of Home) Questionnaire to construct a close approximation of the instrument. The questions are all good starting points for discussion of all dimensions of home: physical/spatial, emotional, and social.

Culture shock, a consequence of the shattering of one cultural foundation and a sudden transformation into another environment, has not been addressed otherwise in this book. The transition to homelessness can certainly qualify as a source of culture shock. Yet most available culture shock questionnaires focus on transitions of students or professionals from one country to another.

DOI: 10.4324/9781003300380-81

The "Hobson's Choice" game by the Vincentian Formation (Vincentian Formation, n.d.) is an interactive site illustrating various pre-homelessness scenarios (e.g., losing a job because of illness) and giving options for each. Choosing an option leads to other options, some frustrating and some lucky, and describes many typical paths into and out of homelessness. It can be played singly or in pairs or groups, and there is a backup site for the simulation published by SERC (Science Education Research Center at Carleton College, Northfield, Minnesota) with background and pedagogical suggestions (Rowell, 2020). There are lots of sites with practical tips for preparing for becoming homeless, supposing that it is not the abrupt homelessness of disaster. Discuss and make plans; compare these with the contents of homeless-prep sites. Compare both the contents of "Hobson's Choice" and homelessness-prep sites with Shain and Gardiner's interviews of 30 people who have experienced homelessness (Shain & Gardiner, 2023). Their site provides their interview protocol and allows for interaction via email with both the authors and those interviewed.

References and Suggested Readings

American Psychological Association. (2015). *APA Dictionary of Psychology* (2nd ed.) (Online reference source: Entry for 'homelessness'). Washington, DC: American Psychological Association. Retrieved from https://dictionary.apa.org/homelessness

Andersson, N., Nilsson, M. H., Slaug, B., Oswald, F., & Iwarsson, S. (2020, December 7). The Meaning of Home Questionnaire revisited: Psychometric analyses among people with Parkinson's disease reveals new dimensions. *PLOS One*. Retrieved from https://journals.plos.org/plosone/article?id=10.1371/journal.pone.0242792 (https://doi.org/10.1371/journal.pone.0242792).

Beck, J. (2011, December 30). The psychology of home: Why where you live means so much. *The Atlantic*. Retrieved from www.theatlantic.com/health/archive/2011/12/the-psychology-of-home-why-where-you-live-means-so-much/249800/

Cepa, K., & Furstenberg, F. (2021). Reaching adulthood: Persistent beliefs about the importance and timing of adult milestones. *Journal of Family Issues*, *42*(1). Retrieved from https://journals.sagepub.com/doi/10.1177/0192513X20918612

Frost, R. (1915). *North of Boston* (2nd ed.). New York, NY: Henry Holt.

Ravenhill, M. (2008). *The culture of homelessness* (1st ed.). London, England and New York, NY: Routledge.

Rowell, K. R. (2020, November 12). Hobson's Choice: A game simulation about homelessness. *Pedagogy in Action: The SERC Portal for Educators* (online educational resource). Retrieved from https://serc.carleton.edu/sp/library/simulations/examples/36427.html#:~:text=Hobson's%20choice%20is%20a%20game,and%20possibilities%20that%20are%20possible

Shain, S., & Gardiner, A. (Interviewers). (2023, February 12). What's homelessness really like? Thirty people answer questions and share their experiences. *The New York Times* (online newspaper). Retrieved from https://nyti.ms/3xbW9WP

The New York Times. (2023, February 3). 582,462 and counting. *The New York Times* (online newspaper). Retrieved from https://nyti.ms/3HTnwuF

Vincentian Formation. (n.d.). Hobson's choice. *Interactive Video Game Simulating Homelessness*. Retrieved from https://vinformation.org/en/vincentian-formation-resources/presentations-media-games/hobsons-choice/

Private and Commercial Transportation

Transportation, a complex subject, divides roughly into halves: private or individual transportation, from walking and Segways to cars and (comparatively few) private airplanes, and commercial transportation, involving either human passengers or other sorts of freight. A complication of this last category is that some part of commercial transportation is a highly subsidized public convenience or good while other parts of it are for-profit. The line between public and private blurs further when, for instance, national airlines (e.g., the Air France-KLM combination) enter into partnerships with commercial carriers inside and outside of their home countries (Hepher & Trompiz, 2022).

The prototypical form of individual transportation is the personal automobile. Much has been said about US "car culture" for many years (Flink, 1976); few regions in the world are immune to this (Mainwaring, 2018). Economic, space, resource, and other factors have determined that some cultures will favor smaller versions of the car or even smaller individual conveyances—for instance, the motorbike, the tuk-tuk, and the bicycle. In some places, the motorbike was the first vehicle to thoroughly motorize the culture (e.g., Vietnam) and is still prevalent. Cultural preferences for motor vehicles are reinforced, not only in Los Angeles but also in Malaysia, by the lack of sidewalks; only 7 percent of the roads in Malaysia have walkable paths alongside them (Cochrane, 2017). In many rapidly modernizing countries, traffic forced onto inadequate roads can become picturesquely chaotic.

Cars demand resources: space for parking as well as driving and—almost exclusively—fossil fuels. Transportation uses about 28 percent of the total energy available in the United States with about three-quarters of that proportion gasoline and diesel fuel (USEIA, 2022). Cars are also expensive. Initial vehicle cost usually must be amortized worldwide, and further outlays are necessary for maintenance and insurance. Thus, many people in the world are priced out of auto culture; even in the United States, about 1 household in 12 does not own a car (Nealon, 2023). Some local movements toward two-wheeled independence have emerged in the United States (Lugo, Golub, Hoffman, & Sandoval, 2016), but they are counteracted in other places by the continual growth of car culture in places where bicycling was previously dominant. For instance, China, which quickly developed a strong bicycle culture after 1949, experienced steep downturns in commuter cycling as cars became more prevalent (Lusk, Xiu, & Lijun, 2014). There is still a tradition of bike riding in China, though, and short-distance bike commuting as well as recreational biking may be making a comeback (Hongyu, 2022). Northern European cultures are leaders not only in cycle commuting but also in accessible and frequent public passenger transportation. Trams, for instance, are beloved enough to have museums and even rodeos featuring tram

DOI: 10.4324/9781003300380-82

bowling, where tram drivers compete to knock down inflatable pins with large inflatable balls (Giaimo, 2017).

Turning to commercial transportation, air transportation has become the overwhelming means of getting people between widely different cultures. Air transport is a prime area for promotion of safety culture, which sometimes conflicts with cultural traditions of longer standing. Cultural differences—for instance, power distance and communication style in Korean culture—may have played roles in several aircraft accidents (Wee, 2013). Roads have been as important as rivers in bringing cultures together; the Roman roads and the Silk Road (Harrison, 2016) are historical examples. Trucks mix with cars in traffic worldwide; the legendary phrase "Horn OK Please" is an Indian cultural tagline, painted in folk style and color on the tailgates of trucks. Small trucks are the transport of choice for both farmers and terrorists (Engel, 2015). Long-haul trucking—a culture that is itself undergoing substantial change in the United States (Goodman, 2022)—intersects with immigration as a source of both immigrant jobs (Gonzalez, 2016) and exploitation and, sadly, as a part of the pipeline of extra-legal immigration, visible when an occasional trailer-load of hopeful travelers suffocates in a parking lot (Montgomery, Fernandez, & Joseph, 2017). Sea transportation is another multicultural area.

Exposition, Confrontation, and Simulation

Transportation can be integrated into lots of different cross-cultural subjects. Experiences with long-distance air travel can be discussed, and the question can be raised as to whether airports—boundary nodes—themselves share a common culture (Eriksen, 1992) or whether they are cultural vacuums, a home only for the stateless (Beardsley, 2022). Many statistical sources are available to conduct comparisons between the modes of transport of countries and regions. YouTube videos of trains from the cab as well as the passenger compartments and platforms are widely available. Free flight simulators (Lennox, 2023) might be employed in a simulation of some aspects of power distance's effect on cockpit communication. (Actually, any kind of kibitzing could probably be adapted to demonstrating teamwork-friendly vs. teamwork-resistant environments.) Try setting up an appointment for car service in Mumbai or Jakarta; there are lots of sites to do this. Simulate the situation facing a Nigerian city bus driver (Olapoju, 2016). It's not only cellphones that can distract a driver but also swarming crowds; narrow streets; crazy traffic; and having to collect fares, monitor stops, and scan for passengers that present a safety challenge worldwide. Suggested: set up a driving simulator, and have individuals play the role of the driver while the rest of the group creates various mayhem; use scrap cardboard for bus doors, and bring lots of party horns. Regarding commercial transport, at least on a small scale: read Daniel Herriges's (2020) account of furnishing an apartment in Quito, and figure out a way to create an "inefficient but smart" (and inexpensive) method using multiple small operators to facilitate transportation of large goods between stores and homes in the United States.

References and Suggested Readings

Beardsley, E. (2022, November 14). The man who inspired "The Terminal" died at the airport where he lived for 18 years. *NPR (National Public Radio) Website*. Retrieved from www.npr.org/2022/11/14/1136604970/the-man-who-inspired-the-terminal-died-at-the-airport-where-he-lived-for-18-year

Cochrane, J. (2017, August 20). Jakarta, the city where nobody wants to walk. *The New York Times* (online newspaper). Retrieved from www.nytimes.com/2017/08/20/world/asia/jakarta-walking-study-sidewalks.html?mcubz=3&_r=0

Engel, P. (2015, October 7). These Toyota trucks are popular with terrorists worldwide: Here's why. *Business Insider* (online magazine). Retrieved from www.businessinsider.com/why-isis-uses-toyota-trucks-2015-10

Eriksen, T. H. (1992). In limbo: Notes on the culture of airports. *Squarespace Website*. Retrieved from https://static1.squarespace.com/static/5c03b76b96e76fd25bee32fe/t/5c374d03032be474ef1ef397/1547128071934/In+limbo-+Notes+on+the+culture+of+airports.pdf

Flink, J. (1976). *The car culture*. Cambridge, MA: MIT Press.

Giaimo, C. (2017, June 8). Europe holds an annual tram-driver Olympics. *Atlas Obscura* (online magazine). Retrieved from www.atlasobscura.com/articles/tram-olympics-europe-bowling

Gonzalez, S. (2016, April 21). America's trucking industry faces a shortage: Meet the immigrants helping fill the gap. *The World Website* (radio broadcast transcript). Retrieved from https://theworld.org/stories/2016-04-21/america-s-trucking-industry-faces-shortage-meet-immigrants-helping-fill-gap

Goodman, P. (2022, February 9). The real reason America doesn't have enough truck drivers. *The New York Times* (online newspaper). Retrieved from www.nytimes.com/2022/02/09/business/truck-driver-shortage.html

Harrison, K. (2016). *Mongols on the silk road: Trade, transportation, and cross-cultural exchange in the Mongol empire*. New York, NY: Rosen Young Adult

Hepher, T., & Trompiz, G. (2022, May 18). Air France-KLM agrees cargo deal with French shipping firm CMA CGM. *Reuters Website* (online news source). Retrieved from www.reuters.com/markets/europe/cma-cgm-take-stake-air-france-klm-part-new-cargo-partnership-2022–05–18/

Herriges, D. (2020, June 5). Inefficient, but smart. *Strong Towns Website*. Retrieved from www.strongtowns.org/journal/2020/6/5/inefficient-but-smart

Hongyu, L. J. (2022, May 30). Biking becomes new lifestyle trend among Chinese people. *People's Daily Online* (online newspaper). Retrieved from http://en.people.cn/n3/2022/0530/c90000-10103092.html

Lennox, J. (2023, February 25). The best free flight simulators. *Digital Trends Website*. Retrieved from www.digitaltrends.com/gaming/best-free-flight-simulators/

Lugo, A., Golub, A., Hoffman, M., & Sandoval, G. (Eds.). (2016). *Bicycle justice and urban transformation: Biking for all?* New York, NY: Routledge.

Lusk, A. C., Xu, W., & Lijun, Z. (2014). Gender and used/preferred differences of bicycle routes, parking, intersection signals, and bicycle type: Professional middle class preferences in Hangzhou, China. *Journal of Transport and Health*, *1*(2), 124–133.

Mainwaring, B. (2018, August 8). Car culture around the globe. *National Motorists Association Blog*. Retrieved from https://ww2.motorists.org/blog/car-culture-around-the-globe/

Montgomery, D., Fernandez, M., & Joseph, Y. (2017, July 23). Journey fatal for 9 migrants found in truck in a San Antonio parking lot. *The New York Times* (Online newspaper). Retrieved from www.nytimes.com/2017/07/23/us/san-antonio-truck-walmart-trafficking.html?mcubz=3&_r=0

Nealon, L. (2023, February 10). 2023 car ownership statistics. *Bankrate Website*. Retrieved from www.bankrate.com/insurance/car/car-ownership-statistics/

Olapoju, O. M. (2016). Culture of distracted driving among intra-city commercial bus drivers in Ile-Ife, South-Western Nigeria. *Transportation Research Part F: Traffic Psychology and Behaviour*, *42*(3), 425–432.

USEIA. (2022). Use of energy in the United States, explained. *United States Energy Information Administration Website*. Retrieved from www.eia.gov/energyexplained/use-of-energy/transportation.php

Wee, H. (2013, July 9). *Korean culture may offer clues in Asiana crash*. *CNBC* (online news source). Retrieved from www.cnbc.com/id/100869966

Sustainability and Population

As defined on the *Circular Ecology* website (Circular Ecology, 2023), *sustainability* is actually a composite of three different elements: economic sustainability, meaning the maintenance of an ongoing positive balance sheet between all aspects of production and consumption; environmental sustainability, meaning the conservation (and, so far as, possible the increase) of natural resources; and social sustainability, or the ability of groups to manage their resources to produce a stable level of well-being. Often, discussions of sustainability focus on one or another of these elements and most often (at least in the United States at present) on the environmental ones, for which the evidence of imbalance is steadily mounting in the form of gradual temperature increases, sea level rises, and other effects of changing climate. At the core of the question of sustainability—apart from the question of what is to be sustained (Current levels of economic growth? Current levels of military expenditures? Current levels of automotive production? Current lifestyles and levels of consumption?)—is a clash between two different worldviews or, one might also say, between two cultures. On one side are groups that see resources as limited and endangered and which recommend policies limiting expectations and the extent of economic growth. The other side sees fewer to no limits to growth and reads the evidence for resource depletion as a temporary aberration if not entirely fabricated. These sides do not map neatly onto particular subgroups or regions, and they shift over time. Worldwide attitudinal support for environmental conservation and other sustainability-related beliefs has been documented for several years (Schultz, 2002), and major international accords under the aegis of the United Nations resolving to limit greenhouse gases were recently (in 2016) put in force (United Nations, 2023). However, local politics as well as differing attitudes within diverse demographic groups in different regions (e.g., Bronfman, Cisternas, López-Vázquez, de la Maza, & Oyanedel, 2015) weaken the unanimity of resolve.

Fifty-five years ago, on publication of Garrett Hardin's *The Tragedy of the Commons* (Hardin, 1968), overpopulation was widely seen as an imminent threat. But since that time, the global population has nearly tripled, and increases are projected confidently rather than feared. The world is on track at this writing to reach 10.9 billion people by the end of this century (Ciluffo & Ruiz, 2019) with population growth slowing to a stop at that point. Population growth mirrors the tensions within sustainability debate. As noted earlier in this text in connection with the Family entry, fertility rates vary widely across the globe. Lower fertility rates, some below the replacement level, characterize more affluent and educated regions. The more people become educated and affluent, the fewer children they have and the more resources they direct to each child.

DOI: 10.4324/9781003300380-83

The highest fertility rates are in the poorest areas, and even though infant mortality is also highest in those areas, they are still the most energetic drivers of world population growth.

Population growth correlates with sustainability concerns. Increasing population density connects to deforestation and soil erosion even in otherwise affluent countries; in poorer ones, it leads to food shortages that become acute during periodic droughts. Famine and poverty lead to migration and its consequences. The desire to limit population is strong in most poor countries. However, this aim is impeded by the lack of access to contraception as well as by cultural traditions that insist on women's primary role as child-bearers and caregivers.

It might seem at first that limiting population everywhere in the world is as necessary as limiting fuel use practices that lead to global warming. However, it's sometimes the case that increases in population may also lead to improved living conditions. China's recent reversal of its long-standing one-child policy is said to have occurred in order to have a larger younger working population to support its increasingly aged population, one consequence of too few births coupled with longer lifespans. At the same time, an increase in population in a now highly urbanized and relatively affluent society will lead to a demand for more consumer goods and cars and thus contribute further to threats to environmental sustainability.

Exposition, Confrontation, and Simulation

While sustainability and population growth are usually featured in environmental psychology, addressing these subjects in a cross-cultural psychology context will make it plain that cross-cultural issues are not confined to boardroom behavior or interpersonal dyads. Sustainability and population are transcultural issues that will eventually impact every culture on earth. A starting point for establishing basic terminological and conceptual infrastructure for discussion of both population and sustainability could be the open-source text *Population and Culture* available from the University of Minnesota Libraries (University of Minnesota, 2017). One way to conceive of the relation between sustainability and population is to see each as demanding action to control growth based on different sets of attitudes and habits. At the outset, ask students to imagine that they have to make a decision about (a) buying a car and (b) having a child. In which ways (if any) will sustainability and population concerns be considered in making each decision? Compare results. Search the research literature for comparative data on perceptions of climate change threats in different world regions; a recent article on climate change and its effects in Pakistan also contains a chart of the 10 countries most affected by climate change worldwide (Sukhera, 2017).

Culture is often equated with values, and sustainability and other environmental aspects of psychology have a heavy investment in value description and clarification. Examination of overall value systems in an environmental context can be done by taking advantage of the scales provided in Dietz, Fitzgerald, and Shworn (2005). Speculate also on whether human populations have to be as large as they now are in order for humans to be as advanced (i.e., technologically interconnected, knowledge-rich, and interpersonally interactive) as they are now. How large must the world be, in terms of the people in it, to be a complete world? Examine, in this context, the articles available on the website of the Ten Million Club (The Ten Million Club Foundation, 2023).

References and Suggested Readings

Bronfman, N. E., Cisternas, P. C., López-Vázquez, E., de la Maza, C., & Oyanedel, J. C. (2015). Understanding attitudes and pro-environmental behaviors in a Chilean community. *Sustainability, 7*(10), 14133–14152. Retrieved from https://doi.org/10.3390/su71014133

Ciluffo, A., & Ruiz, N. G. (2019, June 17). World's population is projected to nearly stop growing by the end of the century. *Pew Research Center Website*. Retrieved from www.pewresearch.org/fact-tank/2019/06/17/worlds-population-is-projected-to-nearly-stop-growing-by-the-end-of-the-century/

Circular Ecology. (2023). What is sustainability and what is sustainable development? *Sustainable Ecology website* (online resource). Retrieved from www.circularecology.com/sustainability-and-sustainable-development.html#.WbRZ_eQUjIU

Dietz, T., Fitzgerald, A., & Shworn, R. (2005). Environmental values. *Annual Review of Environment and Resources, 30*(1), 335–372. Retrieved from www.annualreviews.org/doi/full/10.1146/annurev.energy.30.050504.144444

Hardin, G. (1968). The tragedy of the commons. *Science, 162*(3859), 1243–1248.

Schultz, P. W. (2002). Environmental attitudes and behaviors across cultures. *Online Readings in Psychology and Culture, 8*(1) (Online resource, International Association for Cross-Cultural Psychology. Retrieved from https://scholarworks.gvsu.edu/orpc/vol8/iss1/4/

Sukhera, N. (2017, March 27). The perils of inaction on climate change in Pakistan. *Dawn* (online newspaper). Retrieved from www.dawn.com/news/1322335

The Ten Million Club. (2023). *The Ten Million Club Foundation website* (online). Retrieved from www.overpopulationawareness.org/en/articles/

United Nations. (2023). What is the Paris Agreement? *UNFCC Website*. Retrieved from https://unfccc.int/process-and-meetings/the-paris-agreement

University of Minnesota. (2017). *Chapter 1.3: World regional geography: People, places, and globalization* (population and culture). Minneapolis, MN: University of Minnesota Libraries Publishing (online). Retrieved from https://open.lib.umn.edu/worldgeography/chapter/1-3-population-and-culture/

Technology and Connectedness

Technology is one of the intellectual roots of cultural studies, evidenced by the connection of the term *technology* specifically to culture (in the title—*Technology and Culture*—of the journal of SHOT, the Society for the History of Technology) and to civilization (Mumford, 1934/2010). Up until comparatively recently, the term *technology* was virtually equivalent to *mechanization* (e.g., Giedion, 1948/ 2013). Gradually, over the past two decades especially, technology has risen to equivalence with the mathematized sciences in the field of education, evidenced by the current acronym STEM, standing for Science, Technology, Engineering, and Mathematics. It has also become equated in the popular mind with digitization and its outcomes and consequences, from robotics to the dominance of the computer and the internet in human affairs. Any technology—medical, food, or manufacturing—could be considered from a comparative cultural and historical perspective (for instance, the persistence of bullock and donkey carts in India and Africa alongside modern transportation in the context of transportation in culture, Iyer, 2017). For the following examples of potential interactives, the focus will be on what is probably the most ubiquitous element of digital technology in use worldwide today: the cellphone.

Exposition, Confrontation, and Simulation

Cellphone use parallels the historic growth of trade along transportation routes. In Burkina Faso, for example, much of the population has access to cellphones (though not to computers or the internet), and that growth is centered on main highways (NPerf, 2023). Search, display, and compare relative availability of power grid and cellphone coverage worldwide, using data from sites such as Open Signal (Open Signal Corporation, 2023). Investigate the electricity gap, a major constraint on expansion of digital applications (Gronewold, 2009. The concept of digital nativity, which has been advanced as an explanation of cross-cultural differences in technology adoption and acceptance (Zhao & Zhao, 2021), can be explored by means of the DDS index (Janschitz & Penker, 2022). Cyberbullying is one of the less pleasant cross-culturally relevant consequences of electronic technology use; for background for the discussion of this, consult Barlett et al. (2014). Finally, it would be engaging and fun to replicate, as far as possible, the studies of Ma, Yang, and Wilson (2017), who have found differences between Chinese and British selfie takers in both composition and redaction (image editing) related to underlying cultural characteristics.

DOI: 10.4324/9781003300380-84

References and Suggested Readings

Barlett, C. P., Gentile, D. A., Anderson, C. A., Suzuki, K., Sakamoto, Y. A., & Katsura, R. (2014). Cross-cultural differences in cyberbullying behavior. *Journal of Cross-Cultural Psychology, 45*(2), 300–313.

Giedion, S. (2013). *Mechanization takes command* (Reprint ed.). Minneapolis, MN: University of Minnesota Press (Originally published in New York by Oxford University Press, 1948).

Gronewold, N. (2009, November 24). One-quarter of world's population lacks electricity. *Scientific American* (web magazine). Retrieved from www.scientificamerican.com/article/electricity-gap-developing-countries-energy-wood-charcoal/

Iyer, S. (2017, June 16). From bullock cart to bullet train: Transportation in India has indeed come a long way! *India.com* (online news source). Retrieved from www.india.com/news/india/from-bullock-cart-to-bullet-train-transportation-in-india-has-indeed-come-a-long-way-1403645/

Janschitz, G., & Penker, M. (2022, January 24). How digital are 'digital natives' actually? Developing an instrument to measure the degree of digitalisation of university students—the DDS-Index. *Bulletin of Sociological Methodology, 153*(1). Retrieved from https://journals.sagepub.com/doi/full/10.1177/07591063211061760

Ma, J. W., Yang, Y., & Wilson, J. A. J. (2017). A window to the ideal self: A study of UK Twitter and Chinese SinaWeibo selfie-takers and the implications for marketers. *Journal of Business Research, 74*, 139–142.

Mumford, L. (2010). *Technics and civilization* (Reprint ed.). Chicago, IL: University of Chicago Press (originally published in London UK by Routledge Kegan Paul in 1934).

NPerf. (2023). 3G/4G/5G coverage map, Burkina Faso. *NPerf Website*. Retrieved from www.nperf.com/en/map/BF/-/-/signal/?ll=12.260238031382267&lg=-1.5599999999999885&zoom=7

OpenSignal Corporation. (2023). *OpenSignal website* (online). Retrieved from www.opensignal.com/

Zhao, C., & Zhao, L. (2021, September 21). Digital nativity, computer self-efficacy, and technology adoption: A study among university faculties in China. *Frontiers in Psychology (Sec. Educational Psychology), 12*. Retrieved from www.frontiersin.org/articles/10.3389/fpsyg.2021.746292/full

Vandalism

Vandalism—briefly, the defacement or destruction of property—began to be studied seriously by psychologists in the 1950s in connection with juvenile delinquency. Later, in the late 1960s and early 1970s, Philip Zimbardo, among others, examined the power of environmental situations to influence (anti)social behavior by setting up conditions for vandalism to occur (Zimbardo, 1973). Vandalism since that time has usually been considered a species of petty crime. In criminology, vandalism was a stimulant to the creation of an influential theory of policing, "broken windows theory" (Kelling & Wilson, 1982), which viewed acts like property destruction as the tinder for neighborhood deterioration and increases in major crime levels and recommended that law enforcement focus attention on small-scale destructive activity. This form of policing, which has disproportionately targeted poor and marginalized people and cultures (Legal Aid Society, 2022), is largely discredited (Vedantam et al., 2016).

In psychology, vandalism continues to be viewed as a marker of adolescent maladjustment, but it is a more complex concept socially and cross-culturally. The threat of vandalism may be a pretext for repressing adolescent girls' development of identity and autonomy in street culture (Bottrell, 2008). Stickers with wry comments (e.g., "Press Until Shiok"), pasted on pedestrian traffic signals in Singapore by Samantha Lo, resulted in her arrest for vandalism under strict Singaporean law. This notoriety fueled her development into a recognized urban artist (Ubersnap, 2015).

The term *cultural vandalism* is used to describe anticultural acts. These are similar to antisocial behavior but aimed at cultural products. One example of this is *elginism*, a term coined for the practice of expropriation of significant cultural products, based on the removal of the marble sculptures from the Parthenon in Greece to Great Britain by Lord Elgin between 1801 and 1812. A blog with this name (Various, 2002–2022) has had 245 pages of commentary since 2002; negotiations are ongoing between Great Britain and Greece regarding the return of the marbles, which the British maintain were legally acquired and the Greeks perceive as looted (Marshall, 2023). Other recent examples are the destruction of ancient sites in Syria during the recent civil war there and the passage of laws denying access to information necessary to counteract the effects of climate change, viewed as an attack on science (Crease, 2015).

Exposition, Confrontation, and Simulation

Since this issue is redolent of at least minor criminality, confession will be good for the soul at the outset—but strictly anonymously! Survey to see whether acts of vandalism have been committed, and analyze for intent vs. negligence, creative destruction vs. the

DOI: 10.4324/9781003300380-85

other sort, and so on. No culture is immune to vandalism, and a further expedition can be made to gather as many instances as are necessary to demonstrate the breadth and diversity of vandalism worldwide. As case studies, consider graffiti; is the widespread decoration of building surfaces in Berlin (Arms, 2011) expressive art or a crime? Tours are available (Tours By Locals, 2023). Is the recent vandalism of the Tejas Express in India (Bhattacharya, 2017) or of New York City subway cars (Zaveri, 2020) really *vandalism*, or was it thoughtlessness or an expression of frustration? Following the research of Philipps, Scholzel, and Richter (2016), draw a mustache or other decoration on a portrait of a local politician: disrespectful or deserved?

References and Suggested Readings

Arms, S. (2011, July 13). The heritage of Berlin street art and graffiti scene. *Smashing Magazine* (online magazine). Retrieved from www.smashingmagazine.com/2011/07/the-heritage-of-berlin-street-art-and-graffiti-scene/

Bhattacharya, R. (2017, May 22). The vandalism of the Tejas Express proves that we Indians just don't deserve good things. *ScoopWhoop* (online news magazine). Retrieved from www.scoopwhoop.com/reads/why-we-dont-deserve-good-things/

Bottrell, D. (2008). TGG: Girls, street culture, and identity. In A. Harris (Ed.), *Next wave cultures: Feminism, subcultures, activism* (pp. 37–62). New York, NY and London, England: Routledge.

Crease, R. P. (2015, September 3). Cultural vandalism in America. *Project Syndicate* (online magazine). Retrieved from www.project-syndicate.org/commentary/lamar-smith-us-congress-war-on-science-by-robert-p--crease-2015–09

Kelling, G. L., & Wilson, J. Q. (1982). Broken windows: The police and neighborhood safety. *Atlantic Monthly*, *249*(3), 29–38.

Legal Aid Society. (2022, May 29). Broken windows, broken trust: The NYPD's racially discriminatory quality-of-life policing. *Legal Aid Society (NY)*. Retrieved from https://legalaidnyc.org/wp-content/uploads/2022/03/LAS_Report-on-Racial-Disparities-in-Broken-Windows-Policing_3.29.2022.pdf

Marshall, A. (2023, January 17). After 220 years, the fate of the Parthenon marbles rests in secret talks. *The New York Times* (online newspaper). Retrieved from www.nytimes.com/2023/01/17/arts/design/parthenon-sculptures-elgin-marbles-negotiations.html

Philipps, A., Scholzel, H., & Richter, R. (2016). Defaced election posters: Between culture jamming and moral outrage. *Communication, Politics, and Culture*, *49*(1), 86–109. Retrieved from www.researchgate.net/publication/323446259_Defaced_election_posters_Between_culture_jamming_and_moral_outrage_A_case_study

Tours By Locals. (2023). Street art is talking: A walking tour in Berlin. *Tours By Locals* (commercial website). Retrieved from www.toursbylocals.com/berlin-street-art-private-tour?gclid=CjwKCAjw5dqgBhBNEiwA7PryaHG9ap2nygg1CfdoLLTS_Nihwcazgm2eMCJve6Y9eWzwYnh29KeScBoC7IAQAvD_BwE&gclsrc=aw.ds

Ubersnap. (2015, November 27). Sam Lo: Life after "Sticker Lady". *Vulcan Post* (online magazine). Retrieved from https://vulcanpost.com/463621/sam-lo-sticker-lady-interview/

Various. (2002/2022). *Elginism* (online blog). Retrieved from www.elginism.com/

Vedantam, S., Benderev, C., Boyle, T., Klahr, R., Penman, M., & Schmidt, J. (2016, November 1). How a theory of crime and policing was born, and went horribly wrong. *NPR (National Public Radio) Website*. Retrieved from www.npr.org/2016/11/01/500104506/broken-windows-policing-and-the-origins-of-stop-and-frisk-and-how-it-went-wrong

Zaveri, M. (2020, August 23). Smashed windows on subway cars have cost the M. T. A. $300,000. *The New York Times* (online newspaper). Retrieved from www.nytimes.com/2020/08/23/nyregion/nyc-subway-vandalism.html

Zimbardo, P. G. (1973). A field experiment in auto shaping. In C. Ward (Ed.), *Vandalism* (pp. 85–90). London, England: The Architectural Press.

Animals and Other Species

DOI: 10.4324/9781003300380-86

Animals

Historically, animals have been deified, and they continue to be symbolic in many ways as sports totems, as allegorical characters, and as deliverers of alternative points of view on the human experience, e.g., the narrator in *War Horse* (Malone & Jackman, 2016). Practically speaking, animals integrate at all levels with human society and with many of the topics in this book. They are utilized as beasts of burden and food, combated as pests, loved as pets, hunted for sport, exhibited in zoos, empathized with in pain and suffering (Specia, 2017), and utilized in many other ways. Animals do not have a specific presence at the core of cross-cultural psychology, but anthropologists in the specific area of anthrozoology have filled this gap, revealed by recent work on the human–animal connection (Hurn, 2012; Murray, 2016). Likewise, comparative psychologists have pursued the question of whether animals themselves, individually or collectively, form cultures (Laland & Galef, 2009) and, along with philosophers, have probed the degree to which they are to be included in human moral systems (Gluck, 2016; Fitzpatrick & Andrews, 2022).

Exposition, Confrontation, and Simulation

The chapter titles in Hurn (2012) identify the following areas among others as important sites of animal–human cultural interaction: "The West and the Rest," "Domestication," "Food," "Pets," "Communication," "Intersubjectivity," "Humans and Other Primates," "Science and Medicine," "Conservation," "Hunting and Blood Sports," and "Animal Rights and Wrongs." These could form the basis of an inventory and discussion of the multiple cultural roles of animals in the immediate environment and could be treated individually in interactive presentations. Individual stories of human–animal connectedness can be solicited and shared.

On the principle that a culture is a system that confers particular rights on its members, examination and discussion of various initiatives for animal rights could be introduced. Neumann (2012) provides the text of both the 1978 UNESCO Universal Declaration of Animal Rights and its later revisions along with a comprehensive historical account of the development of formal proclamations of animal rights. A draft of a Bill of Animal Rights could be undertaken in a class and then compared to these texts.

Actual involvement with animals, while it could be extraordinarily revealing of layers of culture, needs to be crafted with some care. Official policy demands that any activity involving animals be passed through an Institutional Animal Care and Use Committee, similar to a human participants review committee (National Institutes of Health, 2021). Perhaps some semblance of the interaction of human and animal can be gained by the

DOI: 10.4324/9781003300380-87

employment of virtual pets. Perhaps recent research (Aguiar & Taylor, 2015) suggesting that children detect different affordances from stuffed animals (friendship) vs. virtual pet animals (entertainment) could be replicated with a cross-cultural component if circumstances permit.

References and Suggested Readings

Aguiar, N. R., & Taylor, M. (2015, April). Children's concepts of the social affordances of a virtual dog and a stuffed dog. *Cognitive Development*, *34*, 16–27.

Fitzpatrick, S., & Andrews, K. (2022, December). Animal culture and animal welfare. *Philosophy of Science*, *89(5)*, 1104–1113. Retrieved from https://static1.squarespace.com/static/622640a26edfa473c2f303bb/t/6268eef56f3751239f2d246e/1651044086240/Fitzpatrick+and+Andrews+2022_Animal+Culture+and+Animal+Welfare.pdf

Gluck, J. P. (2016). *Voracious science and vulnerable animals: A primate scientist's ethical journey*. Chicago, IL: University of Chicago Press.

Hurn, S. (2012). *Humans and other animals: Cross-cultural perspectives on human-animal interactions*. London, England: Pluto Press.

Laland, K. N., & Galef, B. G. (Eds.). (2009). *The question of animal culture*. Cambridge, MA: Harvard University Press.

Malone, T., & Jackman, C. (2016). *Adapting war horse: Cognition, the spectator, and a sense of play*. London, England: Palgrave Macmillan.

Murray, L. (2016). Animals and anthropology. *AnthroPod: The SCA Podcast* (Cultural Anthropology website). Retrieved from https://culanth.org/fieldsights/animals-and-anthropology-laura-murray

National Institutes of Health. (2021, October 22). The institutional animal care and use committee. *NIH Office of Laboratory Animal Welfare Website*. Retrieved from https://olaw.nih.gov/resources/tutorial/iacuc.htm

Neumann, J. M. (2012). The Universal Declaration of Animal Rights or the creation of a new equilibrium between species. *Animal Law Review of the Lewis & Clark University*, *19*(1), 359–396. Retrieved from https://law.lclark.edu/live/files/22931-191-neumannpdf

Specia, M. (2017, July 27). Animals, abandoned and starving, are evacuated from zoo in Syria. *The New York Times* (online). Retrieved from www.nytimes.com/2017/07/27/world/middleeast/syria-zoo-animals-rescued-aleppo.html?_r=0

Pest Control

From far back in history, humans have been at war with nature in the form of other species called pests. These include crop eaters, disease vectors, and people biters. The history of physical and chemical combat of agrarian and domestic pests stretches back far before the ancient Greeks to the beginnings of cultivation and medicine. Sumerians used sulfur compounds for insect control while, in China circa 2000 BC, arsenic and mercury are said to have been used on lice (Unsworth, 2010). The recent history of pest control leads through the development of DDT and other synthetic insecticides, the bad consequences of which led to the development of less toxic varieties as well as heightening consciousness of the effects of humans on the environment.

The similar ways that humans combat the worldwide distribution of rodents, insects, and microorganisms reflects the struggle of human culture against other cultures—and not only non-human ones—that may have been the impetus for the pessimistic views of both William James and Sigmund Freud on the likelihood of the eradication of war. In terms of current psychological theory, "cultural pest control," which technically means establishing alliances with other organisms (bacteria, insects, and predators) to eradicate organisms we don't like, opens a wider window on the cultural forces carving out our human niche.

Exposition, Confrontation, and Simulation

Joseph Henrich, among others, sees evolution originating in cultural adaptations transmitted by imitation and learning (Henrich, 2011). Discussion could focus on Henrich's theory in which cultural practices begin as adaptations to environmental conditions, pass through a stage of cultural evolution, and lead to an interaction between genes and culture that produces both a more culturally capable human and one that becomes more diffusely integrated with its environment over time. Bottom line: every action we take with regard to the environment will result in automatic coadaptation (think pesticide resistance or the gradual decrease in antibiotic effectiveness). Bedbugs and mosquitoes themselves are far more stimulating for discussion than theory, so one could start with surveys of local pest control and branch outward to see the marvelous similarity between cultures worldwide in terms of the regionally specific pests they combat. Pest exterminators are employed on every continent, and, according to their websites, most drive panel trucks!

For a simulation, consider raising the issue of the cultural meaning of *pests*. An example from Australia involving a plan to reduce a water buffalo herd believed to be a vector of tuberculosis and brucellosis met strong resistance from Indigenous populations

DOI: 10.4324/9781003300380-88

who saw the buffalo in a very different light (Robinson & Whitehead, 2003). In the US context, game management might be easier to simulate and promote the same interaction of different cultural views. And, while otherwise little is said directly about agriculture in this book, the combating of agricultural pests can be a foothold for discussion of the larger cultural issues surrounding agriculture, society, and sustainability. To add to the speculation, consider the possibility of encountering alien microorganisms in space (Netea et al., 2020); will this lead to assimilation or extermination?

References and Suggested Readings

Henrich, J. (2011, November). A cultural species: How culture drove human evolution. *APA Psychological Science Agenda* (online resource). Retrieved from www.apa.org/science/about/psa/2011/11/human-evolution

Netea, M. G., Dominguez-Andrés, J., Eleveld, M., Op den Camp, H. J. M., van der Meer, J. W. M., Gow, N. A. R., & de Jonge, M. I. (2020, January 30). Immune recognition of putative alien microbial structures: Host-pathogen interactions in the age of space travel. *PLoS Pathogens*, *16*(1). Retrieved from www.ncbi.nlm.nih.gov/pmc/articles/PMC6991955/

Robinson, C. J., & Whitehead, P. (2003). Cross-cultural management of pest animal damage: A case study of feral buffalo control in Australia's Kakadu National Park. *Environmental Management*, *32*(4), 445–458. Retrieved from www.ncbi.nlm.nih.gov/pubmed/14986894

University of Wisconsin. (2023). Cultural control. *University of Wisconsin Vegetable Crop Entomology Extension and Research Website*. Retrieved from https://vegento.russell.wisc.edu/ipm/cultural-control/

Unsworth, J. (2010). History of pesticide use. *IUPAC (International Union of Pure and Applied Chemistry) website: Agrochemicals* (online). Retrieved from https://agrochemicals.iupac.org/index.php?option=com_sobi2&sobi2Task=sobi2Details&catid=3&sobi2Id=31

Pets

This entry and its recommendations focus specifically on animals as pets in contrast to animals considered in other ways, treated earlier in this section. Domestication of animals progressed to animals being kept solely for their value as companions. This change of function is explained, psychologically, in terms of animals being recognized for their emotional connection, valued as sources of unconditional positive regard or solace, and even accepted as family members (McConnell, Lloyd, & Buchanan, 2016). Some claim that animals may be important adjuncts in psychotherapy, but, according to stringent research, this may be overstating the case (see e.g., Lilienfeld & Arkowitz, 2008; Jones, Rice, & Cotton, 2019).

Only very recently has an effort been made to summarize the cross-cultural presence of pets. Gray and Young (2011), using a probability sample drawn from the Human Relations Area Files (Yale University), accessed a great deal of detailed information about the presence, treatment (including living conditions and feeding), and ultimate disposition of pets and presented it in tabular form. Dogs, cats, and birds are, not surprisingly, the most commonly kept pets worldwide, ever more frequently since they take up less room in a world under pressure of population increase and land loss. (Horses, for instance, need much more room.) Pets are also a marker of economic advance. Formerly the privilege of the rich in mostly European settings, pets, especially dogs, now accompany the rapid reconfiguration of Chinese society into a heavily urbanized one. Gray and Young also note many anthropologically interesting pet sidelights such as human breastfeeding of dogs and the relation of dogs and cats to the spirit world.

Exposition, Confrontation, and Simulation

Oddly, Gray and Young (2011) do not tabulate fish as pets, although their presence is widespread in US culture. (Any Walmart has a bank of fish tanks in its pet section.) Discussion might focus not only on this omission but on the vagaries of using a large database containing an indiscriminate mix of very old and very modern data as an information source. Another line of discussion might focus on the enculturation of certain types of pets (e.g., very small ornamental dogs in specific urban neighborhoods; particularly aggressive breeds favored by similarly aggressive people; or the personality characteristics of individuals who might keep armadillos or wallabies as pets). The question of the emotional connection between pets and humans might be introduced in context with the question of eating cats and dogs, considered by Gray and Young and also by Podberscek (2009). A mordant simulation might involve recreating the situation faced by Victor Klemperer, a scholar-professor who survived the period of 1933 through 1945 as

DOI: 10.4324/9781003300380-89

an assimilated (he thought) Jew in Dresden, Germany, keeping a diary of his successive stages of dehumanization. In May 1942, he tragically decided that he would euthanize his and his wife's pet cat since it would no longer be allowed to have any official food rations (Klemperer, 2001). This could be a springboard for discussion not only of the human–pet bond but also of the particular inhumanity of the Nazi *Kultur* of that time (Mosse, 2003). Klemperer's ordeal, as described in his diaries, has also been adapted into a full-length play (Bartenieff & Malpede, n.d.).

References and Suggested Readings

Bartenieff, G., & Malpede, K. (n.d.). *I will bear witness: The diaries of Victor Klemperer. Stage play, adapted from the nonfiction work of the same title*. Brooklyn, NY: Theatre Three Collaborative. Retrieved from www.theaterthreecollaborative.org/i-will-bear-witness

Gray, P. B., & Young, S. M. (2011). Human-pet dynamics in cross-cultural perspective. *Anthrozoös*, *24*(1), 17–30.

Jones, M. G., Rice, S. M., & Cotton, S. M. (2019, January 17). Incorporating animal-assisted therapy in mental health treatments for adolescents: A systematic review of canine assisted psychotherapy. *PLoS ONE*, *14*(1). Retrieved from www.ncbi.nlm.nih.gov/pmc/articles/PMC6336278/

Klemperer, V. (2001). *I will bear witness 1942–1945: A diary of the Nazi years*. New York, NY: Modern Library.

Lilienfeld, S., & Arkowitz, H. (2008, June 1). Is animal assisted therapy really the cat's meow? *Scientific American Mind* (online). Retrieved from www.scientificamerican.com/article/is-animal-assisted-therapy/

McConnell, A. R., Lloyd, E. P., & Buchanan, T. M. (2016). Animals as friends: Social psychological implications of human-pet relationships. In M. Hojjat & A. Moyer (Eds.), *Psychology of friendship* (pp. 157–174). New York, NY: Oxford University Press.

Mosse, G. L. (2003). *Nazi culture: Intellectual, cultural, and social life in the Third Reich*. Madison, WI: University of Wisconsin Press (Originally work published by 1966).

Podberscek, A. L. (2009). Good to pet and eat: The keeping and consuming of dogs and cats in South Korea. *Journal of Social Issues*, *65*(3), 615–632 (Cross-reference: Animals).

Robot Culture

Though named *robots* only comparatively recently, mechanical stand-ins for humans have existed for millennia. Currently, robots are used extensively in surgery and are proving superior to humans in this domain (Strickland, 2016), similar to the way in which computer chess programs have outstripped human brain power (Baraniuk, 2015). Almost 20 years ago, Sherry Turkle (2006) explicitly named the developing relation between humans and humanoid machines "cultural,' " and, since that time, robotic companionship has extended from robotic pets and conversing heads to robotic elder-caregivers to robotic sex (Galaitsi, Hendren, Trump, & Linkov, 2019). Robots plus humans are evolving a worldwide superculture as previously labor-intensive complex tasks are progressively automated (Bradsher, 2017). Even psychotherapy may involve robotic components (Costescu, Vanderborght, & David, 2014; Bram, 2022).

Exposition, Confrontation, and Simulation

Two approaches follow. The first one is conceptual. Historian of science Sophia Roosth (2015) suggests that designing synthetic biological systems ultimately reveals new biological knowledge; the synthetic precedes the actual. Consider a chatbot that can simulate any conversation with any human, such as ChatGPT (Open AI, 2023). Should this chatbot be programmed to reflect a particular cultural origin and membership? If so, which culture—and what elements would need to be included? Could ChatGPT develop a cultural persona on its own?

The second approach is practical. An object that might be more available now in teaching settings than it was five years ago would be a 3D printer. The printer could be set up to produce a product that is or could currently be produced in a manufacturing facility involved in injection molding. The steps of injection molding, which itself is dependent on several machines similar in complexity to the printer, can be detailed and the number of individual machine tenders reduced ad lib depending on the number of steps selected. It's recommended to choose a site from a company in China or India (e.g., Aco-Mold, 2023). Collaborate with individuals in computer science and robotics. A clunkier but just as effective demo could involve setting up an assembly line for folding and mailing charity t-shirts. Experiment with ways to make this task more efficient, and tabulate the number of displaced folders and mailers.

Inactivity, as Daniel Lieberman says, is a natural condition, a result of a built-in drive toward entropic stasis or, in evolutionary terms, the need to rest after hunting and gathering (Itkowitz, 2016). Discussion could move to what might replace work or what might occupy leisure for individuals with varying capabilities and talents. Maybe, as Bradsher

DOI: 10.4324/9781003300380-90

(2017) opines, there will be a proliferation of robot factories that will employ all skilled workers who are displaced by machines. (But what will they do?) What will a culture without much physical work at all look like? And is such a culture possible? Some think that it's unlikely (e.g., Fleming, 2018). The question of what cannot be automated is a natural offshoot as well; start with commercial fishing (SmartCatch, 2023).

References and Suggested Readings

AcoMold. (2023). Injection mold making. *AcoMold website* (company website). Retrieved from www.acomold.com/mold-making.html

Baraniuk, C. (2015, December 4). The cyborg chess players that can't be beaten. *BBC Future* (online magazine). Retrieved from www.bbc.com/future/article/20151201-the-cyborg-chess-players-that-cant-be-beaten

Bradsher, K. (2017, May 5). A robot revolution, this time in China. *The New York Times Magazine* (online). Retrieved from www.nytimes.com/2017/05/12/business/a-robot-revolution-this-time-in-china.html?_r=0

Bram, B. (2022, September 27). My therapist, the robot. *The New York Times* (online newspaper). Retrieved from www.nytimes.com/2022/09/27/opinion/chatbot-therapy-mental-health.html

Costescu, C., Vanderborght, B., & David, D. O. (2014). The effects of robot-enhanced psychotherapy: A meta-analysis. *Review of General Psychology*, *18*(2), 127–136.

Fleming, P. (2018, April 4). Robots and organization studies: Why robots might not want to steal your job. *Organization Studies*, *40*(1), 23–38. Retrieved from https://journals.sagepub.com/doi/10.1177/0170840618765568

Galaitsi, S. E., Hendren, C. O., Trump, B., & Linkov, I. (2019, November 29). Sex robots – A harbinger for emerging AI risk. *Frontiers in Artificial Intelligence*, 2. Retrieved from www.frontiersin.org/articles/10.3389/frai.2019.00027/full

Itkowitz, C. (2016, September 15). This Harvard professor explains why we were born to resist working out. *The Washington Post: Inspired Life* (online newspaper). Retrieved from www.washingtonpost.com/news/inspired-life/wp/2016/09/15/this-harvard-professor-knows-why-you-skipped-the-gym-this-morning-it-is-natural-and-normal-to-be-physically-lazy/

Open AI. (2023). *Introducing ChatGPT Website*. Retrieved from https://openai.com/blog/chatgpt

Roosth, S. (2015). *Synthetic: How life got made*. Chicago, IL: University of Chicago Press.

SmartCatch. (2023). DigiCatch: Digital catch monitoring system. *SmartCatch website* (commercial site, online). Retrieved from https://smart-catch.com/#catch_cam

Strickland, E. (2016, May 4). Autonomous robot surgeon bests humans in world first. *IEEE Spectrum* (online magazine). Retrieved from https://spectrum.ieee.org/autonomous-robot-surgeon-bests-human-surgeons-in-world-first

Turkle, S. (2006). A nascent robotics culture: New complicities for companionship. *AAAI Technical Report Series* (online). Retrieved from http://web.mit.edu/sturkle/OldFiles/www/nascentroboticsculture.pdf

Index

For Product Safety Concerns and Information please contact our EU
representative GPSR@taylorandfrancis.com
Taylor & Francis Verlag GmbH, Kaufingerstraße 24, 80331 München, Germany

www.ingramcontent.com/pod-product-compliance
Ingram Content Group UK Ltd.
Pitfield, Milton Keynes, MK11 3LW, UK
UKHW050232200926
475702UK00020B/2996
* 9 7 8 1 0 3 2 2 9 1 8 1 9 *